The

Reverse Mortgage

Book

Everything you Need to Know Explained Simply

By Cindy Holcomb

THE REVERSE MORTGAGE BOOK: EVERYTHING YOU NEED TO KNOW EXPLAINED SIMPLY

Copyright © 2008 by Atlantic Publishing Group, Inc.
1405 SW 6th Ave. • Ocala, Florida 34471 • 800-814-1132 • 352-622-1875–Fax
Web site: www.atlantic-pub.com • E-mail: sales@atlantic-pub.com
SAN Number: 268-1250

ISBN-13: 978-1-60138-213-9   ISBN-10: 1-60138-213-8

Library of Congress Cataloging-in-Publication Data

Holcomb, Cindy, 1965-
 The reverse mortgage book: everything you need to know explained simply / by Cindy Holcomb.
   p. cm.
 Includes bibliographical references and index.
ISBN-13: 978-1-60138-213-9 (alk. paper)
ISBN-10: 1-60138-213-8 (alk. paper)
 1. Mortgage loans, Reverse--United States--Handbooks, manuals, etc. I. Title.
HG2040.5.U5H647 2008
 332.7'22--dc22
                                    2008016617

INTERIOR LAYOUT DESIGN: Nicole Deck ndeck@atlantic-pub.com

Printed in the United States

We recently lost our beloved pet, Bear, who was not only our
best and dearest friend, but who also the "Vice President of
Sunshine" here at Atlantic Publishing. He did not receive a salary,
but worked tirelessly 24 hours a day to please his parents.
Bear was a rescue dog who turned around and showered myself,
my wife Sherri, his grandparents Jean, Bob and Nancy, and every
person and animal he met (maybe not rabbits) with friendship
and love. He made a lot of people smile every day.

We wanted you to know that a portion of the profits of
this book will be donated to the Humane Society
of the United States.

–Douglas & Sherri Brown

THE HUMANE SOCIETY
OF THE UNITED STATES ©

The human-animal bond is as old as human history. We cherish our animal companions for their unconditional affection and acceptance. We feel a thrill when we glimpse wild creatures in their natural habitat or in our own backyard.

Unfortunately, the human-animal bond has, at times, been weakened. Humans have exploited some animal species to the point of extinction.

The Humane Society of the United States makes a difference in the lives of animals here at home and worldwide. The HSUS is dedicated to creating a world where our relationship with animals is guided by compassion. We seek a truly humane society in which animals are respected for their intrinsic value, and where the human-animal bond is strong.

Want to help animals? We have plenty of suggestions. Adopt a pet from a local shelter, join the Humane Society and be a part of our work to help companion animals and wildlife. You will be funding our educational, legislative, investigative and outreach projects in the U.S. and across the globe.

Or perhaps you'd like to make a memorial donation in honor of a pet, friend or relative? You can through our Kindred Spirits program. And if you'd like to contribute in a more structured way, our Planned Giving Office has suggestions about estate planning, annuities, and even gifts of stock that avoid capital gains taxes.

Maybe you have land that you would like to preserve as a lasting habitat for wildlife. Our Wildlife Land Trust can help you. Perhaps the land you want to share is a backyard—that's enough. Our Urban Wildlife Sanctuary Program will show you how to create a habitat for your wild neighbors.

So you see, it's easy to help animals. And the HSUS is here to help.

The Humane Society of the United States
2100 L Street NW
Washington, DC 20037
202-452-1100
www.hsus.org

Acknowledgements

R eaching any important point in life is a group effort. If you stop to think about it, there is always someone to thank for contributing to what you have become and what you have achieved. Success begins at birth and is achieved when you understand that each encounter has led you to this point and are willing to acknowledge the people that have made a difference in your life.

I would like to thank Angela Adams at Atlantic Publishing for giving me this opportunity, and for all the advice and help I have received throughout the writing of this book.

Thanks to my husband, Keith, and my beautiful daughters, Shonda and Rebecca, for their love and support throughout this project. Thanks for all the glasses of iced tea delivered to my desk and for just being here for me. Thanks to my daughter, Leann, for believing in me and encouraging me always. And, thanks to my granddaughters, Karmen and Riley, for being the precious angels you are.

A very special thanks to my parents, Richard and Trena Williams, for giving me the kind of childhood that every child deserves and always allowing me the freedom to be all that I could be. To my Mom: Thanks for always encouraging me to reach for more and for teaching me that learning is the most exciting part of life, for taking teachers to task when they couldn't understand my need to know the "hows" and the "whys" rather than taking the facts at face value. I love you!

To my Dad: Although you are not with me on this earth, you are always with me in spirit. Thank you for always supporting me and for always being my solid ground as I travel through this shaky world. Thank you for teaching me the lessons about love and family that I will carry with me throughout my life. I love you!

To my grandmother, Gladys Watson, who, with only a third-grade education is the most intelligent person I have ever met: Thank you for teaching me that learning is not only for the classroom — that life is all about learning. Thank you for always challenging me and teaching me that words are more than just letters — words are an expression of life.

To my grandmother, Nellie Williams Wright: Thank you for always believing in me and encouraging my poetry. Thank you for being proud of each accomplishment — no matter how small it may be. I love you!

There are so many people who have made a difference in my life — Kelley, Buffy, and Ricky, who shared my wonderful childhood and were my partners-in-crime on many wonderful childhood adventures. Lisa Summers, my best friend since 7th grade — thanks for all the fun times we have had and for always being my biggest fan. Ryan Hinton, for encouraging me to take the first step and "get out there" and show the world what I have to offer. Herman Jensen, for letting me experience a reverse mortgage firsthand as I researched and wrote this book. My mother-in-law, June Holcomb for everything you do to help me take care of the girls when I am writing. And, my friends at Online Business Alliance — thanks for always supporting me and encouraging me to reach for more.

Table of Contents

Introduction

The reverse mortgage has been around for a long time. As a matter of fact, the first reverse mortgage loan was made in 1961 by the Deering Savings & Loan, in Portland, Maine. Imagine that one simple act could have changed how millions of senior citizens viewed their retirement years! Of course, that was not the plan at all. The only goal Nelson Haynes had in mind was to help the widow of his high school football coach find a way to survive after the loss of her husband. Can you imagine the looks on the faces of Haynes's colleagues when he told them he would like to issue a loan that did not have to be paid until the homeowner died? That was simply unheard of. How does a company make a profit if they issue loans that do not come with monthly payments? Somehow, Haynes convinced his colleagues that the loan would eventually benefit the company, and Nellie Young became the first person to benefit from the terms of a reverse mortgage. Nelson Haynes became the man who lit the fire that has rescued many senior citizens and offered them a less stressful and worry-free retirement.

Slowly, the idea of the reverse mortgage began to take shape, and it was not until the 80s that the reverse mortgage drew national attention. The first federal statutory recognition of reverse mortgages occurred in 1982 with the passing of the Garn-St. Germain Depository Institutions Act. The act opened the doors for what has become one of the most popular loans for people over the age of 62 in recent years. Even as late as the 90s, there were few reverse mortgages taken out. With the real estate boom and the increased value of homes, the reverse mortgage became the go-to plan for elderly people in the early 2000s and has been on the rise since, with some years showing an increase of as much as 109 percent over the previous year. And it all started because one man had the heart to assist his former football coach's widow.

What makes the reverse mortgage such a popular loan? The main point is there are no payments to make as long as a party to the loan lives in the home. For some, this is the answer to the retirement question that has puzzled people for many years. While raising a family, our earnings are used to provide a home for our family, and a quality education for our children to provide a better life for them. Often this does not leave much for our own retirement.

For many, a reverse mortgage is the solution. A reverse mortgage is a line of credit that allows people over the age of 62 to use the equity in their homes to finance their retirement, whether it be taking care of monthly expenses or taking a long-awaited trip abroad.

The reverse mortgage loan is repaid when the owner either sells the home or, at the owner's death, the estate repays the loan. This is the major difference between a reverse mortgage and other types of home equity loans.

The reverse mortgage has offered a retirement solution for millions of Americans. As with most things, there are advantages as well as disadvantages. In this book, we take a detailed look at the reverse mortgage;

the advantages and disadvantages; the qualifications of both the borrower and the home; and the effect a reverse mortgage may have on your heirs. You will be able to make an informed decision about whether or not a reverse mortgage is right for you.

CASE STUDY: NANCY MILLER

Academy Mortgage, LLC
9748 Stephen Decatur Highway
Ocean City, MD 21842
www.oc-reversemortgage.com
e-mail: nmiller@academyloans.com
voice: (410) 213-9215
fax: (410) 213-7894

Nancy Miller — Reverse Mortgage Specialist

Many senior Americans are in the position that their homes have appreciated in value while their incomes have failed to keep up with rising healthcare costs, property taxes, and other expenses. A reverse mortgage is a safe, smart, and easy way to achieve financial independence and gain peace of mind. This program will enable the borrower to increase their current retirement income with no income or credit requirements, and best of all without making monthly payments.

Academy Mortgage has specialized in reverse mortgages since 1988. We specialize in reverse mortgages and understand that these programs can seem complicated. As a result, we will meet with our clients in the comfort of their own homes to review and explain all the information in detail.

For me, it is very rewarding to assist clients lighten their monthly financial burden or be able to accomplish a goal otherwise unobtainable. We have been able to provide peace of mind to many senior homeowners, and that is something you don't get to do in many businesses. Probably the hardest part of my job is overcoming the misconceptions of the program. Once I sit down with them and give them the facts, they are usually surprised in a positive way.

For the families of seniors, they can rest assured that this program will enable their parents to live in their homes for the rest of their lives, retaining full title to their home and having the financial independence they need.

1

What Is a Reverse Mortgage?

A reverse mortgage is just what the name implies: a mortgage in reverse. When you take out a loan to buy a home, the money is used for the purchase of the home. Then you make monthly payments to repay the loan. At this point, you have no equity in your home. As you make monthly payments and the principal lowers, you begin to build equity in your home. Many times, a person sells his or her home to use the equity that has built up over the years. A reverse mortgage makes it possible for a person over the age of 62 to use the equity without giving up his or her home.

Reverse Mortgage versus Regular Mortgage

While both a reverse mortgage and a regular mortgage provide you with money for a certain purpose, there are some differences. Here is a comparison of the two types of mortgages:

REVERSE MORTGAGE	REGULAR MORTGAGE
A reverse mortgage is a loan.	A regular mortgage is a loan.
A reverse mortgage has to be repaid.	A regular mortgage has to be repaid.
A reverse mortgage is not repaid via monthly payments.	A regular mortgage is repaid via monthly payments.

REVERSE MORTGAGE	REGULAR MORTGAGE
Repayment is not due as long as any party to the mortgage lives in the home.	Payment begins within two months of acquiring the loan in the form of monthly mortgage payments.
The homeowner is free to use the money for anything he or she wishes.	Money is used to purchase the home from the current owner.
Payments to the borrower deplete the equity in the home.	Payments to the lender build equity in the home.

As you can see, almost everything about the reverse mortgage is the opposite of a regular mortgage. In summary, a reverse mortgage allows someone over the age of 62 to take advantage of the equity built up in the home to pay monthly expenses, pay large bills (such as credit card bills that have high interest), or improve his or her lifestyle during retirement.

What a Reverse Mortgage Can Be Used For

A reverse mortgage can be used for almost anything the borrower wishes. Depending on the person's financial situation, a reverse mortgage can mean the difference between having enough money during retirement, having enough money to live a carefree life during retirement, or having enough money to afford luxuries the person has long dreamed of. Each situation is different; therefore, each person has a better idea of where the money from the reverse mortgage is needed. Whether poor or rich, the main factor that ties people who get reverse mortgages together is that each person has more house than money. Most people want to stay in their homes as long as possible. In many cases, a reverse mortgage allows this to happen. Here are some of the ways a reverse mortgage can help a person during retirement:

- A reverse mortgage can be used to pay off the existing mortgage on the home, if the amount is small enough to be covered by a portion of the home's value.

- A reverse mortgage can be used to make changes to the home that enable the person to remain in the home for a longer period, such as making the home wheelchair accessible.

- A reverse mortgage can be used to pay off other debts, such as credit cards, store accounts, or a vehicle loan, thus freeing the borrower from monthly installments that take away from retirement funds.

- A reverse mortgage can be used to help offset monthly living expenses.

- A reverse mortgage can be used to improve a person's lifestyle; for example, more dinners out and more trips.

- A reverse mortgage can be used to purchase a summer or winter home, as long as the home does not become the borrower's primary residence.

- A reverse mortgage can be used to take a long-dreamed-of trip.

- A reverse mortgage can be used as a safety net for emergency situations; for example, you can place the money you receive from a reverse mortgage in a savings account so it is readily available should an emergency arise.

- A reverse mortgage can be used to offset the cost of long-term care, as long as the borrower remains in the home. For instance, funds from a reverse mortgage can be used to pay someone to "sit" with the borrower should he or she need round-the-clock care.

What a Reverse Mortgage Cannot Be Used For

As you saw above, a reverse mortgage can be used for almost anything the borrower wishes. There are, however, a few things that funds from a reverse mortgage cannot or should not be used for.

- A reverse mortgage cannot be used to buy another permanent residence. The home, with the reverse mortgage attached, must be the permanent residence. If the borrower does not live in the home for a period of more than 12 months, the loan becomes due.

- Funds from a reverse mortgage cannot be used to pay anyone that gave you advice during the process of obtaining the reverse mortgage. The government provides counselors who can assist you during the reverse mortgage process.

Advantages of a Reverse Mortgage

There are many advantages to a reverse mortgage. The most compelling advantage is that you are using your available assets rather than letting them sit unused. It does not help anyone to have more house than money when the funds tied up in the equity could be used to make life easier during the years when you may need it most. Another great advantage is you do not have to give up your home to use the equity you worked so hard to build up; ownership of the home remains in your hands, as does use of the home. As a matter of fact, one of the requirements of a reverse mortgage is that the home must be your primary residence.

Additionally, the use of the equity in your home is available without monthly payments. Simply refinancing your home causes you to have an additional monthly payment. You may use the funds from refinancing to consolidate your bills into one payment, but you still have a payment to make each month. With the reverse mortgage, you can do the exact same thing; in addition, you can eliminate those payments, and do so without gaining a mortgage payment. That fact alone can help you to increase your quality of life during your retirement years.

A reverse mortgage could also make it possible for someone to stay in his or her own home during a long illness by supplying the funds for round-the-clock nursing care or sitter fees. As long as the person on the deed is living in the home, the loan does not become due. Even if you do not require long-term care, other medical expenses can add up, and the funds obtained from a reverse mortgage can offset these costs and allow you to maintain the lifestyle that you are accustomed to.

Look at some real-life situations that could occur and see how a reverse mortgage can help in these situations:

- Carrie has worked hard all of her life. She raised three kids on her own, and while she provided well for her kids and was able to send them to college, she never had the needed funds to put away a nest egg for herself. She purchased her home through a government program and owes only a small amount of the original loan. Carrie retired from her job six months ago at the age of 65. She has a home she can live in and she can meet her basic needs. But Carrie has always dreamed of taking a summer tour of Europe, something that was not possible while raising three kids alone. Carrie seeks counseling and decides a reverse mortgage is right for her. Once she has her funds available, she pays off her remaining mortgage (which eliminates a monthly expense for her), pays off her high-interest credit cards (which eliminates additional monthly payments), and prepares for her trip to Europe. Upon her return, Carrie puts the remainder of her funds into a savings account so that, should an emergency arise, she has immediate access to the money. Carrie has taken the trip of her dreams plus eliminated most of her monthly expenses, which results in a better quality of life for her during her retirement years, enabling her to enjoy her time with her children and grandchildren.

- Sam worked his entire life at different labor jobs. He never had a lot in terms of material things, but he provided a home for his wife and kids, as well as all of the basic needs. Sometimes they had extras, especially if he and his wife pinched pennies and saved for them. His children are grown and have families of their own, and he and his wife are ready for their retirement years together. However, Sam has been diagnosed with cancer. He has insurance, but it is not enough. Sam's cancer requires many medical treatments as well as medications. He and his wife discuss selling their home to meet the expected expenses, but their daughter has another solution. Since Sam paid off his mortgage five years before he retired, he should take out a reverse mortgage. Sam and his wife look into the reverse mortgage, and their only misgiving is not being able to pass the home down to one of the children. But, they do need the funds that the reverse mortgage would provide. They call the children together, discuss the ins and outs of the reverse mortgage, including when the repayment for the loan is due. Together, as a family, they decide the reverse mortgage is the best option for Sam and his wife, because it provides the needed funds for medical care and to hire help, should Sam require round-the-clock care; and should Mom be left alone, she would not have to worry about having a home to live in.

- Martin and Susanne have been married for 50 years. Both are from wealthy families and have never had to worry about the basics. Their lifestyle has been one of privilege. They live in a fancy house, drive exotic cars, and travel on occasion. They have enough money to meet their basic needs and more during their retirement, but their dream has always been to take a world cruise together, just the two of them celebrating their lifelong love. Martin and Susanne have two children, both of whom are married, have great careers, and own substantial homes of their own. Things are set for Martin and Susanne to enjoy their retirement together. While they could probably afford to pay for the cruise, or could use their available credit lines to pay for the cruise, Martin and Susanne believe it is smarter to use the equity they have built up in their home to fund the cruise. Their children will not need anything they have to leave them, so why not use something they have worked hard for to fulfill their dream of a world cruise?

- John purchased his home when he was a young, newly married farmer. He farmed the land all his life, never working any job away from the farm. His wife, Charlotte, never worked outside the home; she took care of the kids and helped John on the farm. Together, they worked hard and provided for their family. Now, all they have is the home they purchased. Their monthly government stipend barely meets their basic needs and each month is harder on the couple. What do they have that could ease their burden? They have a home that was paid off 30 years ago and has been building equity. Although their children help as much as possible, they have their own families to provide for, and John's pride keeps him from asking for things that he and Charlotte need. Their children discuss a reverse mortgage amongst themselves before approaching John and Charlotte with the idea. Charlotte has a hard time grasping that they could get a loan that requires no monthly payments. John does not understand how they could use the equity in their home without having to give up their home. After all, they have lived in this home together since they were married; this is where they belong and where they want to remain. Their children, with the help of a counselor, finally convince both John and Charlotte that a reverse mortgage could provide all the necessities for them, and, as long as one of them lives in the home, they would never have to make payments. After years of hard work, John and Charlotte can live out their remaining years in comfort and in their own home.

As you can see, there are many circumstances in which a reverse mortgage can be used to ease the burden of meeting monthly expenses as well as providing a means of long-term healthcare. A reverse mortgage can be used to raise your standard of living or to fulfill a once-in-a-lifetime dream that forever resides in the back of your mind. Reverse mortgages are not only for people in dire situations looking for a way out of the dark; they are for anyone who possesses more house than money. Whether a person is poor, middle class, or rich, a reverse mortgage could be the answer he or she is looking for. Keep in mind, though, there are disadvantages to a reverse mortgage (which we explore next), and all options should be weighed before making a decision on whether or not a reverse mortgage is the answer you have been seeking.

Disadvantages of a Reverse Mortgage

While the advantages of a reverse mortgage are many, there are also disadvantages that should also be considered. As you will see, the advantages of the reverse mortgage far outweigh the disadvantages, if you are the right age and have the right amount of equity in your home (these factors are discussed in detail in Chapter 9).

The most significant disadvantage of a reverse mortgage is the fees involved with obtaining the loan. Closing costs, appraisals, and other fees can add up quickly; however, some of these costs can be put into the loan as with a traditional mortgage. Another disadvantage is that the homeowner is responsible for items such as taxes and insurance on the home. The homeowner never loses possession of the deed; therefore, these costs remain the homeowner's responsibility. One of the few ways the homeowner can lose his or her home with a reverse mortgage is by letting the taxes on the home fall behind.

Another disadvantage is the estate is responsible for repayment of the loan. However, this is not always a bad thing, and the lender does not always end up with the home. Some elderly people worry about not having anything to leave their children or that their children will owe money when the loan becomes due. In most cases, this is not true. First, the reverse mortgage is a non-recourse loan, which means the lender can never collect more than the value of the home. In the same vein, the loan is only a portion of what the home is worth. In most cases, the value of the home continues to appreciate; so, if the estate sells the home, there is enough money to repay the loan and, in most cases, money left over. As the original loan is only a portion of the value, should the heir wish to keep the home, he or she will be able to obtain a regular mortgage that repays the reverse mortgage.

Interest is considered another disadvantage to the reverse mortgage. Unlike the interest with a regular mortgage, the interest on a reverse mortgage is not tax-deductible until a part or the entire loan is paid off. Also, the loan increases over time, because the interest is added onto the principal each month, which means that, as the principal grows larger, so does the interest. Again, you must keep in mind that the lender cannot collect more than the value of the home. Since the original loan is only a portion of the home's value, this offsets the additional amount of the principal caused by the interest being added.

Wrapping It Up

As you can see, there are many advantages to a reverse mortgage loan. As shown in this chapter, sometimes the reverse mortgage can be the answer you are looking for to make your retirement years less stressful and more carefree. You should never feel guilty about obtaining a reverse mortgage; after all, you are only taking advantage of the equity you worked hard to create. You are not taking anything away from anyone; you are putting to use the assets you gained through hard work and dedication to your family and your home.

A reverse mortgage can help you take control of your future, manage your retirement, and avoid having to depend on others when you prefer to take care of yourself. Millions of Americans have benefited from funds that a reverse mortgage has made available to them, whether they need help with monthly living expenses or they want to take the trip of a lifetime. Whatever your financial situation, if you are a homeowner over the age of 62 and have built enough equity in your home, there is an option available to you.

CASE STUDY: NEIL GARFINKEL

Abrams Garfinkel Margolis Bergson LLP
237 W. 35th Street
New York, NY 10001
212-201-1173
www.agmblaw.com

Neil Garfinkel — Attorney at Law, specializing in Reverse Mortgages

CLASSIFIED CASE STUDIES ™
directly from the experts

CASE STUDY: NEIL GARFINKEL

I have been an attorney for 15 years. There are many complications involved in real estate law — special situations and special needs. The most rewarding aspect of my career has been reverse mortgages. No area of real estate law gives you the satisfaction that comes from knowing that you have helped someone change his or her life. I have cases every day that result in life-changing experiences.

For many people, a reverse mortgage is truly a lifesaver. I have had cases in which the client truly felt that all was hopeless — and with the reverse mortgage, we were able to turn their lives around and give new meaning to their lives. There are many clients with special situations such as trust funds or other estate issues. In many cases, we can find solutions that will enable the client to get a reverse mortgage — and the results can make a real difference.

One of the things that I like best about helping people with reverse mortgages is the gratitude once the job is complete. We don't get that sort of gratitude from clients with forward mortgages, but when you help someone who thinks they have no options available, and show them how they can use the equity in their home to make their retirement years the best they can be, the gratitude you receive is the true reward! Working with the reverse mortgage is a very fulfilling career.

While the reverse mortgage can be a lifesaver for many, it is not for everyone. It is important that anyone considering a reverse mortgage meets with a trusted advisor and discusses all options to find the one that best suits the situation. However, if someone has a lot of equity and plans to stay on the property or is looking for a way to stay in their home, the reverse mortgage may be the answer they are seeking.

The greatest problems with the reverse mortgage are the misconceptions and myths that surround it. Any time you have something that does not work in the normal way, misconceptions and myths tend to abound. The single most important thing people who are considering a reverse mortgage can do is to educate themselves — learn what a reverse mortgage is, how it works, and the effect it will have on their lives as well as their property.

This is the reason it is so important to seek the advice of a trusted advisor. They know the product, know how it works, and know what safeguards are in place to protect the client. The great thing about the reverse mortgage is that there are safeguards in place. These safeguards are there to protect both the client and the lender — and help make reverse mortgages possible.

I would highly recommend the reverse mortgage to those that have more house than liquid assets. I would also highly recommend that, before making the final decision, they learn everything they can about the reverse mortgage and consult with a trusted financial advisor.

2

Home Equity Conversion Mortgage

There are three major types of reverse mortgages in America: the Home Equity Conversion Mortgage (HECM) from the U.S. Department of Housing and Urban Development (HUD), the Fannie Mae Home Keeper Loan, and the Financial Freedom Cash Account Advantage Plan. For those living in Canada, the Canadian Home Income Plan (CHIP) is available. In this chapter, we will explore each of these loans in-depth to provide you with the information necessary to decide which loan is right for your circumstances.

Home Equity Conversion Mortgage

Representing more than 90 percent of reverse mortgage loans today, the HECM (Home Equity Conversion Mortgage) has long been the most popular reverse mortgage choice. One reason for this is because the federal government backs the HECM. The HECM reverse mortgage is backed by HUD and is insured by the Federal Housing Authority (FHA). An act passed in 1987, gave HUD control over the HECM and appropriated FHA as the insurer.

Here is a look at some of the reasons that the HECM is the most popular reverse mortgage:

- Backing by the federal government means you can never owe more than your house is worth.

- Being federally insured means that, should your originator go out of business or if your home loses value, the FHA protects you. This means if you are receiving monthly payments, and your lender defaults, the FHA continues your monthly payments.

- In retrospect, the FHA also guarantees the lender full repayment of the loan balance. What this means is that, should your loan amount exceed the value of your home, you or your heirs are only required to pay the amount that represents the value of your home. The FHA pays the rest.

- HECM loans are readily available in every state as well as the District of Columbia and Puerto Rico.

- All Fannie Mae approved lenders are required to offer the HECM loan.

- HECM loans often offer a higher cash amount along with lower loan origination fees, meaning more of the home's equity ends up in your hands.

What Are the Requirements for the HECM?

Of course, you just cannot walk into an FHA approved lender with your deed and walk out with a reverse mortgage loan. Although the HECM reverse mortgage is one of the easiest loans to get and, unlike a regular mortgage, your credit score does not determine your eligibility, there are certain requirements you must meet to qualify. These requirements include:

- You must be at least 62 years old — this includes each person listed on the deed. If more than one person is listed on the deed, and one is under the age of 62, this disqualifies you for the HECM.

- You must be the homeowner and have some equity built up in the home.

- Your home must qualify. There are standards, discussed in a later chapter, your home must meet.

- The home must be your primary residence. If you live somewhere other than your home for more than 12 months, the loan becomes due.

- It is a requirement that before you apply for the HECM reverse mortgage, you talk to a HUD-approved counselor. The counselor issues you a certificate to present at the time of your loan application.

- Because the loan is federally insured, you cannot be delinquent on any federal debt, such as taxes or school loans.

How Much Cash Can I Get?

As with any government program, there are limits. The limits for the HECM may be lower than the limits for other types of reverse mortgage loans, but the cash amount you receive is often larger than with other types. This is because the loan is federally insured, which guarantees both the borrower and the lender are protected. The lending limits for the HECM are called "203-b" lending limits. The reason for this is simple: This is where the limits are found within the National Housing Act (the Act that regulates the HECM reverse mortgage). The limits may vary from state to state or from county to county, because the limits are based on the statistics acquired by HUD regarding the average sale price of homes in different counties. This means the same type of home may have different lending limits depending on the average sale prices in your county.

Along with "203-b" spending limits, there are also personal lending limits. Your personal lending limit will be determined by three factors:

1. **Age**. Age plays an important role in the amount of money you can get from the HECM loan. Whether you are single or married does not play a role in this amount as it does in other types of reverse mortgage loans For instance, the Fannie Mae Home Keeper Loan offers less money to married couples simply because studies have shown that married couples live longer; and the longer you live, the longer the life of your loan. With the HECM loan, a single person or a married couple could be allowed the same amount of money. This is because the HECM bases its limit on the age of the youngest person on the loan; the younger you are, the lower the limit. The reason for this is the same for the Fannie Mae marriage factor. The younger the person, the longer the life of the loan. A longer loan life means more costs to the lender for servicing the loan and means that there is a greater chance the loan exceeds the value of the home. For example, you could have a single person who is 63 apply for a loan and get the same amount as a married couple in which one person is 68 and the other is 63. Because the loan is not payable as long as any person on the loan lives in the home, the youngest person on the loan becomes the determining factor. How does HUD use age to determine the loan limit? In all probability, you have taken out a life insurance policy. Your insurance representative used a chart to determine how much coverage you were allowed and how much your monthly payment would be. These charts are called actuarial tables and are tables that predict the life span of people taking into consideration certain factors. Unlike the actuarial tables used by insurance companies, the tables used by HUD do not add in lifestyle factors, such as occupation, or smoker or non-smoker. The actuarial tables used by HUD are based solely on the current age of the youngest borrower on the loan and are much more generous than insurance tables.

2. **Maximum Claim Amount.** This amount is based on the value of your home. There are certain factors that determine the value of your home. One factor is geographical location. The maximum claim amount for the same home could be different if the homes are in different locations. For instance, a three-bedroom home located in a rural area of Mississippi would not have the same value as a three-bedroom home located in Atlanta, Georgia. Since the cost of living is lower in a rural area, the price of housing is lower as well. And, since the cost of living is higher in large cities such as Atlanta, the price of housing is higher as well. Therefore, your maximum claim amount is based on the lesser of these two factors: the value of your home determined by appraisal, or the maximum loan amount FHA insures in the geographical area (county) in which the home is located. Accordingly, the limit varies from county to county; homes in urban communities are allowed higher limits than homes in rural communities.

3. **Interest Rates.** As with any loan, interest rates play a role. A HECM reverse mortgage loan is not different. The current interest rate affects the amount of money you can get in a couple of ways. Unlike a regular mortgage where interest rates are deducted from your monthly payment and the remainder applied to the principal, the interest on a reverse mortgage loan is added onto the loan amount each month, so your original loan amount grows over the life of your loan. HUD bases the interest rates on HECM loans on the one-year U.S. Treasury Securities rate, which is a percentage figure that changes on a weekly basis. The originator of your loan adds the Treasury Securities rate to a margin to formulate the amount of interest you pay. The FHA places margin limits on these loans to prevent the originator from charging rates that are excessively high or excessively low. This forces the loan originators to charge fair interest rates determined by the one-year Treasury Securities rate. If you choose the monthly payment option for your

loan, the interest rate does not affect the amount of the payment. The interest rate affects the amount you can borrow: the lower the margin, the higher your original loan amount; the higher the margin, the lower your original loan amount.

More on Interest Rates

The interest rates for an HECM loan are adjustable-rate mortgages, or ARMs. There are two types of ARMs available: monthly or annual. It is your choice as to which rate you want applied to your loan. An adjustable-rate mortgage means the interest rate changes on a regular basis: either once a month or once a year. The interval you choose can affect the amount of the initial loan. Let us explore each type and see how each one can affect the amount of cash available to you at the beginning of your loan.

- **Monthly ARM.** As the name indicates, the interest rate for the monthly ARM changes each month. The interest rate could go up or down, but usually does not change any more than a fraction of a percent. For example, at the beginning of your loan, the interest rate may be 3.75 percent — the next month, the interest rate could change to 3.5 percent or even 3.9 percent. Small changes usually do not have a huge impact on your loan. Something that can have a huge impact on your loan is if, over a period of time, the interest rate climbs to a much higher percentage. No matter what amount the interest rate may climb to — 8 percent, 10 percent, even 12 percent or higher — until the interest rate changes one way or the other, that is the interest rate you are charged. The rise and fall in interest rates does not affect the amount you can get on the loan (that is determined by the current interest rate on the day of closing), this fluctuation in interest affects the amount owed when the loan becomes due. The interest is added to the loan amount each month. If the ARM rises and stays at a high rate, this could tremendously increase the amount owed when the loan comes due.

If you choose the monthly payment method of receiving your loan, the rate could affect the length of the payments if the loan you chose has a cap on the loan balance. Once the loan reaches the cap, payments stop. One of the greatest advantages of the monthly ARM on an HECM loan is that over the life of the loan, the interest rate cannot be more than 10 percent of your original interest rate. This means that, should interest rates rise over the course of years, once the rate hits the cap of 10 percent over your initial rate, the rate stays the same until it drops below the cap.

- **Annual ARM.** The annual ARM changes only once per year. There are advantages and disadvantages to this. Two of the most compelling advantages involve caps set in place by FHA: Your interest rate cannot go up more than 5 percent over the life of your loan and your interest rate cannot go up more than 2 percent each year. Let us look at how this can affect your interest rate. Suppose the initial interest rate of your loan is 3.75 percent, and, over the course of the year, the interest rates rise dramatically so that by the end of your year, interest rates are 8.25 percent. Because of the cap put in place by FHA, the interest on your loan can only go up to 5.75 percent. This could also backfire, however. Suppose your interest rate was locked in for the year at 5.75 percent, and, over the course of several months, interest rates dropped drastically to 3 percent. For the remainder of your annual term, you would still be locked in at the rate of 5.75 percent. This brings us to one of the disadvantages of the annual ARM: No matter how many times the interest rate may drop over the course of the year, you cannot take advantage of the decrease until your annual term is over. The biggest disadvantage to the annual ARM is the initial interest rates for an HECM loan with an annual ARM are usually higher than with a monthly ARM, which can mean you receive less cash initially.

How Much Will It Cost Me?

As with any loan, there are fees involved. In a later chapter, we take an in-depth look at the fees involved in obtaining a reverse mortgage loan. Some of these fees occur at the origination of the loan and can include: closing costs; cost of obtaining a credit report; various certifications and inspections such as flood, pest, and title; and an appraisal of the home. There are also ongoing fees associated with a reverse mortgage that include servicing fees and mortgage insurance premiums.

Of course, HUD recognizes that most people in search of a reverse mortgage are in no position to pay for these fees out-of-pocket. Unlike a regular mortgage where all such fees are payable up-front before the closing date, the fees incurred in the origination of the HECM loan can be rolled back into the loan. In most cases, the only exception is the cost of the appraisal, which must be paid for out-of-pocket. The average cost for an appraisal is between $300 and $400. In many cases, this may be the only payment you make before the closing of your loan.

While reverse mortgages are generally expensive loans to obtain, the good thing about the HECM is that almost all of the fees can be added to the amount due at repayment. If you choose the monthly payment option, adding these fees back into the loan can slightly decrease the amount of your monthly stipend. The ongoing fees are added to your account balance each month along with the interest. This can play a factor in the amount of your original loan, as anything added to your loan balance is taken into consideration when determining the initial amount you are allowed.

Where Is My Money?

Once all of the factors have been considered and decisions have been made concerning interest rates and how the fees will be handled, it is time to think about the options available to you in regard to how you wish to receive the funds from your HECM loan. You have several options to choose from (these are discussed in greater detail in Chapter 3). With any of these options, you need to weigh your particular situation and find the best option for you. The HECM offers two monthly payment options: term and tenure. The term loan allows you to choose how long you wish to receive monthly payments. For instance, if you choose a short-term loan, you receive larger monthly payments over a shorter amount of time. If you choose a long-term loan, you receive smaller monthly payments over a longer period of time. With the tenure loan, you receive monthly checks until the last surviving homeowner either moves out of the home or dies. This may mean smaller monthly amounts, but you have the added security of knowing you have a monthly income for the rest of your life.

The HECM also offers a line of credit option. This works just like a bank account. The entire amount of the loan is placed into an account and you can withdraw money as the need arises. There are two major benefits to the line of credit option: you are only charged interest on the amount of money you withdraw, and the amount that remains in the account earns interest. The more you leave in the account, the faster your money grows.

Depending on your situation, you may need the bulk of your loan immediately. In this case, you can choose the lump sum option. The lump sum option puts the entire amount of your loan into your hands immediately. If you choose the lump sum option, you should plan well for the future, because once you have the entire amount of your loan in hand, your options are up. If you happen to not use the entire amount, you could put the remaining funds into a savings account and earn interest on the amount until you need it.

Since the HECM is about providing the best solution for your monetary needs during retirement, the FHA has a plan that allows you to combine the payment options to best meet your needs. For instance, if you have a large debt that needs to be taken care of immediately, but you do not need the entire amount of your loan, you could choose to receive a lump sum for the amount needed, and have the remainder of the loan amount placed into a line of credit account or divided into monthly payments. The combination package can be tailored to fit your individual needs.

Paying Back the Loan

Unlike a regular mortgage, you do not have monthly payments with a reverse mortgage. As a matter of fact, the loan is not payable until:

- The last surviving party to the loan dies.

- The home is no longer considered to be the primary residence. Either the homeowner has established another primary residence or he or she has not occupied the home for a period that exceeds 12 consecutive months.

- The borrower does not uphold the terms of the loan agreement.

The lender has the right to initiate foreclosure in certain circumstances. Since the HECM is designed to help seniors in need, everything possible is done to avoid foreclosure proceedings. For instance, one of the ways in which a borrower can fail to uphold the terms of the loan agreement is by allowing the taxes on the home to become delinquent. In this case, the lender has the option of using the remaining funds available on the loan to pay the delinquent taxes, returning the loan to good standing. There are few cases in which foreclosure proceedings take place on HECM loans.

If the borrower moves and the home can no longer be considered the primary residence, the borrower has the option of selling the home and using the proceeds to repay the loan. The borrower also has the option of repaying the loan at any time, either in full or a partial repayment. Should your financial situation change and you wish to repay the loan in full, there is one thing that you should consider: Once the loan is paid in full, if you need funds in the future, you would have to go through the entire process of obtaining a new loan. In this case, you may want to consider making a partial repayment, which leaves the loan open for future use and the amount you repay is added back into the available funds balance. For instance, if your loan is a line of credit loan, and you decide to repay a portion of the loan, the repayment is added to your line of credit account, increasing your available funds and earning interest as long as it remains in the account. If you receive monthly payments, a partial repayment of the loan could increase the amount of your monthly payments.

When the borrower dies, the loan becomes due and payable by the estate. At this time, the entire balance is due. Your heirs or the executor of your estate will have a few options. The home can be sold and the proceeds used to repay the full amount of the loan. Should your heir wish to retain the home; a regular mortgage can be obtained to repay the loan. Or your heir or executor can repay the loan with other available funds. Once the loan becomes due and payable, the heirs have six months to sell the home or make other arrangements before foreclosure proceedings begin.

As we discussed earlier in this chapter, the HECM loan is a non-recourse loan, which ensures that the amount of the repayment is never more than the value of the home. If the loan balance is more than the value of the home, the lender has to accept the market value as repayment and cannot make your heirs pay more to clear the loan. HECM lenders are required to follow the guidelines established by FHA and HUD. These guidelines are set in place to protect the borrower, the borrower's heirs, and the lender.

The HECM reverse mortgage loan is one of the most popular alternatives for seniors and provides seniors with a means of living comfortably when it counts the most. To find a list of HUD-approved lenders, visit the HUD Web site at **www.hud.gov**.

CASE STUDY: AMERICAN MORTGAGE PROFESSIONALS, INC.

Telephone: 800-481-9999 Ext. 119
E-mail: ken@ampy.com
Web sites: **www.fhareversemortgages.com**
www.houserichandcashpoor.com

Kenneth W. Terrill, President

Reverse mortgages were a relatively new concept when we signed up for the program in 1994. We became aware of the program through our local HUD office. American Mortgage Professionals was one of the few lenders in our area that had a HUD/FHA approval at the time. A HUD representative called and asked me if I would be willing to offer the FHA Reverse Mortgage Loan since there was no lender in the area actively offering the product at that time. After doing some research, I decided there was a definite need for reverse mortgages in Southern California so I signed up to offer the program.

In 1994, the program was not nearly as good as it is today. For the first few years most of the reverse mortgages we provided were the result of referrals from the local HUD office. In the beginning, I handled all the reverse mortgage cases personally. For many of my customers, the reverse mortgage literally changed their lives. I met with widows who were trying to squeeze by on $400 to $500 a month in social security while they were living in homes worth from $200,000 to $500,000. They were definitely "House Rich and Cash Poor." The reverse mortgage could double or even triple their monthly incomes, give them cash to repair their homes, buy medications, get their teeth fixed, help a child or grandchild. The list goes on and on but you get the idea. The reverse mortgage was changing people's lives and I was a part of it. The most common reaction was, "This is too good to be true!" In the early days convincing seniors that the reverse mortgage wasn't some kind of sinister government plot to steal their homes was one of the biggest challenges.

In the 90s, most senior citizens had never heard of the reverse mortgage program. If they had heard of it, most of what they "knew" was wrong. Most seniors thought they were signing their homes over to the government if they took out a reverse mortgage. They believed the government could take their homes and kick them out into the street. In fact, that is still a common belief today, even though it has never been true. In the early years, my job was as much one of educating seniors as it was providing reverse mortgages. I could see there would be a growing demand for reverse mortgages in the future. Figuring out how to best educate seniors about what could be accomplished using the reverse mortgage was my biggest challenge.

CASE STUDY: AMERICAN MORTGAGE PROFESSIONALS, INC.

To an old home loan professional like myself, the reverse mortgage contradicted every rule I'd followed since starting in the mortgage business in 1964. Here was a Government Guaranteed Mortgage Loan for senior citizens that they didn't have to qualify for, didn't have to pay back for as long as they lived, and had no restrictions on how they used the money. Credit rating, income, and assets didn't matter. If the senior was old enough and had sufficient equity in the property, the loan was approved. The senior could be in foreclosure and they could get a reverse mortgage. The reverse mortgage was like no other program I had ever seen or heard of before. The real problem was making people believe it wasn't too good to be true. There had to be a catch somewhere. Why would a lender even offer a program like this? It could be 10, 20, and 30 years or more before the lender got any money. To many old timers, that just did not make sense.

Make sense or not, the program was there just waiting to be taken advantage of by those in need. Lawyers, CPAs, financial planners, stock brokers, bankers, and savings and loan people all seemed have a bias against the program. There had to be catch in there someplace, right? Of course, there is a catch. The senior citizens are spending their children's inheritance when they get a reverse mortgage. They are diluting the value of their estates in return for a better life for themselves. How selfish of them to do a thing like that. On the other hand, many of these 70-, 80-, and 90-year-olds had worked hard to put their children through college, helped them buy homes of their own, or start them in business. Maybe it was time for Grandma and Grandpa to spend a little of the money they'd worked so hard to accumulate.

There are many heart-wrenching stories about seniors who have benefited from the reverse mortgage program. Widows have saved their homes from foreclosure after borrowing money from a loan shark to supplement their income. Delinquent taxes have been paid. Leaky roofs have been repaired. Broken-down vehicles have been replaced. Tired or worn out furnaces, kitchen appliances, and bathroom fixtures have been replaced. Elevators and ramps have been installed for disabled senior citizens. All of these things may be done after the reverse mortgage has closed. Seniors struggling to make payments on an existing mortgage have had it paid off and gotten a guaranteed monthly income for life when they obtained a reverse mortgage. Even a $200 or $300 mortgage payment can be a huge burden when a senior citizen is trying to get by on less than $1000 per month in Social Security. This list could go on and on, but you get the idea. Reverse mortgages solve problems and improve lives.

I've had little old ladies break down in tears when I explained what we could do for them. Some of the stories you hear about seniors living on pet food are true. There is nothing more rewarding than changing someone's life for the better.

3

Fannie Mae Home Keeper Loan

To take advantage of larger limits, some people turn to loans funded by private lenders. The one thing you give up is the security found by going with a reverse mortgage insured by the government, but for some people, the advantages of going with a private lender outweigh the risks. One private lender is Fannie Mae. Many people have the misconception that Fannie Mae loans are government-backed loans. In actuality, Fannie Mae started as a federally funded program, the Federal National Mortgage Association. However, the company became a private company in 1968 and is listed on the New York Stock Exchange.

Even though Fannie Mae is a private company, it functions in accordance with a congressional charter, which directs its focus on providing financial services to low- and middle-income consumers. Since Fannie Mae is not a bank, rather than lending money directly to borrowers, the company insures reverse mortgages and works closely with lenders to provide these loans.

Fannie Mae has two types of reverse mortgage loans available: the Fannie Mae Home Keeper loan and the Fannie Mae Home Keeper for Purchase loan. As you can tell from the names, the Home Keeper loan is for those who wish to remain in their current homes and the Keeper for Purchase is for those who wish to use the funds to purchase new homes.

The Fannie Mae Home Keeper loans have many similarities to the HECM loan. This loan allows the borrower to remain in his or her current home, and there are no monthly mortgage payments to make. The Home Keeper loan also has the added security of being insured by Fannie Mae, who ensures that the borrower receives all payments due even in the event the lender defaults on the loan.

The Home Keeper for Purchase Loan

This loan is designed for seniors who want to use the equity in their home to purchase another home that fits their new lifestyle. Some people may want a smaller home if their children are gone; some may require a home that is wheelchair accessible or only one story. Whatever you may need in a home, the Home Keeper for Purchase can meet your needs.

The Home Keeper for Purchase works a little differently. The main reason is the amount of the loan is used to purchase the new home, rather than receiving cash in hand. The upside is you have a new home, one that meets your needs, and you have no monthly payments on this new mortgage for as long as you live in the home.

To qualify for the Home Keeper for Purchase loan, you must own your home free and clear of any debt, or if you are close to that point, the remainder of your current mortgage can be rolled into the new loan. If you still owe a small amount on your current home, Fannie Mae will give you the money right away to pay off the mortgage.

There are several reasons you may choose to purchase a new home. As mentioned above, you may require a home that offers wheelchair accessibility or a home with only one story to avoid climbing stairs. You may want a smaller home or wish to move to a warmer or drier climate for health reasons.

There are a few downsides to the Home Keeper for Purchase loan, but if your goal is to purchase the home of your dreams to enjoy during your retirement years, these points should not have much effect on your decision. In most instances, your loan is not as much as a regular loan, and the money is used for the purchase of the new home. You receive no monthly payments and no lump sum of cash.

Unlike the HECM, the Home Keeper for Purchase loan requires you have money up front. You have to show you have enough money for a down payment on the new home. Depending on your age, the amount of the down payment may be vary. The younger you are, the higher the percentage of the down payment. Many people are ready to get a reverse mortgage the minute they have their 62nd birthday, but because the younger you are, the less you get, it is beneficial to wait a few years.

Requirements for Home Keeper Loans

Both Home Keeper loans have the same requirements and repayment plans, so we will finish this chapter by discussing both loans. Since the Home Keeper loans are reverse mortgages, they also have the same requirements as the HECM:

- You or the youngest person on the deed must be at least 62 years old.

- You must own your home outright, or close to it, and have some equity built up in the home.

- The home must be a qualifying home (covered in a later chapter) and the home must be your primary residence.

- Just as with an HECM, you are required to meet with a Fannie Mae-approved counselor.

How Much Cash or Home Can I Get?

Since there are two types of Home Keeper loans, there are differences in the amount of money you can get. Additionally, Fannie Mae has higher lending limits than HUD, so it is possible to get more money from your home than you would with the HECM. As with the HECM, certain factors come into play when determining the amount of your loan. These include:

- **Age.** Just as with the HECM, your age plays an important role in the amount of your loan. The younger you are, the less money you are able to get. The older you are, the more money you get. Because the loan has ongoing servicing fees, younger borrowers generally have more months in which the servicing fees are added to the loan balance. This is taken into consideration when determining the initial loan amount.

- **Marital Status.** As mentioned in the previous chapter, Fannie Mae takes into account more than your age. Your marital status is also a factor in determining the amount you qualify for. Studies show that married couples live longer. With this in mind, Fannie Mae gives a lower amount to married couples than to single homeowners. The reason for this is the same as for the age factor: the longer you have your loan, the more servicing charges are applied to the account balance.

- **Number of Borrowers.** Fannie Mae does something different from other reverse mortgages. With other reverse mortgages, there can be two borrowers on the loan and the loan is based on the age of the youngest borrower. Fannie Mae allows up to three borrowers to be listed on the loan. Of course, all three have to be at least the minimum age of 62. But, consider this: Suppose you are a widow of 64 and your parents are still alive. To cut costs and to care for your parents, you move into the home with them. To protect their assets, they may have added you onto the deed. In this case, the amount you can borrow is based on the younger of the two youngest borrowers.

- **Value of Your Home.** The value of your home plays a role in determining the amount you qualify for. Unlike the HECM, which uses home sale prices from within your county, Fannie Mae uses a national average. The actual value of your home is compared to the national average home value. Fannie Mae's lending limits are based on the national average home price as well. If you live in a rural area where the HECM limits are much lower than the actual value of your home, the Home Keeper loan may be the best option for you to get the most money.

- **Interest Rate.** Interest rate has a role in any loan. Being able to charge an interest rate is how lenders make a profit and are able to lend to others. Like the HECM, the Home Keeper loan is an adjustable rate mortgage. Since the ARM is covered in depth in the previous chapter, we need only touch on it here. Unlike the HECM, you do not have a choice between annual and monthly; the interest rate for the Home Keeper loan is based on the monthly ARM. The limits placed on the interest rate for the Home Keeper loan are also different. While Fannie Mae has an interest rate cap on the term of your loan — the rate cap can never go higher than 12 percent of your original interest rate — Fannie Mae does not have a rate cap on the month-to-month changes. This means that if the interest rate for a home with the same value as your own rises 6 percent in a three-month time span, you are required to pay the higher interest. The only way you would not have to pay is if it reached the 12 percent cap within those three months, which is highly unlikely. The initial interest rates for you loan are also figured a little differently. Fannie Mae figures the amount of your interest on two factors: the most current average of secondary market interest rates on one-month CDs and a maximum margin of 3.4 percent that the lender can tack on to your interest rate.

How Much Will It Cost Me?

As with any reverse mortgage, certain fees apply. These fees can include origination fees; costs to get a copy of your credit report; certifications and inspections such as flood, insect, and title; and an appraisal. The Home Keeper loan also has recurring monthly service fees. The recurring fees are added to the account balance each month, while some, if not all of the closing costs (with the exception of the appraisal) can be added back into the loan. So, while all reverse mortgages come with fees, and sometimes-higher fees than regular loans, most of the time, these do not have to come out-of-pocket. Keep in mind, though, that the more fees that are added back into the loan, the less available cash you have.

How Do I Get the Money?

All reverse mortgage loans offer you options when it comes to how you get your money. Of course, if you are applying for a Home Keeper for Purchase loan, the only two options available are money to pay off your current mortgage and the purchase of your new home. The Home Keeper loan offers three choices for getting your money: monthly payments, line of credit, or a combination of the two. The Home Keeper loan does not give you the option of a lump sum payment. Additionally, you only have one option for your monthly payment: the tenure plan. The tenure plan offers you the security of knowing you have a steady income for the rest of your life. Another advantage of the monthly tenure plan is you have the ability to invest your money any way you choose once you have it in hand. Another feature that may come in handy is the ability to stop your payments temporarily. Your loan remains open, and interest and servicing fees continue to build, but if it becomes necessary to suspend payments to qualify for certain programs such as SSI or Medicaid, your payments can be stopped and started again when you are ready. Note: It is legal to stop these payments to meet financial qualifications for these programs.

There are also a couple of disadvantages to the tenure plan. The first disadvantage is the ability to make large purchases. If you do not have time to save up for a purchase or if you cannot save up for a purchase because monthly expenses use all of your payments, it may be better to choose the line of credit option. The other disadvantage is once your monthly payments are set, they remain the same without ever changing. With the cost of living rising each year, the monthly payments may not be enough to meet your needs a few years down the road.

The line of credit option works in the same way as the line of credit for the HECM. The balance of your loan is placed into an account and you are free to draw money out of the account as the need arises. This makes it easier for you to make large purchases when necessary. You also have the option of paying back any portion of the money you use to earn interest off the balance.

The last option you have with the Home Keeper loan is a combination of the two previous options. Fannie Mae calls this the modified tenure plan. This is the perfect option if you need to make a large purchase that does not use the bulk of your loan amount. You decide how you want the money split. Should your situation ever change, for a fee, you have the option of changing how your money is distributed. This fee is never more than $50 and, as with other fees, you have the option of adding the fee onto the account balance.

How Do I Repay My Home Keeper Loan?

Repayment of your Home Keeper loan is like the repayment options of the HECM. The loan does not become due until the last surviving borrower dies or moves out of the home, the home is sold, or the borrower defaults on the loan. As with the HECM, the only way a borrower can default on the loan is by not paying taxes and insurance on the property, in which case the lender can use any remaining funds available to pay these to avoid the foreclosure process. At your death, your heirs or executor have six months to repay the loan and can choose from several repayment options, such as obtaining a regular mortgage, using available funds, or selling the home. Home Keeper loans are also non-recourse loans, so you do not have to worry about your heirs having to pay more than the value of the home.

Although Fannie Mae reverse mortgage loans are not federally funded, Fannie Mae does offer you some of the same securities as a HUD loan. The Fannie Mae Home Keeper loan may be the perfect solution for you if your home's value is higher than the lending limit applied to the HECM, especially if you live in a rural area where the cost of living and property values are low. You can apply for a Fannie Mae Home Keeper loan online, or get a list of Fannie Mae-approved lenders, by visiting **www.fanniemae. com.**

4

Financial Freedom Cash Account

 wned by Indymac Bank, Financial Freedom offers the only reverse mortgage with no lending limits. This is the perfect solution for those who have homes that exceed both the HUD and the Fannie Mae lending limits. These loans are ideal for people in the upper income range, especially those who live in Manhattan, Aspen, and Santa Barbara, where home values tend to be much higher than the national average.

While Financial Freedom does offer both the HECM and Home Keeper loans, their main target is the Cash Account Advantage Plan, which provides reverse mortgages for homes with a value of more than $450,000. Some people may think they have no choice when it comes to the reverse mortgage if they own a high-value home, but there are many lenders that offer standard reverse mortgages as well as jumbo cash accounts. Financial Freedom has set the standard for the high-end market by implementing the following practices to ensure borrowers are treated fairly and can make informed decisions about a reverse mortgage:

- All borrowers must be given a disclosure document showing all of the reverse mortgage options available.

- Financial Freedom encourages meetings between the loan originator and the borrower's representatives, including both personal and financial advisors.

- Financial Freedom provides special training for their employees and all affiliate originators with an emphasis on protecting the interests of the borrower.

- Financial Freedom uses HUD-approved counselors to provide counseling for borrowers before they make the final decision.

- Financial Freedom conducts a secondary review at the underwriting center before the loan is finalized.

- Financial Freedom submits a customer-satisfaction survey to all borrowers to obtain important feedback to ensure all customers are satisfied with the services provided.

What Are the Qualifications?

Since the Cash Account Advantage Plan is a reverse mortgage, this loan has the same qualifications as the HECM and the Home Keeper loans. These include:

- Youngest borrower on the loan must be at least 62 years of age.

- Borrower must own, or be close to owning, the home and have some equity built up. The home must also be the primary residence of the borrower.

- The home must be a qualifying property.

- The borrower is required to meet with a Financial Freedom-approved counselor.

Since there are differences in the lending limits of the Cash Account Advantage Plan, co-ops are allowed. Neither the HECM nor the Home Keeper allows co-ops and there is no limit on the number of condominiums that are allowed (the HECM only allows 10 percent of the condos in the building to be attached to a reverse mortgage). Another difference in the Cash Account Advantage Plan is Financial Freedom allows rental properties, although the owner must reside in one of the units. As you can see, in addition to no lending limits, Financial Freedom offers a wider selection of homes that can be used for a reverse mortgage loan.

Although the Cash Account Advantage Plan offers more choices for the borrower with high-value property, the biggest drawback to the loan is that it is not available in as many places as the HECM and the Home Keeper. If you live in the state of Texas, you cannot get a Cash Account Advantage Plan, because the only way of disbursement is a line of credit, and Texas does not allow a line of credit-type loan.

How Much Money Can I Get?

Some of the same factors play a role in the amount you get with the Cash Account Advantage Plan: age of the youngest borrower and value of property. What makes this loan different from the HECM and the Home Keeper is there are almost no lending limits. This means seniors with high-value homes can get a higher percentage of their equity as cash-in-hand. The Cash Account Advantage Plan is a Jumbo loan, which means these loans typically start off where the other two leave off, and the result is that seniors get a higher percentage of their equity.

Before July 2006, Financial Freedom offered Jumbo Cash Accounts. Then, the Cash Account Advantage Plan came on the scene. The Cash Account Advantage Plan has the highest lending limits in the industry. In the right circumstances, a borrower could receive up to 75 percent more equity than with the Jumbo Cash Account. This is a huge step in helping homeowners of high-value homes make the most of their equity.

The Cash Account Advantage Plan comes with a unique feature that helps to protect the equity in your home. You can choose to place a cap on the amount of equity used for your loan to preserve some equity for when the loan becomes payable. This means a couple of things for you. The downside is that your initial loan amount is smaller if you place a cap on the loan. The upside is that, at the time of repayment, either you or your heirs retain a percentage of the equity in the home.

Interest Rate

The interest rate for the Cash Account Advantage Plan is the same type that the other reverse mortgages use: the ARM. However, Financial Freedom uses the 6-month LIBOR (London Interbank Offered Rate) plus a margin (3.5 percent). The LIBOR index represents the rate at which banks in London lend money to one another; but the LIBOR index also plays a large role in American financial markets. Your interest rate is determined by the rate that the LIBOR index is using on the closing day of your loan plus 3.5 percent — so, if the LIBOR index is at 4 percent, Financial Freedom adds 3.5 percent to that and your beginning interest rate is 7.5 percent. Rather than a monthly or annual ARM, your interest rate is adjusted every 6 months (semiannually). There is no cap on the six-month rate increase, but there is a cap of 6 percent over the lifetime of your loan. Thus, if your loan starts out at 7.5 percent, you never pay more than 13.5 percent, no matter how high the rate may go during the life of your loan.

How Much Will It Cost Me?

All loans have fees. The fees for the Cash Account Advantage Plan are similar to the fees associated with the HECM and the Home Keeper loans. These include an origination fee; closing costs; costs for inspections and certifications such as flood, insect, and title; and appraisal costs. Unlike the other two loans, some of the fees for the Cash Account Advantage Plan may be waived, depending on which payout plan you choose. If you choose the combo option and withdraw the required amount at closing, the origination fees are waived. If you choose the cash-out option and withdraw the required amount at closing, both the origination fees and the closing fees are waived. This is an incentive offered by the lenders to entice borrowers to choose the loans with the least amount of servicing needed.

How Do I Get My Money?

As mentioned previously when discussing Texas and the reason the Cash Account Advantage Plan is not available there, you only have one option for receiving your funds: a line of credit. A line of credit means the amount of your loan is put into an account that you can withdraw from as needed. You do not pay interest on any of the money — until you withdraw it, and then you only pay interest on the amount that is withdrawn. While the money sits in the line of credit account, it earns interest. So, if you take out a Cash Account Advantage Plan and do not use the money right away, the equity you have gained from the purchase and upkeep of your home continues to grow. Although the line of credit loan may seem limiting, there are options you can choose within the line of credit itself. These options include:

- **Credit Line Option.** This is the most flexible of the three choices and works like a revolving line of credit. This means you are free to take the money out or put the money back in at any time. Once the money is returned to your account balance, you are free to use the money again. Each withdrawal must be a minimum of $500. The amount of the loan that remains in the account earns 5 percent interest each year. There are no penalties for prepaying a partial amount of the loan or for prepaying the loan in full.

- **Combo Option.** If you choose this option, you have to withdraw at least 75 percent of the available funds at closing. After this point, each withdrawal must be at least $500. Like the credit line option, the portion of the loan that remains in the account earns 5 percent interest each year. There are no penalties for full prepayment of the loan. However, you cannot make partial prepayments on the initial withdrawal for 5 years. For instance, if your initial withdrawal is $300,000, you cannot repay $100,000 back into the account until after 5 years.

- **Cash Out Option.** Just as the name implies, this option requires that you cash out 100 percent of the loan amount at closing. If you need a large amount of cash right away for an emergency, this is your best option; but, if you do not need the entire amount, one of the other two options may be better for you. The drawback for this type of payout is that any unused portion of the funds does not earn the 5 percent annual interest the other options offer. And, since you cannot partially prepay the loan amount for 5 years, if you choose not to prepay the full amount of the loan, it takes 5 years before your money can start growing.

How Do I Repay My Loan?

Repayment of the Cash Account Advantage Plan is the same as the previous two loans. The loan is not due until the last remaining borrower either dies or sells the home, or unless the borrower defaults on the loan by not keeping the taxes current. The heirs have the same options for repaying the loan as with the HECM and the Home Keeper: Sell the home and repay the loan, take out a regular mortgage and repay the loan, or repay the loan from other funds. To find out more about the Cash Account Advantage Plan from Financial Freedom, visit the Web site at **www.financialfreedom.com**.

5

CHIP Reverse Mortgage

The CHIP (Canadian Home Income Plan) reverse mortgage is Canada's version of the reverse mortgage. Unlike the United States, which has several options for reverse mortgages, Canada only has one: the CHIP reverse mortgage. It works the same as the reverse mortgages in the U.S. with some slight differences. The main function of the CHIP is the same as the American version in that the CHIP helps seniors to take advantage of the equity in their home without adding an extra mortgage payment, and it is tax-free.

Who Qualifies for the CHIP?

The Qualifications for the CHIP reverse mortgage are the same for other reverse mortgages, except for one difference — the age of the homeowner. To qualify for the CHIP reverse mortgage, the homeowner must be 60 or over (rather than 62). If the homeowner is married or has a common-law spouse and the spouse is a party to the loan, the spouse must also be 60 or over. In other words, anyone on the loan must be at least 60.

The other qualifications are the same as the HECM, Home Keeper, and Cash Account Advantage Plan. The home must be a qualifying home and must serve as the primary residence.

How Much Money Can I Get?

The amount of money you can get with the CHIP reverse mortgage is from $20,000 (the minimum loan amount) up to 40 percent of the value of your home. The amount is specific to each individual homeowner and is based on the age of the homeowner (as well as the homeowner's spouse), the value of the home, the type of home you own, and the location of the home. Depending on these factors, the amount you receive from the CHIP reverse mortgage could be as low as $20,000 or as high as $500,000 (the maximum loan amount).

How Much Will It Cost?

As with any other type loan, the CHIP reverse mortgage requires a few out-of-pocket expenses. The homeowner is responsible for the cost of an independent home appraisal, which runs between $175 and $400. The borrower is also responsible for the cost of independent legal advice, which can run between $300 and $600. However, the legal and closing costs of an estimated $1, 285 can be deducted from the available funds of your CHIP reverse mortgage and are not an out-of-pocket expense.

Interest Rate

The interest rate for the CHIP reverse mortgage is slightly different from its American counterparts. Borrowers have more of a choice when it comes to interest rates. A borrower can choose a fixed or variable rate. The variable rate option does not have a fixed term and the rate is based on the current bank prime rate at the closing of your loan. With the fixed term rate, you have the option of 6 months, 1 year, 3 years, or 5 years.

The CHIP reverse mortgage also offers interest rate discounts to help you lower the costs of your loan. The long-term escalating discount occurs once you have had your loan for a period of three years. Upon the three-year anniversary of your loan, the rate of interest is discounted by 0.25 percent, and is discounted an additional 0.25 percent each year until the maximum of 1 percent is met. The interest payment discount is available if you choose to pay your full annual interest. In this case, your interest rate is discounted by 1 percent for the following year. Your annual interest can be paid in a lump sum or divided into 12 monthly payments. To get the largest discount, you can take advantage of both and receive a discount up to 1.5 percent.

What Are My Payment Options?

The CHIP reverse mortgage offers several payment options. You have the option of receiving your available funds in a lump sum payment at the closing of the loan. You also have the option of taking a portion of your loan and getting the remainder at a later date. Or you can set up planned advances over a period of time: monthly, every 6 months, yearly, and so forth. The CHIP loan also gives you the option of combining the lump sum payment with ongoing advances.

Repayment of the Loan

As with other reverse mortgages, the loan is not payable as long as any borrower listed on the loan is still living in the home. The loan becomes payable at the borrower's death, if the borrower moves out of the home, or if the home is sold. You have the option of paying the interest on the loan rather than adding it to the account balance. This can be done in a yearly lump sum payment or monthly payments. You can repay the loan at any time. However, if you repay the loan within the first three years of the loan term, you are charged a prepayment penalty. This penalty could be waived if the homeowner dies during this period, or if the homeowner has to move to a long-term care facility or retirement home. You or your heirs have the option of repaying the loan by selling the home, obtaining a regular mortgage to repay the loan, or repaying the loan from other available funds.

6
Types of Payment Plans

As you have seen, reverse mortgages come with a variety of payment plans. In some cases, you may choose a lump sum option, a line of credit option, or a monthly payment option. You may also be able to choose a combination of these. Your payment choice depends on what your needs are as well as what the particular loan you obtain allows. Before you decide which type of reverse mortgage to choose, study the types of payments available for each one and find the option that best suits your needs — both present and future. In this chapter, we will take an in-depth look at the different options available to you.

Lump Sum Payment

As the name implies, you receive the funds from your reverse mortgage in a lump sum at the closing of your loan. In some cases, you can divide the amount of the loan into several lump sum amounts and receive these at certain intervals. You also have the option of combining a lump sum payment with other options, such as monthly payments. You may need a lump sum that is not as large as the amount of the loan for an immediate need or purchase, then choose to receive the remainder of the loan in smaller monthly payments.

Credit Line Option

The credit line option is like a revolving account at a furniture store. You borrow against the amount you have been approved for and as you make payments on the loan, the payment amounts become available to you so you can make other purchases. The credit line option of the reverse mortgage works in the same way. The funds from your loan are placed in an account and you are allowed to withdraw from this account as the need arises. Just as with a revolving charge account at a furniture store, if you pay back any portion of your loan, this amount becomes available for your use again.

The best feature of the credit line option is that while your funds are in the account not being used, the funds are earning interest. The larger the amount of money in your account, the more interest you earn. In essence, you are taking the equity built up in your home and placing it into an account in which it can grow more. This option can also be combined with other options to best meet your needs. You could choose to receive a portion of your loan amount in a lump sum payment at closing, and place the remainder into a credit line account where it is easily accessible and it continues to grow. Or you can choose to place a portion of your loan amount into a credit line account and receive the remainder in monthly payments. Depending on the amount of your loan, you may be able to combine all three in some instances.

Monthly Payments

The monthly payment option is one of the most popular options. The greatest benefit to this option is that it gives you the security of knowing you have an income for the rest of your life, unless there is a cap on the amount you can receive. Monthly payments can be combined with other payment options as well. There are several types of monthly payments options available. These include:

- **Tenure.** This option provides equal monthly payment throughout the life of the loan. The loan ends when the borrower dies, lives outside of the home for more than 12 consecutive months (which terminates the residence as the primary residence), or sells the home. The tenure option offers security by providing a monthly income for the rest of your life. An added benefit of the tenure option is that you can stop the payments for a specified amount of time, and once that time is over, the payments continue as before. This comes in handy for those who receive benefits such as SSI (Supplemental Security Income) and Medicaid, both government sponsored programs that are dependent on your income. It is legal to stop your loan payments to remain at or below the income requirement for these programs. No matter how many years you live after the closing of the loan, you continue to receive equal monthly payments. The amounts of the payments are determined during the loan process and remain the same throughout the life of the loan.

- **Term.** The term option allows you to receive monthly payments for a specified amount of time. The borrower determines the amount of time these payments are received. One example of how the term option can come in handy is if you have plans to move into a retirement facility within a certain period of time. In the meantime, the term payments can help improve your quality of life while you are living in your home. Another example would be if you had plans to move in with one of your children within a specified amount of time and need the monthly payments to help make ends meet until such time. One thing to consider with the term option is, although the payments are usually higher because they are for a shorter time span, once the term is up, the payments stop. If you choose the term option, it is important to plan ahead and place a portion of your monthly payment into a savings account for emergency use down the road.

- **Modified Tenure.** This option combines the line of credit option with equal monthly payments for the life of the loan. Again, the life of the loan ends when the borrower dies, moves, or sells the home. Since a portion of your loan amount is placed into the line of credit account, the monthly payments are smaller than they would be with a regular tenure plan. However, you have the added security of the line of credit account. You can withdraw from the line of credit account should the need arise. In some cases, you may have to withdraw money from the line of credit account during months when the monthly payment does not cover all of your expenses or when emergencies such as car repairs and other repairs occur. One benefit to the modified tenure option is that you have a regular monthly check to offset living expenses, and a line of credit is available to you, to help offset seasonal expenses such as winterizing your home and vehicle.

- **Modified Term.** Similar to the modified tenure, the modified term combines a line of credit account with a set term of equal monthly payments. This option works well with either of the examples given for the term option. If you are planning to move to a retirement community or move in with a relative in a specific time frame, the monthly payments would be available to help you with living expenses until that time arrives. Once monthly payments have terminated, you have the line of credit available for emergencies.

7

Costs Involved with the Reverse Mortgage

As with any loan, you incur expenses during the process of obtaining the loan. A reverse mortgage is one of the most expensive loans to obtain. However, since reverse mortgages are designed to assist seniors at a time when they may need it the most, some of the expenses can be financed or added to the loan. In most cases, the one expense not added back into the loan is the appraisal. This has to be paid out-of-pocket by the borrower. Some mortgages have options available that, if chosen, waive certain of these fees, such as originator fees and closing costs.

In this chapter, we take a closer look at the fees involved with attaining a reverse mortgage loan, the purpose of the fees, and we discuss which fees can be added back into the loan and which fees must be paid up front.

Origination Fee

As the name implies, origination fees occur at the origin of the loan, in the beginning process. This fee is designed to cover expenses that may be incurred by the lender, such as preparation of your paperwork and the processing of your loan. A portion of the origination fee can also go to cover the lender's operating costs such as overhead expenses and other operating costs.

Each type of loan has regulations that limit the amount lenders can charge for origination fees. The limits put in place by HUD for the HECM state that the origination fee can be no greater than $2000 plus 2 percent of the home's value or 2 percent of the county's 203b limit, whichever is less. The limits put in place by FHA for the Home Keeper loans state that the origination fee can be no greater than $2000 or 2 percent of the adjusted property value, whichever is greater. The limits put in place by Financial Freedom for the Cash Account Advantage Plan states that the origination fee can be no greater than $2,500 or 2 percent of the maximum initial loan amount, whichever is greater. Since the Cash Account Advantage Plan focuses on more expensive homes, the origination fees for these loans are greater.

The origination fee can be rolled back into the loan. To offset the costs the borrower incurs in obtaining a reverse mortgage, Financial Freedom offers two ways in which the origination fee can be waived: if the borrower chooses the combo option of payment and withdraws the required amount on closing; or if the borrower chooses the cash out option and withdraws the required amount on closing. Both of these options decrease the amount of ongoing processing the lender is responsible for, and the savings are passed on to the customer.

Appraisal Fee

The appraisal of the home plays a major role in determining the amount of the loan. An appraiser is a professional responsible for figuring out the current market value for a home. An appraiser may use several methods to determine the current market value: cost of replacement, value as a function of income produced by the property, or market comparison with similar properties. The appraiser may use one of these methods or a combination of the methods. Ultimately, the appraised value of a home is the price a buyer would most likely be willing to pay and a seller would be willing to accept. The appraiser also determines whether or not the home is in need of any structural repairs, and ensures the home will meet all safety and building codes. The price of an appraisal can range from $300 to $400. In cases where repairs need to be made before the home qualifies, the borrower may be required to pay an additional $50 to $75 for the appraiser to conduct a follow-up inspection. The appraisal fee is one of the most necessary fees you incur and, in most cases, this fee has to be paid out-of-pocket by the borrower.

Credit Report Fee

Although your credit score plays no role in determining your eligibility for a reverse mortgage loan, the lender obtains a credit report to determine if there are any tax liens or other judgments that have the home tied up. Your home must be free and clear of any liens to qualify. The credit report costs around $20 and can be added back into the loan.

Tax Service Fee

The one thing that holds precedent over the lenders lien is a tax lien. The tax service fee covers the cost of hiring a tax service agency that determines if your home is free and clear of any tax liens and monitors the tax rolls for the life of your loan. The tax service agency is responsible for alerting the lender if your taxes ever become delinquent. In some cases, if the borrower is in default on the property taxes, the lender pays these fees to maintain the prominent lien on the property. The tax service fee costs between $50 and $100 and can be rolled back into the loan.

Recording Fee

This fee is used to pay the court fee incurred when filing a record of the mortgage lien with your county recorder's office. This fee is between $50 and $100 and can be rolled back into the loan.

Tax Stamps

The Tax Stamp fee covers the cost of city, county, and state tax stamps. These stamps are affixed to the deed and show the amount of transfer tax that has been paid. In many cases, the state stamps the deed rather than attaching a stamp. Some cities and counties charge a transfer tax each time a property changes hands, and some states charge a mortgage tax each time a new mortgage is recorded. These fees may vary from location to location and can be rolled back into the loan.

Repair Administration Fee

The repair administration fee is charged only when a property requires repairs after the closing of the loan to meet HUD requirements. The purpose of the fee is to reimburse the lender for administrative duties related to the repair work. The limit on the repair administration fee is 1.5 percent of the amount advanced for the repairs or $50.

Servicing Fee

This is a monthly fee added onto the balance of your loan along with the interest. The fee covers the lender's duties in the upkeep of your loan after closing. The servicing fee is usually around $20 per month and, as stated above, is added directly to your loan balance.

Hazard Insurance

Among the homeowner's ongoing responsibilities is maintaining hazard insurance throughout the life of the loan. This is to ensure the lender is able to collect on your home should something happen, such as a fire or other damage to the home.

Mortgage Insurance Premium

The Mortgage Insurance Premium applies only to the HECM loan and was created by the FHA to protect the borrower, the borrower's heirs, and FHA. This mortgage insurance protects the borrower and borrower's heirs by ensuring the repayment never exceeds the value of the loan. Mortgage insurance also protects the borrower by ensuring that if anything happens to the originator of your loan, and you are receiving monthly payments, these payments continue. This insurance is also used to protect the lender from losing out when the loan balance exceeds the amount required to be paid back by the borrower or his or her heirs. This fee is added into the loan and is not an out-of-pocket expense. Mortgage insurance premiums require an up-front payment as well as a yearly payment, both of which can be added back into the loan. The up-front payment is 2 percent of your home's appraised value and can be rolled back into your loan at the time of origination. An annual premium equal to 0.5 percent of the mortgage balance for that year is added onto the loan balance.

Title Insurance

Title insurance is purchased to protect the lender or the buyer from any loss that may occur as a result of disputes over true ownership of the property. The cost of this insurance varies according to the size of the loan — the larger the loan, the higher the cost of insurance. This fee can be rolled back into the loan.

Flood Insurance

As many people have found out during the hurricanes that have hammered the Gulf Coast in recent years, normal hazard insurance does not cover floods. If you live in an area considered a flood zone, you may be required to purchase and maintain flood insurance to protect both yourself and the borrower from losses due to flooding.

Title Examination or Title Search

This includes an examination of court records to determine who the rightful owner is as well as the property's legal status. This search ensures the borrower owns the home free and clear of any liens attached to the title. The fee is usually rolled back into the loan.

Septic, Well, and Gas Line Inspection

This expense occurs if the appraiser notices a problem with any of these utilities. If the appraiser notices a problem, an inspection of the utility in question is required to be inspected by a professional. The cost of these inspections varies from place to place and can be added back into the loan.

Termite Clearance Letter

Just as the name implies, this letter states that a professional has inspected your home for termites and has found the property to be free and clear of the insects. Almost every county in the nation requires a clear termite clearance letter. The fees may vary and can be added back into the loan.

8
Borrower Protection

Since the reverse mortgage is designed with the borrower's needs in mind, there are features in place to protect the borrower. With the rising popularity of the Internet, it is easier for people to fall for scams presented by legitimate-acting businesspeople. Over the years, criminals who have gone door-to-door selling fake insurance policies and investments have scammed people. Once the telephone became a household item, these criminals moved to the wires to trick people out of their money. Now that the Internet can be found in most homes, scams are easier than ever to pull off. It only takes tech-savvy criminals minutes to create a Web site that looks almost identical to the real one. And, while the speed of the Internet has made things easier for us, we can never be too careful. With these cautions in mind, here are a few of the consumer safeguards created to protect seniors against illegal and unethical practices by lenders and criminals posing as lenders.

Payment Guarantee

This safeguard ensures that no matter what happens, the borrower receives the payments he or she is due. The protection comes in the form of insurance provided either by the government or by private institutions. The three major agencies providing reverse mortgages have guarantees that the borrower receives the full amount of the loan, even if the lender defaults on the loan. The federal government (HUD) provides the guarantee for the HECM. FHA provides the guarantee for the Home Keeper, and Financial Freedom provides the guarantee for the Cash Account Advantage Plan. No matter what may happen — even if your lender closes shop and skips town a week after your closing date — you are guaranteed to receive every payment that is owed.

Non Recourse Loan

The one thing that is indefinite about the reverse mortgage is the life of the loan. You may get a reverse mortgage and live 20 years after the closing of the loan. In this case, if you have chosen a tenure payment option, the number of payments, the interest added to your balance monthly, and the servicing fees added to your balance monthly could cause your loan balance to exceed the market value of your home. A reverse mortgage is a non recourse loan, which guarantees you never have to repay an amount that is more than what your home is worth. This also means that collateral for the loan cannot be based on any other personal assets or property; the collateral for the debt is based entirely on the value of your home. This protects you should you ever decide to sell your home and repay the loan. And, it protects your heirs from owing more on the home than what the home is worth. There are many factors that can contribute to the growth of the account balance if the loan has a long life cycle, the amount of the loan could exceed the value of the home. But all you or your heirs are required to pay is the value of your home.

Three Day Right of Rescission

In many legal dealings, a person is given a certain amount of time to change his or her mind about the contract. With reverse mortgage loans, you are given three days in which to change your mind and cancel the loan. The only time you cannot change your mind and get out of the commitment is when you are using the funds to purchase a new home. But, you must be careful if you decide you would like to cancel the loan. If you phone your lender or show up in your lender's office and tell him or her you are no longer interested in the reverse mortgage and do not want to go through with it, you are obligated to fulfill your part in the loan. The only way you can legally cancel a reverse mortgage once it has closed is to provide your lender with a written statement by letter, fax, or telegram. The only exception is if your lender gives you a form to fill out. To cancel the contract for the reverse mortgage loan, you have to have the letter to your lender before midnight on the third business day. Once this point has passed, you are liable for the loan.

Capped Interest Rates

Most reverse mortgage loans have caps on the amount the interest rate on your loan can go up. These rate caps are put in place to help you avoid paying exorbitant interest rates at the whim of the market. Each of the three major reverse mortgage loans has a cap on the interest rate.

HUD has rate caps in place for both the monthly and the annual ARM. The rate cap for the monthly ARM guarantees that your interest rate can never go up more than 10 percent over the life of your loan and can never rise more than 3.2 percent per month. The annual ARM can never go higher than 5 percent over your original rate over the life of your loan. FHA has a rate cap on the Home Keeper loans that guarantees your interest rate never goes more than 12 percent higher than the original interest rate over the life of your loan. FHA does not have a rate cap on the monthly rate. Financial Freedom has a 6 percent rate cap on the interest rate for the Cash Account Advantage Plan, which means your interest rate can never exceed more than 6 percent of your original rate over the life of your loan.

Counseling

All applicants for a reverse mortgage loan are required by law to participate in a counseling session with an approved counselor. The reason behind this law is that the reverse mortgage is hard to understand, and before anyone commits to a loan, they should be able to make an informed decision. Since the reverse mortgage is geared toward seniors, the government wants to be sure that lenders and originators treat them fairly. The counselor discusses with you the advantages and disadvantages of each type of loan. The counselor also asks you if you have signed any contracts or paid any fees to an estate-planning firm in connection with the reverse mortgage loan. Seniors have long been targeted by unscrupulous businesses, and one purpose of the counseling session is to make sure that no one is trying to pull a scam on you. The other purpose is to help you make the most informed decision you can in regard to your reverse mortgage. Your support team of family, friends, and your financial advisor are encouraged to participate in this counseling session if they so desire. The more everyone involved understands about the reverse mortgage, the more beneficial it is to you.

Total Annual Cost Disclosures

There are three main factors involved in defining the true total annual loan cost of your reverse mortgage. These are: the length of your reverse mortgage, the appreciation rate of your home, and the types of advances you choose. Each year, your lender is required to provide you with the Total Annual Loan Cost for your mortgage. Your lender uses a certain calculation that takes all of the costs and fees of maintaining your mortgage and turns it into one annual average rate. This rate changes over the course of your loan as different things affect your mortgage. The longer the term of your reverse mortgage and the more your home appreciates, the lower your rate.

9

Are You and Your Home Qualified?

There are qualifications that must be met for any loan, and the reverse mortgage has a few slightly different qualifications than regular mortgages. In this chapter, we take a closer look at the qualifications that you must meet as well as the qualifications your home must meet.

Do You Have the Right Qualifications?

Remember when you got your regular home mortgage? You had to go through a pretty tough screening process. Your credit score was a big factor, along with your job record. The lender went over your life with a fine-toothed comb. Well, do not worry! That will not happen to you with the reverse mortgage. Your credit score does not have a role to play in this loan. So, what qualifies you for the reverse mortgage? The three basic qualifications you must meet to qualify for a reverse mortgage are:

1. You and your spouse (if he or she is listed on the deed) must be at least 62 years old or older.

2. You must be a homeowner.

3. You must be the owner of a qualifying home and the home must be your primary residence.

Your Age

Qualifying for a reverse mortgage is a case of the older, the better. Not only do you have to be 62 or older — there are no exceptions to this rule — every party to the reverse mortgage loan has to be 62 or over. If two people are listed on the loan, one person cannot be over 62 and one person under 62; this disqualifies you from the loan. However, if one of you is under the age of 62, there is a solution. Change the deed into the name of the person that is over 62. Once that is done, that person can apply for a reverse mortgage loan. Unless you are in desperate need of the money right away, however, the best thing is to wait until you are both at least 62. The reason is simple. When you get a reverse mortgage loan, one of the greatest advantages is that you never have to make a payment as long as any of the borrowers live in the home. This means that, if you wait until you both qualify, neither of you has to worry about the other one losing the home if you pass away first. That should give you some added piece of mind. The other person does not have to pay back the loan, either. The loan is not payable as long as either of you lives in the home.

And, if you can hold out a few more years, it is even better. If you choose the monthly payment option, the lender is required to send you a monthly check for the rest of your life (unless you move or sell your home). This means that, the younger you are, the less money you get because the lender knows that the life of the loan will be longer. And, the loan is determined by the age of the youngest person on the loan.

So, even though you qualify for the loan the day you turn 62, the best option is to wait a few more years beyond that to get the most out of your loan. We discussed in an earlier chapter the method used to determine the amount of your loan. Lenders use the same type of charts that insurance companies use to determine the cost of your life insurance. The only difference is the actuarial tables for the reverse mortgage loan only take one thing into consideration: your age. Nothing else factors in. It does not make any difference if you go rock-climbing three times a week or how many packages of cigarettes you smoke a day. The only thing that factors in at this stage is the age of the youngest person on the loan.

While marital status has no bearing on the HECM or the Cash Account Advantage Plan, it makes a difference when applying for the Fannie Mae Home Keeper loan. It does not disqualify you, but Fannie Mae factors in your marital status as well as your age. The reason they do this is because studies have shown that married couples tend to live longer; so, married couples qualify for the loan, but they often receive a lesser amount than a single person the same age.

Do You Own Your Home?

To qualify for a reverse mortgage loan, you must own your home free and clear of any type of lien, or as close to this as you can possibly get. If you almost have your mortgage paid off, you can qualify for a reverse mortgage, but the first thing that needs to happen with the funds from your loan is you must pay off the existing mortgage. This works out for many people, with the only downside being that you have less cash in hand. On the bright side, though, you no longer have any mortgage payments for the rest of your life.

Not only must your home be free and clear of any debt, the home must also be your primary residence, which means you have to live in your home. The whole purpose behind the reverse mortgage loan is to ensure you can stay in your home as long as you are able or as long as you want. You can travel, go on vacations, or spend the winter in a warmer climate, but if you are away from your home for more than 12 consecutive months, your loan ends and must be paid. This means you cannot move out of your home and rent it out, even to family members. You have to physically reside in your home to keep the life of the loan going. As long as one person listed on the loan lives in the home, the loan is not due. If you move out or sell your home, then the loan ends and must be repaid in full.

Does Your Home Qualify?

Now that you have met the first two qualifications, it is time to see if your home qualifies for a reverse mortgage loan. First, look at what types of homes do not qualify; these include:

- Motor homes

- Mobile home or trailers

- House boats or yachts (even if you live on them)

- Manufactured homes built before 1976

- Timeshares

- Multi-family properties with more than four units

- Barns (even if you live in them)

- Any other impermanent structure

Now, look at the types of homes that do qualify. Keep in mind, though, even if the home is on the qualifying list, it must meet FHA and HUD standards to qualify. Your house must be in good condition and must not need extensive repairs that cost more than the amount of the loan. The plumbing and wiring must be up to code. Your home must be free of lead paint and other hazardous conditions. And, of course, you must live in the home. Qualifying homes can include the following:

1. **Single-family homes.** This includes any home that is detached from other dwellings. If you own a home and a plot of land surrounding the home, this qualifies as a single-family dwelling.

2. **Condos and townhouses.** Sometimes these are included and certain loans have different rules about which condos and townhouses are eligible for a reverse mortgage. If you live in a condo or townhouse, check each individual loan's requirements regarding this type of dwelling before choosing the loan you want to apply for. Some loans have a limit to the number of rental units in a neighborhood, and this can sometimes make it difficult to get a reverse mortgage loan on your condo or townhouse, even if you own your unit.

3. **Manufactured homes.** It is possible to get an HECM or a Home Keeper loan on a manufactured home, but the home has to have been built after 1976 and the home must meet FHA/HUD standards. You must also own the land the manufactured home is affixed to. If you live in a manufactured home built after 1976, talk to a loan originator and see if your home qualifies.

4. **Multi-family homes.** Multi-family homes with up to four units can qualify for a reverse mortgage loan as long as one of the units is your primary residence.

10

Determining Your Needs

One important task in determining your needs is thinking about your plans for the future. If you plan to move to a different location within three to five years, a reverse mortgage is probably not for you. As we discussed earlier, a reverse mortgage loan does not become due unless the home is no longer your primary residence. This means, if you move or if you need to be placed in a long-term care facility, your loan becomes due and payable. No one can predict what tomorrow will bring, but there are certain factors you can take into consideration when planning for your future.

Long-Term Healthcare

Nobody likes to think about having to rely on long-term healthcare, but this could play an important factor in whether or not you decide to get a reverse mortgage. The cost of healthcare is one of the main reasons people get reverse mortgages. About one-third of adults over the age of 75 require long-term care due to a chronic illness. If you have to meet many of your obligations out-of-pocket, it will not take long to drain your resources. If you suffer from a chronic illness, but are able to live in your home with some assistance, a reverse mortgage may be the answer. It can provide the much-needed funds to cover the expenses of long-term care; as long as you are living in your home, you are not required to make any payments. One thing to consider is the length of time you are able to remain in your home. If you may have to turn to a long-term care facility within a couple of years, the reverse mortgage may not work for you unless you plan to sell your home. In that case, you could take advantage of the reverse mortgage, and once you were ready to move into a long-term care facility, you could sell your home and repay the loan. Those are two of the many options available to help you meet your needs if you suffer from a chronic illness.

How Will a Reverse Mortgage Affect Government Benefits?

The need for government benefits is something to be taken into consideration. Some benefits, such as SSI and Medicaid, have eligibility requirements based on your income. If you receive either of these benefits, and the reverse mortgage did not relieve your dependency on them, you may want to reconsider the loan. One solution is that if you choose the monthly payment option, you can have your payments stopped during the qualifying period for these programs — and then have them start back up after you qualify. If you are retired and drawing Social Security (SS) the income from the reverse mortgage does not affect your SS benefits.

Proceeds from a reverse mortgage are ideal for supplementing your income if you are on Social Security. And since Social Security does not have income limits, there is no problem receiving your loan payments on schedule.

Determining What You Need

The reverse mortgage was designed for people who are house rich and cash poor. The income from a reverse mortgage could be just what you need to ease your mind about the future, because as long as you live in your home, you have no payments. The best thing to do before you decide on a reverse mortgage is to sit down and make a list of your short-term and long-term needs. Try to imagine where you will be a few years down the road.

One of the first things that should be done when you get a reverse mortgage is to pay any debt you may owe. Once you have eliminated as much debt as possible, you can plan your future needs more easily.

Tools for Calculating Loan Advances

Most Web sites that offer reverse mortgage loans utilize tools that allow you to guess how much money you can receive from your loan. These tools make it possible for you to get a ballpark figure on the amount of resources available. A great way to look at the options available to you is to use the tools on each Web site to make a comparison chart that can help you decide which loan program you need to participate in. When you are researching the reverse mortgage, think ahead to the future. Try to anticipate your future needs so you can use funds from the reverse mortgage to help meet your needs. That is first and foremost: Make sure your needs are met without spending too much of the money at once.

CASE STUDY: DAVID AND VANDA KENNEDY

Reverse Mortgage Consultant.Net
700 Rosaer Circle
Virginia Beach, VA 23464
Phone: (877) 817-6941 (toll-free)
(757) 322-0746 (local)
Web site: **www.reversemortgageconsultant.net**
David and Vanda Kennedy
— Reverse Mortgage Consultants

I was attracted to reverse mortgages because it is a great concept and has the ability to improve a senior's lifestyle significantly. It can be used to supplement monthly income; cover healthcare costs, thus avoiding a nursing home; fixing up a home; or simply gaining peace of mind. Whatever the specific goals, a reverse mortgage can go a long way toward helping seniors maintain their financial independence. The feedback from those who are able to benefit from reverse mortgages makes it a wonderful, fulfilling, and purposeful profession.

The availability of reverse mortgage is sufficient, but the quality of the services being provided sometimes is not up to par. These days you have everyone from A to Z trying to offer reverse mortgages. Some just for the monetary gains it provides. They

CASE STUDY: DAVID AND VANDA KENNEDY

often forget that a caring heart is needed when dealing with our senior community. You need patience and understanding to be able to communicate and explain the process involved, and genuinely want to help improve their quality of life. We now have banks and mortgage companies that are suffering due to the lag in the forward mortgage industry jumping on the bandwagon, thus flooding the market, sometimes with misinformation, and opening the door to possible fraudulent practices. It can be very confusing and sometimes misleading to seniors. I do believe, however, there are more credible and ethical providers than not.

I like the fact that reverse mortgages provide seniors with a viable option, where appropriate, to help them meet their financial goals with very little qualifications. It is truly a financial planning tool used by seniors in all walks of life to enhance their financial position during their retirement years. Nothing can replace the satisfaction one feels when looking into the smiling face of a borrower(s) when a reverse mortgage changes his or her life for the better during their golden years.

At first glance, the closing costs involved can appear to be steep to a homeowner, even though they are rolled into the loan and not out-of-pocket expenses. But, if you think about expense, in comparison to . . . what? Nothing out there compares to what a reverse mortgage can offer. Peace of mind in life is priceless. You have a program where you can tap into a portion of your home's equity, while the remaining portion continues to appreciate, and there is no monthly payment for as long as the borrower remains in the home. If used wisely, I feel there isn't much to dislike about the loan, other than the many misconceptions, lack of knowledge, and sometimes, misuse of this dynamic tool.

We have had some very positive and uplifting experiences, and it feels great! Who wouldn't want a career that helps people live out the remainder of their lives in comfort, dispelling worry and fear, and creating a life of independent living? Assisting someone in accessing tax-free cash, which they have earned during their lifetime, to enhance their lifestyle is an incredibly wonderful feeling.

If I can share my advice with people considering a reverse mortgage and their grownchildren, I would offer the following:

1. Follow your heart. In most cases, you are shopping for the representative or specialist you feel comfortable with, not for the cash out. Make sure they are receptive and caring and very knowledgeable about the product and your goals. If someone is pushy or forceful, shop around until you find the right one for you. Genuine customer care is everything!

2. Do not deal with someone trying to use your funds to invest in an annuity, or any other investment solely on their recommendation. A reverse mortgage is

CASE STUDY: DAVID AND VANDA KENNEDY

your equity, and you should use it exactly how you want to. You should not be pressured into giving your money away — period. Investing should be your choice if that is your goal, and seek the advice of a professional advisor if so.

3. A lot of adult children are worried about their inheritance. I personally feel that if you are not paying your parents' bills and they are in need, this program should be at least considered. We love our parents, and if they wish to use their investment (home) to help make ends meet or to assist their retirement, or even just to go on that dream vacation, I say go for it. A reverse mortgage is a non-recourse loan, meaning the possibility of leaving a burden of an unpaid debt to heirs is impossible with this program. Remember, with a reverse mortgage, a portion of the equity is turned into tax-free income, and is not paid off until the borrower sells, moves out permanently, or passes away. The balance will reflect the amount borrowed with interest and is paid when the home is sold by the borrower or out of the estate once the last borrower has passed away. The borrower and heirs always remain in control of the home.

11

Adult Children and Reverse Mortgages

Since your children are your heirs, obtaining a reverse mortgage has an effect on their lives. The best approach is to be straightforward and honest with them when you are considering a reverse mortgage. Having a good support team to help you through the process eases some of the pressure for you. Who better to be your support team than your children? You need to explain what the reverse mortgage does for you — how it makes it possible for you to enjoy your retirement and meet your financial obligations. You also need to discuss with them what happens after your death and the options they have available for repaying the loan.

Since your children will probably end up repaying the loan — either from your estate, from the sale of the home, or through financing — they need to be a part of the decision-making process. This does not mean they should make the ultimate decision; that is yours to make. However, it always helps when you are doing something like a reverse mortgage loan to have all of the help and support that you can get.

It is important that your adult children support you throughout the process. Another great support resource is your friends. Many can give you a more unbiased opinion than your children can. Having the right kind of support from your kids makes it impossible for someone to scam you, because scammers are waiting to be the person that reaches you first.

The remainder of this chapter is devoted to adult children of people considering a reverse mortgage. If you are considering a reverse mortgage and you have adult children, please share this information with them when you discuss the reverse mortgage.

Offering Your Support

At some point in your life, you may realize the tables have turned. The parents who have supported you your entire life may need your support. One thing you need to remember, though, is there is a thin line between supporting your parents and butting in. The goal is to learn how to support them without making them feel as if you are taking over completely. If your parents are of sound mind and capable of making financial decisions, this must be a decision they make themselves, and you support that decision.

However, it is perfectly normal for you to want to educate yourself about the reverse mortgage process for several reasons. First, seniors are among the most targeted people for con artists, so you may want to ensure yourself that the reverse mortgage is not a scam. Secondly, repayment of the reverse mortgage could affect your inheritance, and it is important that you understand how. Thirdly, you probably feel the same way about your parents as they did when you were a child: a sense of responsibility or maybe even the feeling that you know what is best for them. But, it is important that you let your parents make their own decisions as long as possible. Your involvement should not exceed the limits that your parents place on you; if they are perfectly capable of making sound financial decisions, it is your job to step back and let them make this decision, while letting them know that you support their decision.

Determining how much involvement on your part may be needed involves doing something you may not have done in a while: getting to know your parents all over again. While you may know them as the strong, capable people who have always taken care of you, things can sometimes change pretty quickly. If your parents are considering a reverse mortgage, or if you are considering introducing the idea to them, it is important to know their financial capabilities, as well as their ability to understand the reverse mortgage, and emotional and mental capabilities.

If your parents meet the following guidelines, your role should be as a member of the support team. If your parents do not meet the following guidelines, your role in the reverse mortgage process will need to be more involved:

FINANCIAL CAPABILITIES	UNDERSTANDING OF REVERSE MORTGAGE	EMOTIONAL AND MENTAL CAPABILITIES
Pay own bills	Understand the basics	Independent
Keep a balanced checkbook	Understand the finer points such as interest rates and so forth	Rational
Ability to remember where money is — savings, investments, different banks	Comfortable with the idea	Live on their own
Able to keep track of cash and can be trusted with large amounts of money	Understand the costs involved	Cope well with stress
Understand about con artists who target seniors	Know how much they need compared to how much is available	Capable of living on their own for the next few years

Determining Your Parents Financial Needs

Since your parents most likely take care of their own finances, you may not know exactly what their financial needs may be. Your parents might have always tried to protect you from their financial burdens, and this does not change just because you are grown. If you do not live near your parents and do not have the opportunity to visit often, you may not notice if things begin to change financially for your parents.

It is important that, when you discuss a reverse mortgage with your parents, you discuss their financial situation and what the money will be used for. There are many reasons people get reverse mortgages, and it is not always a case of being needy financially. There may be things that your parents "want" to do. Do not assume that your parents are having financial problems because they want to take out a reverse mortgage. They may just have plans to use the equity in their home.

As stated in an earlier chapter, there are many reasons people utilize reverse mortgage. These reasons can include helping with daily living expenses; improving quality of life during retirement; helping cover medical expenses; remodeling, either for safety and accessibility or simply for a change; taking a dream vacation; or providing financial assistance for children or grandchildren. Whatever the reason, your parents should feel comfortable using the equity in their home for these purposes.

Once you have discussed the reverse mortgage with your parents and discovered the reason they want to get one, there are some things for you to think about. Keep in mind a reverse mortgage is not free money; it comes with a price. The price is the equity in your parents' home, plus fees and charges. While most of the fees and charges are not required up-front, they make an impact on repaying the loan down the road.

Do not discourage your parents; however, do consider alternatives. Just as with any major financial decision, it is important to consider the alternatives available to see if there is a better solution, especially if your parents have just reached the age for qualification. As we discussed in an earlier chapter, the longer your parents can wait, the more they can benefit from the reverse mortgage.

Here are a few steps that you can take to delay the reverse mortgage:

- Check to be sure your parents are receiving maximum benefits from healthcare sources such as Medicare, Medicaid, and private insurance (including prescription coverage).

- Check to be sure your parents are receiving maximum benefits from financial resources such as Social Security, Supplementary Security Income (SSI), and other retirement plans.

- Check to see if your parents qualify for state or federal assistance programs. There are many programs that provide assistance with food, medical expenses, prescriptions, and utilities.

As your parents reach a certain age, they may feel out of touch with the changing world. You may find them calling on you more often for your advice on financial, as well as personal, matters. This is why it is important for you to offer your support and help your parents in any way that you can. This may involve explaining how the reverse mortgage works, setting up and attending meetings with the reverse mortgage counselor and originator, and being there with your parents through each step up to the closing of the loan. When your parent approaches you about a reverse mortgage loan, discuss the boundaries that he or she wishes to set concerning your involvement, and respect those boundaries. They may be able to make their own decisions concerning the reverse mortgage, but may just need your moral support. Or they may need you to be more involved. In either case, it is important that your parents feel they have your support throughout the process. Always remember, this is something your parents have worked hard for, and they deserve to reap the benefits.

Understanding the Deed

One of the most common concerns for adult children is "What happens to the deed?" Most people are under the impression that once the papers are signed for the reverse mortgage, the bank owns the home. Rest assured that your parents retain the title to their home, unless they choose to sell it.

The type of deed that your parents will have is called a deed of trust. This type of deed is recorded with the county to secure a loan. It remains in your parents' names. The deed of trust has only one purpose: to record that a loan has been taken out on the property. A deed of trust does not transfer the property to the bank. The deed of trust does not transfer the property to anyone at any time. Therefore, if your parents want to leave the property to you or someone else, it needs to be stipulated in their will.

An important thing to remember is this: As long as the deed remains in your parents' names and the home is your parents' primary resident, no payments have to be made. Should your parents decide to sell the home — even if they sell it to you and they remain in the home — the loan becomes due. Some children purchase their parents' home and allow their parents to live in the home rent-free. This may be one solution to avoid a reverse mortgage; but, once the reverse mortgage has been taken out, the deed must remain in the parents' name.

Another Option for Children

In some cases, a parent may not have the mental capacity to make a decision such as a reverse mortgage. If your parent has Alzheimer's, dementia, or other mental disorders, it is possible for you to help your parents take advantage of the reverse mortgage so that he or she can stay in the home and avoid the unnecessary agitation that would be caused by moving the parent. Even if your parent needs live-in care, he or she can take advantage of the reverse mortgage in order to stay in the home.

If your parent is incapable of making major decisions, you have the option of obtaining a durable power of attorney. A durable power of attorney gives you the power to make financial decisions on behalf of your parent so that he or she can receive the benefits of a reverse mortgage.

Here are a few signs to look for:

- Memory skill worsening

- Sudden changes in personality

- Repeating the same questions

- Repeating the same conversations

- Making harmful decisions, such as traveling long distances on foot in dangerous weather, climbing ladders in dangerous weather, or other things he or she would not normally do

- Confusion about times and places

- Being unable to make a decision

- Misplacing things; losing money

- Unable to make plans for the future, near or far

- Ignoring basic personal hygiene

It is not a pleasant task to have to consider if your parent is becoming mentally incapable. No one wants to realize this is happening. But, it is necessary so that you can offer the support and help that your parents need. Once you have determined that your parents need your assistance, you should meet with an attorney that specializes in situations for seniors. At this meeting, you and your parents can decide the level of durable power of attorney you need.

Before you meet with an attorney, you should discuss this with your parent or parents. Your parents can determine the length of the durable power of attorney; for example, they may only need you to have the power of attorney to acquire the reverse mortgage. If your parents are not at the point where you need to oversee all of their finances, it can be stipulated in the durable power of attorney exactly what your role is.

Your role could include any of the following: applying for the reverse mortgage; opening a bank account; making donations on behalf of your parents; signing tax forms and returns; paying yourself for overseeing your parents finances; or managing your parents existing finances including existing bank accounts, pensions, healthcare, insurance, and other financial or personal concerns.

Your role is as small or as large as you and your parents decide. They may only feel comfortable with you taking control over obtaining the reverse mortgage and overseeing the funds from it. You may not feel comfortable being in control of their total finances, especially if they are still taking care of their everyday financial needs. That is why it is critical to discuss all aspects of the durable power of attorney before deciding to go that route.

A living trust is also an option. As with the durable power of attorney, it can be specified within the trust exactly what the responsibilities are. A living trust can be revocable or irrevocable, meaning that a revocable trust can be changed or canceled, while an irrevocable trust cannot. Also, if your parents are of sound mind at the time the living trust is created, they can be both the trustee and the beneficiary, meaning they retain control over everything until they can no longer manage, at which point, another trustee steps in and takes over. This could be you, another family member, or a friend — whoever is named in the trust. With a revocable trust, if your parents name one person and decide later this person is not suited for the role, they have the option of appointing someone else.

Just as you would with the durable power of attorney, everything needs to be discussed beforehand and indicated within the living trust. For example, if the only property and finances the trustee will manage are the home and the funds from the reverse mortgage, this needs to be stated. If the trustee is expected to manage all finances, this should be explained in detail. Unlike the durable power of attorney, which includes all finances not specified, the finances have to be specified to apply in the living trust. If your parents intend for you to manage their present assets and accounts, a living trust will not allow you to do this unless it is written within the trust. Even if your parent becomes incapacitated, if it is not specifically outlined within the trust, you cannot automatically assume management of other assets.

The Reverse Mortgage and Your Inheritance

Although most people do not like to think about it, one of the first things that comes to mind when the reverse mortgage is mentioned is "What about my inheritance?" Most people would not actually bring the subject up; nevertheless, the thought is there. Maybe you are not thinking in terms of what you get versus getting the necessary funds for your parents. You may be thinking, "I will have to pay back the loan."

It is normal to think about how a reverse mortgage affects your inheritance. After all, if your parents do not sell the home and repay the loan, someone will have to repay it at their death. While nobody likes to think of the death of someone they love, when a reverse mortgage is being discussed, this must be one of the topics: when and how the loan will be repaid.

There are three reasons a reverse mortgage becomes due. The senior moves out of the home; the senior fails to maintain the property, usually the taxes; or the senior dies. If your parents move out of their home, they will probably sell it to pay off the loan. If your parents fail to maintain the home, the loan could become due; however, in some cases, the originator pays the taxes and adds them to the loan. The only time you need to be involved with the repayment of the loan is when your parent dies; and then, only if you are the heir.

Before you panic, remember that with a reverse mortgage, you can never owe more that the home's fair market value. No matter how much the loan is, even if the amount payable is more than the value of the home, the cost of repaying the loan never exceeds the value of the home. However, the loan is usually only a portion of the value of the home. So, the good news is, once you repay the loan, you have (or the named heir has) money left over.

Repaying the Loan

How you repay the loan depends on whether you want to sell the home or keep it. If there is more than one heir (brothers and sisters who each get equal share in the home), this needs to be decided beforehand. This is one reason it is important to discuss the reverse mortgage with everyone involved during the decision-making process. When there is more than one heir, the home is usually sold and the proceeds divided equally among the heirs. This can happen by selling the home outright or by one heir obtaining financing to buy out the others. The same thing can happen if a reverse mortgage is involved; the only difference being the heirs also split the cost of repaying the loan.

Selling the home is the most common way to repay a reverse mortgage. Especially as in the scenario above, when there is more than one heir. Another good reason to sell the home is when the amount of the loan is more than the value of the home, which means the home may be depreciating in value. Remember, if the loan is more than the value, you are only obligated for the fair market value of the home; you do not get stuck paying the difference. That is the biggest advantage of the reverse mortgage.

On the other end of the spectrum, if the value of the home is much higher than the loan amount, you can sell the home, repay the small loan amount, and pocket or divide the remainder, as the case may be. Other instances of when you might sell the home to repay the loan would be if no one in the family wants to live in the home, and the home has no sentimental value to you or anyone in the family.

There are several reasons you or one of the heirs might want to keep the home: if the home has sentimental value (you grew up in it); the home has another significance — maybe it is a historical landmark; a family member would like to live in the home; or the home is in an area with increasing home values or an area in which you could easily rent it for a good price. Whatever the reason, you must now find a way to repay the loan, and the loan cannot be repaid in installments. When the last person on the deed is deceased, the loan is payable in full.

This is why it is important to discuss all facets of the reverse mortgage in the beginning. This allows everyone involved to develop a plan of action for each scenario, whether the parents sell the home, the children sell the home, or the children keep the home. There should be a viable plan.

If you decide to keep the home, there are a few ways in which you can repay the loan. If there are enough funds in your parents' estate, these can be used to repay the loan. If you have enough savings, you can repay the loan out-of-pocket. If you wish to move into the home, you can use the proceeds from the sale of your own home. Or, you can obtain a regular mortgage to repay the loan. This last option works especially well if the loan amount is a lot smaller than the value of the home. Do not rely on the appraisal from the origination of the reverse mortgage. Have the home re-appraised so that you can consider your options with the knowledge of the true value of the home. In some cases, this can make your decisions easier.

Get Everyone Involved

This may be one of the most important things you can do, besides supporting your parents' wishes. If your parent's mention they are considering a reverse mortgage, ask if they would like to discuss it with you and your siblings, when appropriate. Explain to them that you are not trying to butt in, nor are you trying to tell them what to do; but, if you are going to be responsible for repaying the loan, it would be wise to have a family meeting to plan for that time. This may be a touchy area for some. You do not want your parents to think that you are putting your inheritance above their needs; yet it is important for the family to have a plan of action for different scenarios that may arise.

If there is more than one heir, all heirs should be included in the decision. Remember, the ultimate goal is not to discourage your parents from obtaining a reverse mortgage; the goal is to support their decision and plan for the future of the home, namely the repayment of the loan. If your parents do not already have a will, this would be a good time to approach the subject. Once a plan of action has been decided on, your parents could stipulate this in the will.

In a case where a reverse mortgage means the difference between a poor quality of life and a good quality of life, you want your parents to do whatever is necessary to improve their quality of life. However, there are some cases in which the parents have a good quality of life. There may be other reasons they wish to obtain a reverse mortgage. Perhaps they have always dreamed of taking a trip around the world, staying in a warmer climate during the winter months, or perhaps they want to help their children or grandchildren with college tuition or a down payment on a home. They may even just want the security of knowing the money is readily available in times of emergency.

Whatever the reason, one thing to keep in mind is the equity they have built in their home belongs to them, and it is ultimately their decision. It is your job to do what they have always done for you: show your love and support. On the other hand, if your parents have reached a point of needing care, it is in your parents' best interest for you to perform due diligence and research the reverse mortgage so that you can help to support your parents when they needs you most.

The reverse mortgage is a real mortgage, backed by the government in some cases and by private organizations in others. However, there are con artists who prey on seniors. The best way to spot a con artist is if your parents are asked to pay exorbitant fees out-of-pocket. Steer your parents toward a trusted lender, whether it is a local bank or HUD.

CASE STUDY: MAGGIE O'CONNELL

Seniors Reverse Mortgage
144 So. K Street
Livermore, CA 94550
Phone: (800) 489-0986
Fax: (925) 605-1778
Web site: **www.ReverseMortgageStore.com**
E-mail: Maggie@ReverseMortgageStore.com

Maggie O'Connell — Branch Manager

When I first learned about reverse mortgages in the early 1990s I knew I wanted to specialize in the program. After a round of golf with a woman who happily announced she just received a reverse mortgage through Household Senior Services, I contacted them and was interviewed and hired within a month. We were in the education business as no one had heard of reverse mortgages at that time. Reverse mortgages have come a long way since then. Not only are there more programs to choose from, most people have heard of them and many understand how they work. Also different are the attitudes people have towards home equity, inheritance, and lifestyle. The old attitude that the family farm goes to the kids is fading. It started with the bumper sticker on motor homes, "I'm spending my kid's inheritance." The "me" generation has come of age along with incredible appreciation of their homes. The reverse mortgage is rapidly becoming the financial instrument of choice to help people tap into that equity and live the lifestyle they can afford.

High home values have helped people feel more comfortable with tapping into their equity and has lead to the creation of many new "Jumbo" reverse mortgages. The different options allow homeowners to select the program that best suits their circumstance and needs. As a representative of a variety of programs, I can truly call myself a specialist and provide assistance in evaluating my client's needs with the program options available. The FHA-insured HECM continues to be the shining star of reverse mortgages, and with lending limit increases, will become an even more viable option. But as lending limits increase, so do the up-front mortgage insurance fees. I am hopeful the decision-makers at HUD and our government will view reverse mortgages as a program that allows people to take care of themselves with their own assets, and help out by capping or adjusting up-front mortgage insurance. Reverse mortgages are very helpful for seniors and the phrase "sounds too good to be

CASE STUDY: MAGGIE O'CONNELL

true" is often heard. I want to continue to tell people they are very good and it is true.

My career as a reverse mortgage specialist has been very rewarding. I meet very interesting, warm, and caring people on a daily basis. It is a joy to be able to help them enrich their lives. From the elderly gentleman who surprised his wife with a cruise to Alaska, to the widow who remodeled her home and proudly said, "I polish my equity every day," the stories are endless and it's very satisfying to know that people are taking care of themselves and making their lives better. I'm blessed to be a part of that process.

12

Available Resources

There are many resources available to help you make the right decision concerning your reverse mortgage. Many have Web sites you can visit and learn more about the terms of the reverse mortgage. When making a decision of this magnitude, it is best to utilize as many resources as are available to you. The more informed you are, the more likely you are to make a decision that is the most beneficial. Some of these resources include:

- AARP
- BenefitsCheckup.org
- Reverse Mortgage Counselor
- HUD
- National Reverse Mortgage Lender's Association
- Administration on Aging
- Fannie Mae
- Financial Freedom
- Social Security Administration

AARP

AARP is a nonprofit organization that has provided information and resources for seniors for many years. Focusing on all aspects of life to improve the quality of life for people over the age of 50, the AARP has an astounding Web site with information on health issues, personal issues, and financial issues. AARP's Web site has an entire section devoted to the reverse mortgage, a loan specifically for seniors. You can also find information on the site that can help you delay getting a reverse mortgage until you can receive the most benefit from it. AARP's Web site includes information on budgets, government programs available to help with living expenses, and information on different types of reverse mortgages.

"Home Made Money" is a free booklet that can be downloaded from the AARP Web site or sent to your home as a hard copy. The booklet covers the basics of a reverse mortgage as well as different types of reverse mortgages. The "Home Made Money" booklet includes an explanation of the concept of rising debt and falling equity in a language that is easy to understand, and comes complete with charts to make visualization of this concept easier. AARP provides options other than reverse mortgages for comparison, as well as resources to help you find counselors and originators in your area. AARP also provides links to lawyers and financial planners specializing in the needs of seniors. You can visit the Web site at **www.aarp.org/revmort**.

Administration on Aging

The Administration on Aging is a government agency, a division of the Department of Health and Human Resources, which specializes in providing information and resources for America's seniors. The Administration on Aging Web site provides resources for seniors including health, housing, and financial information. The Web site offers resources to help seniors with everyday living expenses such as food, housing, medical expenses, and utilities, complete with links to local, state, and federal agencies.

The Administration on Aging provides a downloadable resource guide on reverse mortgages that includes links to consumer information, federal resources, mortgage information resources, and state and local programs. This report also links to numerous articles and reports about reverse mortgages to help you make the most informed decision you can. You can visit the Administration on Aging Web site at **www.aoa.dhhs.gov** or call 800-677-1116 to request information packets.

BenefitsCheckup.org

The Internet brings a wealth of information right into your home, and much of this information is free. The National Council on Aging sponsors this Web site that helps seniors find local, state, and federal programs to help cover the costs of healthcare, prescriptions, utility bills, housing, meals, and much more. When you visit the site, you can complete a questionnaire that requires yes or no answers. Once you complete the questionnaire, you receive a printable personalized report showing a list of programs that you may qualify for in your area, complete with telephone numbers and directions for signing up for the programs. You can even sign up for some programs directly from the Web site. Some of the partners that make this Web site possible include AARP, Humana, Pfizer, Synergy, and other pharmaceutical, insurance, and utility companies. The site is easy to use and provides lots of information for resources that could possibly help you to wait as long as possible for the reverse mortgage to get the most benefit. You can visit the Web site at **www.benefitcheckup.org.**

Fannie Mae

Fannie Mae started out in 1938 as a government agency established by Franklin D. Roosevelt as a means of helping more families become homeowners during a period when finances were uncertain in every community in the United States. Many people think Fannie Mae is still a government agency, but Fannie Mae was rechartered by Congress in 1968 and is now a shareholder-owned company that is funded with private capital.

Although a privately funded organization, Fannie Mae continues to provide affordable housing to Americans. Fannie Mae has two versions of the reverse mortgage: the Home Keeper and the Home Keeper for Purchase. Both are explained in detail in Chapter 3. Fannie Mae does not actually lend the money for these loans. Much like HUD, Fannie Mae connects lenders and borrowers, and Fannie Mae insures the Home Keeper and Home Keeper for Purchase reverse mortgages.

The Fannie Mae Web site offers several downloadable pamphlets to help you better understand the reverse mortgage and decide which loan is right for you, including a fact sheet for both the Home Keeper reverse mortgage and the Home Equity Conversion Mortgage from HUD. The Web site also offers a downloadable, comprehensive list of lenders in each state who offer both the Home Keeper and the HECM reverse mortgages, and also a section that links you directly to the lenders' Web sites.

Counseling is a requirement for any type of reverse mortgage. The Fannie Mae site has a downloadable consumer's guide called "Money From Home" that is a required counseling tool. This guide gives an in-depth look at the types of reverse mortgages and provides information to help you decide which reverse mortgage is right for you. To take advantage of the information and tools available from Fannie Mae, you can visit their Web site at **www. fanniemae.com** or call 800-732-6643 to request a copy of their literature.

Reverse Mortgage Counselor

A reverse mortgage loan is a major decision in a senior's life. While it is everyone's wish for seniors to enjoy their retirement in comfort, it is also important that seniors have the tools to make the right decisions. For this reason, all reverse mortgage loans require counseling by an approved reverse mortgage counselor. The reverse mortgage counselor's role as a part of your reverse mortgage support team is discussed in-depth in Chapter 13.

Meeting with a reverse mortgage counselor is the first step toward making your reverse mortgage a reality. He or she discusses your needs, which options are available to you, and the impact each one has on your home, finances, and family. The reverse mortgage counselor is not there to tell you what to do or make the decision for you; rather he or she is there to give you an unbiased opinion, help you sort through the options, and make your own decisions.

Financial Freedom

As has been discussed, not all reverse mortgages are backed by government agencies. Some are backed by private agencies such as Financial Freedom (see Chapter 4). While Fannie Mae and HUD offer lending solutions for everyone, each of the reverse mortgages backed by these organizations has lending caps that limit the amount of money you can borrow. Financial Freedom offers both of these products, but they also offer a loan for people who own high-value homes so these people can take advantage of the equity in their homes.

Financial Freedom has been around for a long time. This company participated in the development of the reverse mortgage concept during the 1980s. Financial Freedom specializes only in reverse mortgages; that is the only loan this company offers. This type of specialization makes them one of the most trusted companies for the reverse mortgage.

The Financial Freedom Web site offers a substantial amount of information and literature. The site has answers to frequently asked questions, an explanation of how the process works, consumer safeguards, a special section for the families of seniors, and video success stories from seniors whose lives have been made better because of the reverse mortgage. Financial Freedom also offers a free newsletter as well as a free video to help you decide if a reverse mortgage is right for you. Visit the Financial Freedom Web site at **www.financialfreedom.com.**

HUD

The U. S. Department of Housing and Urban Development (HUD) offers one of the most popular reverse mortgages — the HEC, or Home Equity Conversion Mortgage (see Chapter 2). The HUD Web site offers a vast amount of information covering everything from government agencies that assist seniors with medical, housing, and living expenses to information about the HECM loan for both borrowers and lenders.

The HUD Web site includes a HECM mortgage calculator that you can use to determine how much you may be allowed for your home, as well as an explanation of the HECM loan. The Web site also links you with HUD-approved counselors and lenders, both of which are required for reverse mortgage loans. If you would like information from a live person, the Web site also helps you locate a HUD office near you. To take advantage of the information offered on the HUD Web site, visit **www.hud.gov/buying/ rvrsmort.cfm.**

NOTE: If you suspect that you are a victim of a scam regarding an HECM reverse mortgage, report the incident to HUD by calling 800-358-6216.

NRMLA

The National Reverse Mortgage Lenders Association (NRMLA) is a group of reverse mortgage lenders who have joined together to offer seniors the best possible service. Together, this group stays abreast of changes in laws and any other factors that affect the reverse mortgage. Not only does this group share educational resources with one another, they also have a Web site that provides information for seniors researching the benefits of a reverse mortgage loan.

The NRMLA's Web site, at **www.reversemortgage.org**, offers three downloadable consumer guides for seniors, a reverse mortgage calculator, and links to reverse mortgage news items as well as new developments concerning reverse mortgages. The NRMLA also provides two downloadable pamphlets to help seniors plan for long-term healthcare in the home by using funds from a reverse mortgage. One pamphlet is for seniors who need help now, and one is for seniors who are healthy now but foresee needing care in the future.

One interesting aspect of the NRMLA Web site is the borrower profiles — a section that shows how some borrowers used the funds gained from the reverse mortgage — which contains everything from in-home care to being free of debt to building an airplane!

13

Putting Together Your Support Team

One of the most important aspects of the reverse mortgage process is having an adequate support team. A reverse mortgage is a major decision, and it is always better to face a major decision with information and support from people around you. Your team can include family, friends, your pastor, a reverse mortgage counselor, your attorney, your accountant or financial planner, the lender or originator of the loan, and a broker. All of these people play an important role in helping you determine what your future needs will be, what resources you have available to you now, what you will have available in the future, and what purpose you want to accomplish by getting a reverse mortgage. This is the team you should work closely with until the last details of your loan are in place. In this chapter, we discuss each member and his or her role, and how he or she can help you to make decisions that are right for you and your entire family.

The Most Important Team Member — You

The most important member of your reverse mortgage team is you. It is important to discuss the reverse mortgage with other members of your team; but the ultimate decision is yours to make. This is your home, your equity, and your future. You know what your needs are now and you know what your needs in the future will be; for example, how near or far you are from needing help caring for yourself, what assistance you need with bills, or what you would like to do now that you have the time.

Your Children

Your grown children should be an important part of your team. Although, they probably will not admit it, once you mention the reverse mortgage, their inheritance or how they will pay back the loan may be a concern for them. That is a normal reaction. Your children want what is best for you and they are aware that there are scammers waiting to prey on seniors. While you may think that it is your business and that you are perfectly capable of making your own financial decisions, it is important that you involve your children in the process. You do not have to let them make your decisions for you; but you should discuss the reverse mortgage with them.

Long before you make your final decision and start the process of obtaining a reverse mortgage, you should discuss with your children how it will affect them. During this discussion (or discussions) you need to decide how and when the loan will be repaid, and what your plans are for your home, especially if your children grew up in the home or the home holds some other significant value to your children.

You do not have to let your children make the decision for you if you are capable of making your own financial decisions, but it is important that you involve them in the process and listen to their points of view and understand their feelings. Once you have come to a decision, your children may be the most supportive members of your team.

Your Friends

Whether to include your close friends as a part of your team is a decision that you have to make. You may be able to get a more unbiased opinion from your friends than you can get from your children. Or you may have a friend who has obtained a reverse mortgage, and in this case, discussing it with him or her could provide you with some insight into the process and what you can expect. Your friend may even be able to give you some guidance on how to introduce the subject to your children. We often have resources that can provide information and support at our disposal, and close friends often fall into that category.

Your Pastor

Some pastors offer personal counseling to members of their congregation. If your pastor does, and you like to seek the advice of your spiritual leader before making major decisions, your pastor can offer an unbiased view of the reverse mortgage process and your needs. For those who may think they should feel guilty for using something that would normally be a part of their children's inheritance, your pastor can also offer you advice on how to handle these feelings and do what is in your best interest.

The Reverse Mortgage Counselor

One of the requirements of obtaining a reverse mortgage is a session with a HUD-approved reverse mortgage counselor. The session with the reverse mortgage counselor is free, so it does not require an out-of-pocket expense; and the counseling certificate that the counselor gives you is needed to process the reverse mortgage. HUD-approved counselors specialize in counseling seniors about reverse mortgages. This means the counselor has up-to-date information and can help you determine how the reverse mortgage will affect you, your family, and your home.

An HECM loan requires that certain information be a part of the counseling session and be listed on the certificate your counselor gives you. This information includes alternatives to reverse mortgages, so the borrower can find the best solution to meet his or her needs. The counselor should also discuss other home equity conversion options, such as the Home Keeper and the Financial Freedom Cash Account. The counselor can explain in detail the financial impact of the HECM, and also any effect the loan may have on your taxes, your estate, and your eligibility for state and federal programs, such as Medicaid and food stamps.

An important question your counselor will ask you is if you have signed a contract with someone who charges a fee for information about, access to, or at the closing of an HECM. All information regarding reverse mortgages, including access to counselors and lenders, can be found on the HUD Web site or requested by telephone from HUD free of charge. You should never pay anyone for this information. If anyone does try to charge you a fee for access to this information, you should report the incident to HUD.

Members of your support team, such as your family or friends, are encouraged to attend the counseling session with you. Be aware that your finances will be discussed during this meeting. Be sure that you are comfortable with your support team learning the details of your financial state. In some cases, your children may want you to do what is necessary to ensure a comfortable retirement, but they may have some doubts about a reverse mortgage being the solution. The session with the counselor can help them to better understand the effects the reverse mortgage will have on the home and your future finances, as well as their inheritance and responsibility when the loan becomes due. If your children are being extremely difficult about the reverse mortgage, it may be best to attend the counseling session with a close friend and present the information to your children in a private setting.

As mentioned above, you should only bring someone you do not mind hearing the details of your finances. During the session, the counselor discusses your current finances, the reason you want the reverse mortgage, and the effects it will have on your finances, your home, and your estate. To accomplish this, you need to bring as much of your current financial data as possible. With this information, you and the counselor can find the reverse mortgage option that best fits your needs.

Be ready to provide the following:

- Your monthly expenses — mortgage payment (if any), utilities, drug expenses, and so forth

- Your semi-annual or annual expenses — auto or home insurance, taxes, and so forth

- An accounting of any outstanding debts

- A list of your current financial needs

- A list of projected future financial needs

- The estimated value of your home as well as the condition of your home. At this point, you may not have had an appraisal done, so an estimate is fine.

During the session, the counselor discusses with you how long you intend to stay in your home. If you are not planning to stay in your home for more than a couple of years, the reverse mortgage may not be your best option, because once you are no longer using the home as your primary residence, the loan becomes due and payable. Your reverse mortgage counselor also discusses the reason you want the reverse mortgage loan and provides alternative solutions. The counselor is not trying to talk you out of the loan; rather he or she is there to help you make the most informed decision you can.

Your reverse mortgage counselor looks at all of the facts surrounding your financial situation, your current and future needs, and the value of your home. He or she then recommends a course of action for you. Just as with your family and friends, this is only a recommendation; the ultimate decision is yours to make. However, HUD-approved counselors specialize in reverse mortgage counseling, so it may be in your best interest to take their recommendations seriously.

Once you have completed your counseling session, be sure you sign the counseling certificate and take it with you. Without it, you are not eligible for the HECM or the Home Keeper loan; this certificate is one of the first things your lender will ask for.

CASE STUDY: GREENPATH, INC.

Diane Reichel, certified credit counselor
and regional group manager

Eve Pidgeon, communications manager

I have a great job. As a certified credit counselor at GreenPath, Inc., I help people every day. Whether they are looking to solve financial problems or achieve financial goals, I am always finding a solution, outlining a direction, and serving as a guide to a balanced budget. Sometimes, the path leads to reverse mortgages.

Typically, clients come to GreenPath for help. They need guidance to resolve credit issues, reduce debt, stop collection calls, and succeed in paying their monthly living expenses and credit obligations. While the "answer" is usually in better money management, occasionally, the need is for finding more cash, increasing income to make paying for expenses an easier task. And, since many of our clients are seniors on fixed incomes, the topic of reverse mortgages arises frequently. While they can often be a perfect solution to a big problem, they aren't right for everyone all the time.

In spite of the fact that reverse mortgage counseling in mandatory, people should want to explore the details of these opportunities. There are plenty of counselors out there now and their availability is growing every day. As a result of increased competition for reverse mortgage customers, I believe we will also see more aggressive marketing for these products. Rather than take the ads at face value and just jump in, I hope people will remember that the best choice is an educated choice. After all, a reverse mortgage can be a wonderful opportunity for some, helping them stay in their homes longer. They can also help people balance their budgets so that they can live more comfortably in their later years. But there are financial consequences that they should be aware of as well. Breaking down the facts, myths, risks, and rewards of reverse mortgages helps ensure their decision is based on understanding, not blind hope or simple desperation.

Since GreenPath is certified by HUD as a housing counseling agency, our counselors are obliged ethically, professionally, and legally to ensure seniors are clearly informed of all options, obligations, and requirements when we counsel them about reverse mortgages. We counsel people on a number of points, including the factor of time and the issue of impact on their estate. It usually takes about an hour to review reverse mortgages — and their pros and cons — in detail, analyze the individual's unique situation, and provide them with the facts they need to determine if a reverse mortgage is, indeed, the right choice. It's an hour very well spent.

There is so much people don't realize about reverse mortgages. For instance, all three types of plans (FHA-insured, lender-insured, and uninsured) charge origination

CASE STUDY: GREENPATH, INC.

fees and closing costs. Insured plans also charge insurance premiums, and some plans charge mortgage servicing fees. Additionally, interest is added to the loan balance each month and the total interest owed increases significantly over time as the interest compounds. All of this can eat up a significant part of a home's equity.

A lot of our clients are also surprised to learn that they keep the title to their homes, so they continue to be responsible for taxes, repairs, and maintenance. GreenPath counselors always help clients make sure they will still have room in the budget for these critical expenses. We also make certain that clients understand that the loan becomes due, with interest, when it is no longer their primary residence. So, if you move, sell your home, die, or take a permanent placement in an assisted living facility, someone must repay that debt. If the intention was always to sell the home to repay the loan, then there are no surprises. If the intention was to preserve the home for heirs of the estate, the situation can be problematic.

As a counselor, I want clients to understand the effects of reverse mortgages on both their current financial situation and on their estate's. For that reason, it is really nice when heirs attend counseling sessions, too. That way everyone likely to be involved — now and later — understands the ramifications of the reverse mortgage decision. If the heirs wish to retain the home and they are eligible for a mortgage, the reverse mortgage can be refinanced into a forward mortgage at the time it becomes due. If they are not eligible, though, they'll have to sell the house or repay the debt some other way.

All things considered, the advantages of a reverse mortgage often outweigh the disadvantages. In a lot of cases, just getting out from under a mortgage payment relieves the budget enough to allow someone to meet all of his or her other obligations. I recently counseled a senior who fell behind on her mortgage while juggling that payment with lots of medical bills, credit card debt, and day-to-day living expenses.

Her reverse mortgage stopped a foreclosure, allowed her to remain in her home, and gave her the ability to meet all of her other financial obligations. It gave her financial freedom and that is certainly something to be happy about.

I have also seen cases where the budget balances, but the individual is unable to save monthly for property taxes, insurance, and emergencies. Often they may need to make home repairs, but are unable to fit a loan payment into the monthly budget. If there is not a local government program that can help them with these issues, a reverse mortgage loan or line of credit can be a great source of funds for these activities.

If, during counseling, my clients determine that a reverse mortgage option will work for them, we explore the options of lump sum, line of credit, and monthly payments, and I educate them about potential solutions for their specific needs. If a reverse mortgage is not the answer, I can review other available alternatives with them. The

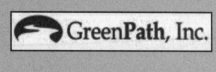
Other Financial and Legal Advisors

Although HUD-approved reverse mortgage counseling is the only legal advice required, some people may prefer to seek the advice of other legal representatives. If you use an attorney to handle financial matters, such as your will, you can seek your attorney's advice concerning your reverse mortgage. He or she can advise you about how the reverse mortgage will affect your estate and what changes, if any, need to be made to your will or other documents.

If your finances and estate are complicated, you may use a financial planner, an accountant, or other professional. In this case, you may want to seek their advice in addition to the advice of the reverse mortgage counselor. These options are not required, but if this is your usual pattern for handling financial dealings, your personal financial planner or accountant may be able to offer you additional insight about how the reverse mortgage will impact your individual situation.

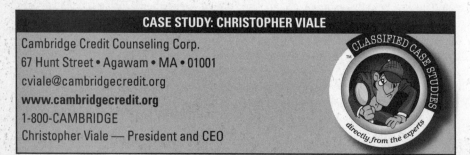

CASE STUDY: CHRISTOPHER VIALE

With higher medical costs and longer life expectancies, people who may have been under-prepared for retirement are turning to reverse mortgages in increasing numbers. Unlike other options to tap home equity, the owner isn't burdened by monthly payments. The reverse mortgage payments the homeowner receives are not considered taxable income; therefore, Social Security benefits shouldn't be affected. Another benefit is that the homeowners' status doesn't change — they maintain ownership of their home. It's also encouraging that counseling applicants receive mandatory counseling prior to securing a reverse mortgage. There may be other financial choices at their disposal that might have been overlooked. Consumers should always be fully aware of the potential benefits and consequences of their choices.

It is important to remember that a reverse mortgage is still a loan, and it does carry some hefty costs. One of the potential costs that can prove to be burdensome is the repayment of any outstanding claims upon the home. Because the reverse mortgage has a growing balance, lenders require that it be recorded as a first mortgage. Lenders will allow that a portion of the reverse mortgage be used for this purpose, but it will greatly reduce the homeowner's access to the funds. The fact that there is a first mortgage may disqualify a homeowner from eligibility altogether. Should an individual's first mortgage and any additional liens, including home equity loans or IRS liens, exceed forty percent of the home's value, they may not be eligible for a reverse mortgage.

As we've seen in the fallout of the sub-prime housing crisis, the amount of interest paid by the homeowner can have a dramatic effect on their monthly finances. Homeowners should attempt to negotiate a favorable fixed interest rate for a reverse mortgage, just as they would with any other type of loan. And just like traditional mortgages, there are other costs that may be associated with a reverse mortgage, such as closing costs or points, and mortgage insurance. Prospective applicants need to consider all of these factors.

In the credit counseling industry, we help a wide variety of people understand their options in dealing with their financial obligations. It is especially gratifying to help senior citizens develop sound financial plans — they've contributed so much to our way of life. Ensuring that seniors can enjoy a worry-free retirement is one reason our counselors come to work every day.

As with any financial move, individuals considering a reverse mortgage should consult a financial professional and, in this case, an attorney. The world of personal finance evolves rapidly, and in the case of senior citizens, there are likely more factors that must be addressed, including trusts, and Medicaid and Social Security eligibility, and so forth. Individuals should receive as much credible input as they can when deciding upon such an expensive and important option.

Lender or Originator

Without a lender, or originator, the reverse mortgage is not possible. When you have your counseling session, your reverse mortgage counselor can provide you with a list of lenders in your area. However, the counselor cannot recommend a lender to you, nor can a lender recommend a counselor to you. Each is only allowed to provide you with a list of possible candidates. You may already have a lender in mind if you have used a certain lender in the past or if a close friend has recommended one. You need to make sure the lender is a HUD-approved lender for reverse mortgages.

If you do not have a particular lender in mind, you can find lists of HUD-approved lenders through most of the resources discussed in Chapter 12. If you have not decided on your lender, shop around, just as you would with any major purchase or decision. Meet with several lenders to find the best lender that fits your needs. Remember, just because you meet with a lender does not mean you owe the lender your business. Choose the lender that gives you the best options to fit your circumstances.

If you have reached the age to qualify for a reverse mortgage, you may have received advertisements from lenders seeking your business. If you belong to a seniors group, a few lenders may have even held seminars. So, finding a lender is not going to be a hard job; however, finding the right lender for you may require a little due diligence on your part.

As has been discussed, the first thing you should do is check to see if the lender is listed on the HUD-approved list of lenders. It might be a good idea to check the National Reverse Mortgage Lenders Association (NRMLA) as well. To become a member of the NRMLA, lenders must agree to uphold a certain code of conduct. While this does not ensure that all lenders on the list uphold this code of conduct — there are always exceptions to the rule — your chances of finding an ethical lender are greater. Another benefit to choosing from the NRMLA list is that the lender must retain a current license in the state they practice to retain membership. Having a license in the state they practice in requires ongoing education, so these lenders have up-to-date information about changes in reverse mortgage laws and practices, which means you get the best possible solutions to meet your financial needs.

Here is a checklist to help you find the best lender to meet your needs:

- Lender is HUD approved.   • Lender is on NRMLA list.

- Lender is licensed in your state.

- Compare length of time each lender has been a reverse mortgage provider.

- Compare which lenders also service the loan (you may get better rates for your servicing fees if the lender services the loan rather than using an outside company).

- Compare origination fees, servicing fees, and closing costs for each lender. A lender may have the lowest fees, but that does not mean that lender is the best choice. Be sure to compare the other points in this list as well.

- Compare how each lender works to meet your specific needs. Weed out lenders that are interested in writing a loan without doing so in a manner that is beneficial to your circumstances. Be sure that you are comfortable with your lender and do not feel pressured into doing things the lender's way.

- Choose a lender that takes the time to explain the loan to you so that you understand every aspect of the loan before you sign. This lender should have materials, such as brochures and pamphlets, to help you better understand the loan.

- Choose a lender that requires background checks for employees and can protect your privacy. Ask each lender about these things. If it offends them, you do not want to use them.

Summing It Up

As mentioned in the beginning of this chapter, a reverse mortgage is a major financial decision that affects not only you; it affects your future finances, your home, and your estate. Always keep in mind that the final decision is yours. Your team's responsibility is to advise you, help you learn everything you need to know, and support your decisions. Each member of your reverse mortgage team is important.

The lender you choose is of utmost importance. Once you make the decision, have the support of family and friends, have attended a counseling session, and are ready to choose a lender, keep in mind that the lender is there for you, and not the other way around.

If you do not feel comfortable with a lender, even after you have signed a loan application, you do not have to go through with the loan. You can stop at any point during the process up until three days after you sign the closing of the loan. Be aware that there are lenders out there who are unethical. This may be rare, especially if you choose a lender from the HUD list or the NRMLA list, but it does happen. If your lender makes promises that seem too good to be true and do not reflect what you have learned about the reverse mortgage, or if your lender is more interested in his or her commission than ensuring you get the most benefit from the reverse mortgage, you can stop the process and find another lender.

Treat the reverse mortgage as you would any major financial decision. Learn all you can, seek the advice of family, friends, or professionals, and know your rights.

14

Step-by-Step Through the Loan Process

This chapter takes you step-by-step through the reverse mortgage process, from the moment you consider a reverse mortgage to closing.

Step One: Become Informed

Before you make the decision about the reverse mortgage, learn everything you can. As outlined in Chapter 12, the resources are numerous. If you have a computer or can access a computer at your local library, visit the Web sites listed in Chapter 12. If you do not have access to a computer or feel more comfortable with written material, contact your local HUD office and request material. You can also call AARP's toll-free number and request information be sent to you.

Step Two: Decide What Your Needs or Wants Are

Most people who decide to get a reverse mortgage have one thing in common: They are house-rich and cash-poor. This affects people in different ways. Some people struggle to make ends meet and cannot meet their basic needs, such as food, utilities, and medical care. Some people can meet their monthly expenses but have trouble paying bills such as property taxes and insurance premiums, or do not have money to meet unexpected emergencies such as car repair and medical bills. Some people can meet their monthly expenses and have money put aside for emergencies, but would like to be free to spend more time with family or do things to help their children, or maybe purchase a new car to replace an undependable car. Some people can meet their needs but wish to live in a warmer climate during the winter months. Some people can meet their needs but would like to take a special trip or be free to travel at leisure. Whatever your needs or wants, you should list these and decide if using the equity in your home is the solution you want to use.

Step Three: Introduce the Idea to Your Children

If you have children, you should introduce the idea to them as soon as possible. This gives everyone time to voice his or her opinions and get comfortable with the idea of the reverse mortgage. Remember, this is a major decision; even though your children will not make the final decision, it is considerate to share your decision with them and decide together how and when the loan is to be repaid and who is responsible for making sure it happens.

Step Four: Counseling

The next step is to find a HUD-approved counselor and make an appointment (see in Chapter 13). When making the appointment, it is important to check with anyone you want to attend so that the appointment is made at a convenient time for everyone involved. Remember to take your financial records with you and to write down any questions you may have so that these can be covered during the counseling session.

Step Five: Decisions

Use the knowledge you have gained and the advice from the counselor to decide what type of mortgage is right for your situation. If your choice is the HECM or the Home Keeper, you need to decide if you want a monthly or annual ARM. Decide how you want to receive the funds: lump sum, monthly payments, credit line, or combination.

CASE STUDY: HERMAN C JENSEN

Herman C Jensen, Retired Truck Driver
Alma, Nebraska

I am a retired truck driver, having retired after selling my last truck in 1996. I am no longer able to work full-time at a decent-paying job. But I still work part-time during the harvest season here in Nebraska, hauling corn, soybeans, and wheat from the field to elevators in nearby towns. Even then, it is hard to make ends meet in today's economy.

In 1995, my wife and I moved to Alma, Nebraska from Colorado. With a population of slightly over 1,200 people, Alma offered the perks of small-town living, the main two being that the cost of living is lower than in a larger town or city and property is reasonably priced. Add to that the fact that most of my wife's children and grandchildren live in Alma and it made this the ideal place for us to spend our retirement. When we moved to Alma, we had enough in savings to pay cash for our home.

When I sold my last truck, we were able to replenish our savings account. However, we decided to loan our son-in-law enough money to start his own business seal-coating asphalt runways at airports. This arrangement worked well until a combination of diabetes and heart trouble resulted in my son-in-law having quintuple (5) bypass surgery, leaving him unable to run his business. Since the repayment of the loan stopped with my son-in-law's illness, and the cost of living continues to rise (even in a small town), I knew we had to do something to ease the financial strain.

Since I paid cash when I purchased our home, there was plenty of equity. After carefully weighing our options and comparing the reverse mortgage with a regular bank mortgage, we decided that the reverse mortgage would best suit our needs. With the increase in property value since we bought our home, the portion of our equity that we were allowed with the reverse mortgage was within a few dollars of what we originally paid for our home. Add to that the fact that we never have to make payments or repay the loan as long as one of us lives in the home, and we now have enough money to pay our bills without fear of losing our home, and it is a win-win situation. Would I recommend the reverse mortgage to other seniors? The answer is yes! I recommend the reverse mortgage to anyone who meets the requirements for a reverse mortgage. It has sure taken a burden off of my shoulders. If you are struggling to make ends meet, I would certainly recommend that you put your equity

CASE STUDY: HERMAN C JENSEN

to use for you. A reverse mortgage can give you peace of mind and can keep you from being a burden on your family because you don't have to ask for help. The reverse mortgage allows you to remain self-sufficient throughout your retirement. As long as you keep the property taxes and insurance paid, keep the home in good repair, and live in the home, you never have to make payments and you have the money to take care of yourself. What more could you ask for?

Step Six: The Loan Process

1. Use the resources outlined in Chapter 12 to find a lender. Remember to shop around if you do not have a particular lender in mind.

2. Set up a meeting with your lender.

3. Apply for your loan. The application process begins by filling out a Residential Loan Application for Reverse Mortgages. Your originator asks you to sign the application for reverse mortgages. At this point, you are not committed to taking out the reverse mortgage; you are only qualifying for the loan. At any time during the process, you can decide that a reverse mortgage is not the solution you are looking for. At this time, you are asked for the one expense that you must pay for out-of-pocket: the appraisal fee. Some questions are simple, such as name, address, and so forth. Be sure to take the following documentation with you so that you have the necessary information to complete the application:

    •　Monthly income

    •　Estimated value of your home (an appraisal comes later)

    •　Social Security card(s)

    •　Copy of deed

    •　Picture ID

- Documentation showing any lien on your home such as existing mortgage

- Counseling certificate

4. Get an appraisal on your home. It is required for federally regulated loans that the appraiser is licensed or certified by the Office of Real Estate Appraisers. Each state requires that appraiser to uphold a code of ethics and meet high standards. Unlike choosing a lender, you do not have to be concerned about finding an appraiser on your own. In most cases, the lender chooses the appraiser and sets up an appointment. It is not required that you be there for the appraisal, but is helpful in case the appraiser needs to see documents pertaining to permits and repairs. The appraiser may also ask you a few questions and point out repairs that need to be made. Before the appraiser arrives, be sure that your home is clean and tidy. The nicer your home looks, the better the result of the appraisal. When the appraiser arrives, do not follow him or her around. Let him or her come to you to ask questions. The appraiser is responsible for placing a fair-market value on your home. To achieve this, he or she considers the condition and safety of your home, and compares your home with others in your neighborhood. The appraiser takes photos of your home and other homes in your neighborhood. These photos become a part of your appraisal report and aid the appraiser in making a fair evaluation of your home. These photos can also be used by the appraiser to point out his or her reasoning should you dispute the result of the report.

5. After the appraisal, you once again meet with your lender. At this meeting, you discuss the results of the appraisal. Your lender tells you if any repairs need to be made for your home to qualify. Your home must meet the safety requirements determined by HUD. If any repairs are needed, your lender works with you to arrange these

repairs. Your lender is also able to tell you how much you can get with your reverse mortgage loan.

6. Once everything is in order, it is time to close your loan. At this meeting, your lender reviews everything about your loan with you. This is information that you have already been over, but must go over one final time before signing the final papers: the type of reverse mortgage you chose, the type of ARM, and the type of payment you chose. The repairs are discussed, if any were needed. If you made arrangements to have the repairs made after the closing of the loan, your lender will ask you to sign a repair addendum. By signing this document, you are agreeing to get the repairs done, and you may be required to get them done by a certain date. If you sign the agreement and fail to get the repairs done as outlined, your lender has the right to terminate your loan. So, be sure you understand the addendum before you sign it and make certain that you follow through. At this meeting, you are presented with a Total Annual Loan Cost (TALC). This document outlines how much you pay for your reverse mortgage. Remember, most of the fees are rolled into the loan and deducted from the amount you actually receive. The TALC outlines the principal loan amount, interest you pay, origination fees, servicing fees, closing costs, and any other fees associated with your reverse mortgage. Once everything is finished, the last step is for you to initial and sign the required documents. Be sure to ask any questions you have and thoroughly understand the documents before signing. If the document requires a notary, your lender will have one present.

7. Once you have signed the closing documents, you have three days to change your mind. This is called your right of rescission.

15
Money in Hand

Now that you have taken the steps necessary to apply for and close your reverse mortgage loan, you have money in hand and are wondering what to do with it. First, eliminate any debt that you can. For instance, now would be a great time to pay off a few credit cards. If possible, the best option would be to eliminate your debts until you are down to the basic needs. Another good idea is to splurge a little. Go out for a nice dinner, go to the theater, go to a live musical, or take a weekend trip to your favorite getaway. Do not get too wild with the money before you make some practical decisions about what you need to spend now and what can wait until later. Be sure to do any repairs that need to be done right away and service your vehicle. Little things like this make it easier on you in the long run.

We discussed in detail in Chapter 6 the types of payment available. In this chapter, we will discuss some of the things you should do with your loan and how the payments work.

Taking Care of Debts

The first thing you should do with your money is to take care of any debt incurred during the process of obtaining the loan and any debt that affects your home. If you have not paid for your appraisal, this is one of the first things that you need to pay. Next, you should pay off any outstanding mortgage on your home. Finally, before you begin spending money, you need to take care of any repairs that were stipulated in the loan. These three things are required before all of your loan can be released. At this point, your available funds may not match your total loan funds. This is because lenders earmark the money needed to complete these three steps. This is to ensure these things are done in a timely manner. The lender deducts the amount of repairs and mortgage from your loan balance and pays for these repairs. Before you receive any funds from your reverse mortgage, your lender makes sure that any outstanding mortgage is paid in full, clearing the deed for the reverse mortgage, and that the repairs are paid for out of the earmarked money. Once any liens are paid off and the required repairs done, any funds left over are added to your available balance.

Lump Sum Payment

The lump sum payment is the quickest way to get your money; however, this type of payment plan may not be wise for everyone. Once all the forms have been signed and the loan has been recorded in the county records, the escrow or title company prepares a check for you for the entire amount of the loan. This check can be mailed to you or can be direct deposited into your bank account.

While the lump sum payment puts more money into your hands, this is the type that can also cause the most trouble. If not handled properly, once your funds are gone, there will not be any more. It is important that you plan ahead if this is the method of payment you choose.

Before you get the lump sum payment, sit down and go over all of your finances. The goal for most people is to get their living expenses down so that monthly expenses include only basic needs: utilities, food, and medicine. Make a list of your monthly expenses as well as credit card and other revolving account expenses.

When you receive your lump sum payment, pay the balance of your credit cards and revolving accounts such as furniture and car payments. You should also have a plan to put a portion of the lump sum payment into savings. Make an appointment with your banker and go over your options. There are many ways you can earn an interest on your money so that the money in savings can grow.

If you can handle some of your financial needs, but have difficulty handling major decisions, you have the option of having a family member oversee your funds and give them to you as needed. In some cases, a family member may have durable power of attorney and can make decisions for you. However, you should use caution when appointing someone to handle your money. The person should be someone you trust completely, and someone you do not mind having access to your finances.

The lump sum option can work well for people who have major debt that needs to be taken care of right away. The key to making the lump sum successful is saving part of the funds for a later date. As mentioned earlier, this is the only payment you receive, and it is your responsibility to use it wisely.

Monthly Payment

The monthly payment is another method of getting money from a reverse mortgage. While it is not ideal for repaying large debts, it does provide a steady monthly income. Should the need arise to make a major purchase; you have to save your monthly checks until you have enough. This is one of the drawbacks of monthly payments; but many people feel knowing the check is going to be there each month outweighs the need to save for special purchases.

There are two ways to receive your monthly payments: paper check in the mail or direct deposit right into your bank account. A lot of people prefer the safety and security offered by direct deposit; many have their social security checks deposited directly to their accounts. This eliminates the need to make a trip to the bank and gives you the security of knowing that the money will be there on a certain date each month.

Some people prefer receiving a check; it makes them feel better to see the money before they deposit it in the bank. Of course, the money ends up in the same place, so direct deposit is a safer alternative. You never have to worry about the check getting lost in the mail and delaying payment, and it saves you a trip to the bank.

The greatest advantage of the monthly check is knowing that, for as long as you keep the loan, the check arrives in your bank account each and every month. If you chose a term loan, the check is deposited each month for the length of the term. Monthly payments give you peace of mind because you know you will have the money each month to help with living expenses or to provide the little extras that will make your retirement more enjoyable.

It is a good idea to start the habit of saving a portion of your monthly check with the first payment. This makes it easier for you to save for large expenses and provides an emergency fund if needed. Be sure to check with your banker to find the best savings plans, so that the money you save earns you the most interest. It is always a smart thing to continue to make your money grow, even though you know you will get a check each month.

Line of Credit

You may have heard of an equity line of credit. In a regular equity line of credit, the homeowner is issued a card that can be used like a credit card. This card gives the homeowner instant access to his or her funds. The reverse mortgage line of credit works a little differently. Instead of having a card that gives you instant access, you have to request a withdrawal in writing. This requires that you plan ahead.

Depending on which loan you choose, the money in your line of credit account could earn interest if you leave it in the account (the HECM). And, when the loan is due, you are only charged for the amount that you actually used. If you are getting a reverse mortgage to have funds to fall back on during an emergency, the line of credit option might work well for you.

You can withdraw a large portion of your money the first time and let the rest sit in the account earning interest until you need it. Your lender can supply you with request forms for your line of credit loan. To get your first withdrawal, fill out the request form and send it to your lender. You can use either fax or mail to send in your request. As with the monthly payment, you can choose a paper check or direct deposit. In most cases, the direct deposit reaches your account faster than a paper check.

Once you have made your first withdrawal, you simply fill out a request form and send it to your lender each time you need to use funds from your line of credit. Be sure to check with your lender during the loan process to learn of any minimums that may be required for each withdrawal.

The line of credit option gives you the freedom to control the funds obtained from your reverse mortgage, plus offers a way for your equity to continue growing. This is why the line of credit option is the most popular option for reverse mortgages.

Combos

Another choice you have is to combine the payment options. If you have a large debt that needs to be paid, but you want the security of monthly payments, you can get a portion of the loan at closing and receive the remainder in equal, monthly installments. The ability to combine the payment options allows you to free yourself from debt at the beginning of your loan, plus have money to fall back on during emergencies.

Splurge, But Carefully

Of course, the reason for obtaining a reverse mortgage is so you can enjoy your retirement without financial worries. You should treat yourself to something special when you get the loan; maybe a vacation or new appliances for your home. There are many ways you can use your money to make life more pleasant for yourself.

How carefree you are with your money depends on your financial situation. If you need the reverse mortgage to provide basic needs, you need to be a little more careful with your money. However, do not let this stop you from spoiling yourself a little. After all, you deserve it. You are the best judge of your financial situation. If you choose to take a vacation — and by all means, you should if you want to — be sure you have the funds available to pay off your debts and make your everyday life more pleasant.

If you want to take the vacation of your dreams, earmark that money and put it into a savings account. Once you have paid off your debts, take a vacation and enjoy yourself. By taking care of your debts first, you are ensuring yourself that once you return from your vacation, your life does not fall back into the constant struggle it was before your reverse mortgage. So, remember: take care of business and have fun.

Frequently Asked Questions

In this chapter, we will look at some of the questions asked most often when it comes to reverse mortgages. The answers can be found in more detail throughout the book, but here you can find basic answers to provide a quick reference about reverse mortgages.

How is a reverse mortgage different from a forward mortgage?

A reverse mortgage does exactly what the name implies; it works exactly opposite from a forward mortgage. A reverse mortgage allows you to borrow against the equity in your home and, instead of you making payments to the lender, the lender makes payments to you.

Can I get a reverse mortgage if I do not have a high credit score?

A reverse mortgage is based on your age, the condition of your home, and the amount of equity in your home. Your credit score has no affect on your qualifying for a reverse mortgage; and, since you have no payments to make, neither does your income.

What if my partner and I are not legally married? Do we qualify for a reverse mortgage?

As long as both of you are listed on the deed and meet the age qualifications, you can qualify for a reverse mortgage. The process works the same; the loan is not due as long as one party to the loan lives in the home.

Who owns my home if I get a reverse mortgage: the bank or me?

When you get a reverse mortgage, you retain title to your home. You are free to live in your home; as a matter of fact, that is one of the requirements of a reverse mortgage. You are also free to sell your home; but keep in mind, if you do, the loan must be repaid.

Can I leave my home to my heirs? And, if so, will I be leaving them a huge debt?

Since you retain ownership of your home, you can certainly leave your home to anyone you choose. At the death of the last surviving person named on the loan, the loan be payable in full. Your estate or heirs will be responsible for repaying the loan. However, they will never pay more than the value of the home, no matter the amount of the loan balance.

Can I lose my home?

It is not impossible, but rare. There are only three ways you can lose your home when you take out a reverse mortgage: move out of the home, let the property taxes get behind, or sell the home. If your home is not your primary residence for more than 12 months, the home no longer qualifies for the reverse mortgage and the loan becomes due. If you let your property taxes get behind, your home is no longer eligible for the reverse mortgage and the loan becomes due. If you see that you are getting behind in your property taxes, talk to your lender and he or she may be able to help you. If you sell your home, the loan becomes due immediately. The reverse mortgage is designed to help seniors enjoy their retirement years; in most cases, the lender will do everything possible to avoid foreclosure. It is your responsibility to work with your lender if a situation arises that could possibly result in foreclosure.

What is one spouse if over 62 but the other is under 62? Will we qualify?

In a case where one spouse is under the required age, you can qualify for a reverse mortgage if the only person listed on the deed is the person who is old enough to qualify. In a case where one spouse is under the required age, it is best to wait, if possible, and get the reverse mortgage once that spouse meets the requirements. The biggest benefit to waiting is to ensure that both of you are covered under the terms of the reverse mortgage. The ideal situation is for both of you to be listed on the loan because the loan does not become due as long as either of you live in the home. If you get the reverse mortgage before both of you qualify, you could risk the chance of leaving your spouse with having to repay the loan. So, if it is possible, it is always best to wait until both of you qualify.

How much does a reverse mortgage cost?

Just as any loan, the reverse mortgage does have fees: the origination fee, closing costs, servicing fees, and interest. Since the reverse mortgage is designed to help seniors, lenders try to keep out-of-pocket expense to a minimum. Unlike a forward mortgage, where you have to pay most of these fees up front, almost all of the fees associated with the reverse mortgage can be "rolled" into the loan. In most cases, the only out-of-pocket expense is the appraisal fee.

How much money can I get?

The amount you receive is based on certain factors: the value of your home, the maximum lending limit for the loan you choose, your age, and the current interest rate. Once the appraisal has been completed and a fair market value placed on your home, your lender uses a formula that factors in the other components to figure out the amount you are eligible for. You cannot borrow an amount that is equal to the value of your home; rather, you will get a percentage of that value. This is done to keep the loan amount from exceeding the value of your home once fees and interest is added.

What can I do with my money?

Once the loan has been closed and you have money in hand, you can spend the money any way you want. The only restrictions are any previous liens on the home must be paid immediately and any repairs that are required must be done immediately. Other than that, you are free to use the money for anything you wish to; it is your money.

Do I have to pay taxes on the money I receive from my reverse mortgage?

Each individual situation is different, so it is best to check with your attorney or financial advisor. In most cases, the money from the equity in your home is tax-free.

Can I get a reverse mortgage on my vacation home?

No, you can only get a reverse mortgage on your primary residence.

Will I lose my public assistance if I get a reverse mortgage?

Reverse mortgages do not usually affect Social Security, Medicare, or pension payments. However, a reverse mortgage could have an affect on public assistance programs where your income cannot be over a certain amount in order to qualify, such as food stamps. You need to check with these programs to find out what the income limits are.

17

Common Mistakes

Gaining knowledge from our mistakes is part of the learning process. Everyone makes mistakes. What counts is when you learn from them. It is much better to learn from other people's mistakes; not that we want other people to make mistakes, but if they have, we can use their mistakes as a learning tool. As the reverse mortgage has grown in popularity, there have been mistakes made by borrowers. That is just the natural process. Here are some of those mistakes and the some of their consequences so you can try to avoid them.

Taking Out a Reverse Mortgage Too Early

While you may qualify for a reverse mortgage at age 62, getting one as soon as you qualify is not always the wisest decision. For one thing, the older you are, the more money you get; so, if you can afford to wait, you could get more benefit from the reverse mortgage. This also applies when one spouse has not reached age 62. Once that person reaches the age of 62, re-evaluate your situation and see how much longer you can put it off because the amount you can receive is based on the age of the youngest person on the loan. Sometimes, this may not be possible, and you may need the reverse mortgage right away. In that case, you should get it. But if you can wait, you could benefit even more.

Taking Out a Reverse Mortgage Too Late

While the consensus is not to take out a reverse mortgage too early, you also do not want to wait too long. The purpose of the reverse mortgage is so you can enjoy your retirement; do not wait until it is too late for you to enjoy the money. While it is true that the older you are, the more you can get, it is important to get the money while you are still physically able to benefit from it. Consider the following scenarios:

- James heard about the reverse mortgage when he was 60 when a friend got a reverse mortgage on his home. His friend took a long-dreamed-of vacation in the Greek islands. James could not wait until he turned 62 so that he could do the same. A couple of months after he turned 62, James took out the loan and he and his wife spent the summer touring Europe. Both James and his wife are in good physical condition and plan to live at least another 20 years. Once home from their trip, they have to manage their remaining money so that it lasts the rest of their lives: once you take out a reverse mortgage and use the funds, the only option you have is to sell your home, repay the loan, and use the remaining equity for your needs.

- Martha had been dreaming of spending the winter months in a warmer climate. She wished to spend each winter in Florida. Martha does not have a lot of available cash, but she does have equity in her home. She wonders if a reverse mortgage could be the solution. Martha researches reverse mortgages on her computer and orders pamphlets and brochures so that she can make an informed decision. As she is studying, she learns that the older you are, the more money you can get. She decides that she can spend a few more winters in the colder climate so she can get the most of her reverse mortgage loan. In her 70s, she will still be young enough to enjoy the loan, yet old enough to get a higher amount.

- Sam just turned 93. While he can still get around reasonably well, his health is deteriorating. He has been waiting to take advantage of the equity in his home. He takes out a reverse mortgage and gets a lot more than he would have 20 years ago. He has always dreamed of spending a summer in Ireland, exploring the place of his ancestors. Because of his reverse mortgage, he has the money to have a wonderful trip, but his declining health keeps him from making his dream come true.

While everyone's situation is different, the key to getting the most out of your reverse mortgage is knowing when to get it and when to wait, and also knowing how long to wait. As with many things in life, it comes down to a matter of timing as well as what your particular situation is. Those in need of the reverse mortgage at age 62 to cover medical care or living expenses should take advantage of it. Not everyone can wait; but, for those who can wait a couple of years, the benefits are greater.

Taking Out a Reverse Mortgage to Pay Off Small Debts

One thing you should remember about the reverse mortgage is, although it works differently from a forward mortgage, and you receive payments rather than make them, it is a loan. Like any other loan, it comes with a price. Before you decide to take a reverse mortgage solely to pay off a few small debts, compare the price of the loan to the debts that you owe. Research other ways of repaying these debts before creating a loan that eventually has to be repaid.

For instance, if you have the money to make ends meet and provide a good quality of life for yourself, but need a few thousand dollars to make repairs to your home; you may be better off finding another solution. If you have good credit, you could probably get a personal loan from your banker that would cost less than taking out a reverse mortgage. This especially makes sense for a family home, a home where you or your children grew up, which you plan to pass down to the next generation. While your children may not have problems repaying the reverse mortgage, you want to consider alternatives before creating a debt against your home.

There are those who are living comfortably and want the reverse mortgage for special trips, a summer home, or a new car. The reverse mortgage can be the solution for you; but you have to remember that it does come with costs and it eventually has to be repaid. Do not be discouraged from getting a reverse mortgage. Just be sure to weigh all options and consequences before taking that step.

Not Planning Ahead

The purpose of the reverse mortgage is to provide you with the security to live out your retirement years in comfort. One of the biggest mistakes people make, just as with any other windfall, is not planning ahead sufficiently. You should enjoy your money; after all, you earned it. However, you should think ahead to the days when you may not be able to take care of your own finances or your own physical needs.

It is understandable that no one wants to think about a time in the future when they may not be able to take care of themselves. And, it may never actually happen. But, it is wise to have a plan in place should it happen. One of the best ways to do this is to establish a living trust.

A living trust can be set up so that you have full control over your finances until such time as you cannot make financial decisions on your own. This gives you the flexibility to decide who you want to handle your finances should that time arrive, and the power to control your finances up to that point.

A living trust can be set up by your attorney (if you use one on a regular basis) or can be set up by an attorney who specialized in issues for seniors.

Check the resources discussed in Chapter 12 for a list of elder attorneys. A living trust is not required to get a reverse mortgage, but if you set one up, you may save yourself and your family a lot of trouble. Plus, should you get to the point that your mental capacity is failing, you will not have the burden of figuring out what to do: it will already be done. Setting up a living trust is a security measure for you and your family, and ensures that your family is in a position to provide for you should the need arise.

Spending Too Fast

When you suddenly get a large amount of money, it is easy to forget the times you had to struggle; therefore, it is easy to spend. The thing to keep in mind, though, is that this money has to last you for the rest of your life, whether it is 5 years or 25. This is it, and you are responsible for making it last.

Of course, you should splurge a little and enjoy yourself. If you take out the reverse mortgage so you can take the trip of a lifetime, do that! Just be sure that once the trip is over, you have the funds to support yourself the rest of your life. This is one of the reasons that combining the payment options is a good idea. Consider a few examples of how you could make it happen. Suppose you want to take a trip when you get your money. You have a couple of choices:

- You can choose a lump sum of a portion of your loan and get the rest in monthly payments. This way, you will have the money for your trip and, once you return, the security of equal monthly installments to help with living expenses.

- You can choose a lump sum of a portion of your loan and have the remainder placed in a line of credit account. You will have the money for your trip, and, once you return, the security of knowing there are funds available for you to withdraw, should you need them.

Since you only have one chance to get a reverse mortgage, it is important that you plan ahead so the money lasts as long as you need it. One of the most common mistakes people make is "spreading the wealth" — purchasing expensive gifts for those we love. Now, this is not meant to discourage you from helping your children or grandchildren (many people actually take out reverse mortgages so they can help provide their children with a down-payment on their own home or help their grandchildren with funds for college); but spreading the wealth too thickly can make you come up short in the end.

So, before you start spending, be sure you have a plan. No one knows what the future holds, but if you use the funds from your reverse mortgage wisely, your future can be financially stable.

Failing to Maintain Your Home

Failing to maintain your home is one of the three ways your loan becomes due and payable; and when your loan becomes due and payable, it is due immediately. There is no negotiation. The other two ways your loan becomes due are if you move out or die. In most instances, you have no control over when you die. But the other two ways are "in your hands." You do have control over them.

Maintaining your home does not require you to "upgrade" every couple of years, but you should keep your home in safe condition and maintain your home's appearance. While your lender is probably not going to visit your home every few months (the lender will probably never visit your home), you should keep in mind that when the loan is due, another appraisal may be done and you want your home to be in the best condition to have a fair market value placed on it. If your children or heirs sell the home to repay the reverse mortgage, a higher value on the home means more money for them once the loan is repaid.

There are a few things that your lender will be checking. One of these is property tax. Since you retain ownership of your home, the property taxes remain your responsibility. This is why it is important for you to have a plan in place regarding the funds you receive from your reverse mortgage. You need to make sure you have the money to maintain the property taxes. There are two options available to you: you can continue paying the taxes on your own, or your property taxes can be taken straight out of your loan and the lender pays the property taxes. While you may be fully capable of handling your financial needs when you take out your reverse mortgage, the second option offers a way for you to be sure your taxes are not forgotten if you get to a point where you need help with your finances. It therefore gives you one less thing to worry about.

Homeowner's insurance is another must-have. Since you are a homeowner already, you are used to making these payments. Just as with the property tax, you have the option of having the insurance premiums taken from your loan and paid by the lender. By taking advantage of this option, you are creating peace of mind and freeing yourself from two financial burdens, and ensuring that neither of these payments will cause you to lose your loan. No matter what happens in the future, your property taxes and homeowner's insurance will be paid. Lenders also like this option because they do not have to worry about their investment; they will get the payments made to protect the investment they have in your home as a lien holder.

As discussed previously, you may be required to complete certain repairs on your home for it to qualify for a reverse mortgage. All homes must meet the safety standards set by HUD. If you chose to complete the repairs after the loan, your lender attached a repair rider to your loan. This rider specifies the repairs that you are promising to make after the loan, and in some cases specifies a certain date by which the repairs should be made. If your loan has a repair rider, it is your responsibility to have the repairs done in a timely manner (even without a specified date). Neglecting these repairs could result in a default of the loan agreement on your part, and the lender could demand repayment in full of any funds received. It is important that these repairs be done before spending the money on other things.

Not Keeping Your Loan Long Enough

One of the questions asked over and over throughout the loan process is "How long do you plan to stay in your home?" Your reverse mortgage counselor will discuss this with you as well as your lender. The length of time you plan to stay in your home should be one of the determining factors of whether or not a reverse mortgage is the right loan for you.

A reverse mortgage loan is, in fact, an expensive loan. Most of the fees involved are added directly into the loan, and each month the loan is charged servicing fees and interest. The longer you keep your loan, the more benefit you receive from your equity. If you are planning to sell your home within the first couple of years, you are better off waiting the couple of years for the money rather than paying the high interest and other fees associated with the reverse mortgage.

A reverse mortgage loan is intended to be a long-term loan and the benefits over cost ratio increases the longer you have the loan. If you keep the loan only a couple of years and repay by selling your home, you end up paying a much higher rate than you would for a forward mortgage or short-term personal loan.

A reverse mortgage loan could be the perfect solution for you if you intend on living in your home for the remainder of your life. But, if you know you will sell your home in a couple of years or move to a different climate, there are other options available that make more sense financially. This is why it is so important that you not only learn as much as possible about the reverse mortgage loan, but also explore other options. Weigh the financial impact each option will have (costs versus benefits), and make the decision that best meets your needs.

18
Current News and Legislation

s the reverse mortgage has grown in popularity, there have been many changes to make the loan as senior-friendly as possible. Loans insured by the government are also regulated by the government.

H.R. 1852 — Expanding American Homeownership Act of 2007

The Expanding American Homeownership Act of 2007 was introduced into the House of Representatives on March 29, 2007. The act was passed by the House of Representatives on September 18, 2007, and was received by the Senate on September 19, 2007. The act was read by the Senate and referred to the Committee on Banking, Housing, and Urban Affairs.

The highlights of this bill that have an impact on reverse mortgages are:

- Increases the lending limit which makes reverse mortgages available to more seniors who live in areas with high-priced housing markets.

- Sets limits on fees associated with reverse mortgage, which could result in lower fees.

- Removes the volume cap on the number of reverse mortgages that can be insured by FHA, which allows more reverse mortgages.

This bill is currently in the Senate, with several different bills created from this act, including:

- S. 2338 — FHA Modernization Act of 2007, which has been passed by the Senate.

- S. 2325 — Expanding American Homeownership Act of 2007, which was introduced in the Senate on November 8, 2007.

- S. 2490 — Reverse Mortgage Proceeds Protection Act, which was introduced in the Senate on December 14, 2007. This act focuses on protecting seniors from predatory lending by allowing HUD to use the Mortgage Premium Insurance to help pay for counseling services, and requires HUD to protect seniors from aggressive marketing tactics by writing new regulations that ensure seniors are not pressured or misled into purchasing unnecessary or unsuitable financial products.

19

Special Situations

As is the case with many financial products, each individual has a different set of circumstances. Each person is different, each home is different, and the rules in each state may be different.

Check Your State

The first thing you want to do is check the rules for your state. Some things may be different, such as lending limits. Lending limits can vary by county, so check the county you live in for the lending limits that apply to you. Hopefully, if the current legislation (see Chapter 18) goes through, the lending limits will be nationwide. If you are thinking of applying for a reverse mortgage, or if you have explored a reverse mortgage and decided to wait a few years, be sure you keep up with the ongoing legislation so that you are aware of all changes. The reverse mortgage concept is constantly being improved so seniors can get the most benefit from the equity in their homes.

If You Live in Texas

If you live in Texas, special rules apply due to differences in state laws. If you live in Texas, the only options available to you are the loans from HUD (HECM) and Fannie Mae (Home Keeper). Texas residents are not allowed to get the Cash Account from Financial Freedom. Because line of credit payment options are not allowed in the state of Texas, not only can you not get Financial Freedom's loan, you are also limited in the HECM and the Home Keeper.

The following payment options are permissible in the state of Texas:

- Lump sum

- Tenure payment plan

- Term plan

- Modified Tenure

- Modified Term

There are also stipulations with these options. For instance, if you choose the lump sum option, you must get the entire amount at closing. You cannot choose a partial lump sum with the remainder to be distributed at a certain date. If you choose the monthly payment plans, all payments are made on the first business day of the month.

An important note about using a power of attorney: If you live in Texas and you wish to use a power of attorney for the closing of a reverse mortgage, the only person that can be named as your power of attorney is your spouse.

Some loans allow you to change the type of payment (requires a fee of around $50). The only type of payment plan change that is allowed in Texas is if you have an HECM, and have prepaid a portion of your loan, you can request a recalculation of your payment amount based on the pre-paid funds. No other payment plan changes are allowed.

Although terms of the reverse mortgage may seem quite limited, you can use the options allowed to take advantage of your equity. Unfortunately, those living in homes with higher values do not have the option at this time.

Special Property Requirements

As mentioned above, each property is different. Some may have special requirements to qualify for a reverse mortgage. Let us look at a few of these special situations:

- **Private Roads and Shared Driveways.** The property must have a surface that allows passable access to both passenger and emergency vehicles; easement rights must be shown on the deed and on file with the county. You are also required to have a legal document that shows a joint maintenance agreement describing how costs of road maintenance are shared and that allows transfer of rights to heirs or future owners.

- **Extra Acreage.** If your deed shows land in excess of what is typical for homes in your area, this land is considered excess and is not included in the appraisal amount for a reverse mortgage loan. For your home to qualify, the value of the excess land itself cannot exceed the value of your home. Once a reverse mortgage has been granted, you cannot sell any land listed on the deed.

- **Wells and Septic Tanks.** If you have a well or septic tank on your property, there are certain rules that apply. Wells should be located 15 feet or more from the home and septic tanks should be located 50 feet or more from the well. If public utilities are available in your area, and the cost is less than 3 percent of the value of your home, you are required to hook up to the public system to qualify for a reverse mortgage. In the chapter on fees, the septic inspection was discussed. This inspection is only necessary if the appraiser finds a problem.

- **Space Heater and Wood Stoves.** If you heat with a space heater or wood stove, this must be typical for your area. The appraiser will check that your heating system is installed properly and is adequate to heat your entire home. The appraiser will also determine if local fire codes are met.

CASE STUDY: EDWARD O'CONNOR

Advanced Funding Solutions Inc.
83 Fire Island Avenue, Suite # 1
Babylon, NY 11702
Telephone: (631) 539-7517
Fax: (631) 539-7518

Not just answers, Solutions!

Edward O'Connor — Reverse Mortgage Specialist

I have been involved in the mortgage industry since about 1997, and gotten involved in reverse mortgages around the year 2000. I have a bachelor's degree in Finance and Economics and I am still an IRS Enrolled Agent. Before getting involved in the mortgage industry, I owned my own tax practice for about 16 years. I am also a retired detective from the Nassau County Police Department, having served 20 years helping the public. Advanced Funding Solutions was formed by me, to help our seniors in the area of reverse mortgages. Ninety-five percent of our business is in reverse mortgages.

I was attracted to reverse mortgages because of the level of financial and psychological comfort and well-being they provide people. When people have lived in their homes for 30 plus years, and a reverse mortgage allows them to continue living there, especially after the death of a spouse — there is no better loan to do, and no better feeling that comes along with it.

As far as the availability of reverse mortgages — it is certainly sufficient at this time. However, we are still seeing and hearing about people who would have benefited from a reverse mortgage, but still did not know about it. Market penetration is at a minimum, and publicity and public awareness still need to be pressed. You can certainly get a reverse mortgage, regardless of where you live, if you know to look for it. Reverse mortgage products are still evolving, so there will certainly be plenty of choices — again, if you know you are looking for a reverse mortgage in the first place.

What I like most about reverse mortgages is the freedom that people get to maintain, when they have taken one. As I said to one person who asked me "how do you know

CASE STUDY: EDWARD O'CONNOR

they are a good thing?" My reply was, "I never got a hug after closing a regular mortgage. Almost routinely, after the closing of a reverse mortgage, I will get a hug or a nice warm handshake."

What I like least about reverse mortgages is the lack of understanding sometimes from the client. They "get" how it works, but sometimes don't understand everything. Also, the proliferation lately of the "regular" mortgage broker into the reverse arena solely because they see dollar signs to be made is troubling. The client must always come first and the product offered should be the one with the lowest costs and lowest interest rates; no questions asked. Yes, there are times when different circumstances warrant a different scenario, but they certainly are limited.

Here are two scenarios I have worked on recently, which are not necessarily the normal and "regular" uses of a reverse mortgage.

1. I have a client right now, whose home is owned in a revocable living trust. She is the owner of the trust, but her disabled daughter is the beneficiary of the proceeds of the trust — the main asset of which is the house she lives in. She is divorced and recently had her hours cut at work. Being of limited work skills, she is hard pressed to find another job, let alone one that pays more than her current employer. So she was forced to stay put, hoping that she might get her hours back. In the meantime, she is falling behind on her bills and her mortgage payments. If she loses the house, her plan of leaving the assets behind in the trust for her daughter will fall by the wayside. By choosing the reverse mortgage, she eliminates her mortgage payments, not to mention the $77,000 in credit card bills that have been accumulated due to her limited income; job cuts notwithstanding. The reverse mortgage has given her peace of mind and financial security, all while allowing her to plan for her disabled daughter's needs into the future.

2. In another scenario, the woman was recently widowed and struggled for three years paying a small mortgage and several other bills left behind. When her husband was alive, they did okay. But living on one-third of the income, she was unable to make the monthly expenses. The interesting part is that she really intended to sell the house — she was just not ready to. There were too many memories and too many things to clean up at this time; she could not bring herself to part with the home, even three years after her husband's death. Every time it was discussed, both through family members and her attorney, that the best thing to do was to sell, she could not bring herself to do it. The reverse mortgage gave her the financial stability to take care of the monthly bills, get herself situated both financially and mentally enough to the point that she could

CASE STUDY: EDWARD O'CONNOR

start to make decisions for herself. Her intent was to stay in the house just for a few more years, but now, five years later, she is happier than ever and sees no reason to sell after all.

When we help seniors meet their financial needs, we also help them psychologically. Independence is key to a long and healthy life. Stress, whether it comes from money issues or day-to-day issues, can cause all sorts of problems. When we are able to help seniors with their problems, there is no better feeling in the world, and it makes us proud to continue giving unbiased advice and help to our clients.

The best advice we can offer to people seeking out a reverse mortgage is to take your time, and ask questions. If you do your research, you will find a reputable company to deal with and a specialist you can trust. There is plenty of information available today about reverse mortgages — read!

Appendix
Reverse Mortgage Counselors

One of the most important steps and the first step you should take, is a visit with a reverse mortgage counselor. Some reverse mortgages require a certificate from a counselor before the loan process begins. Even if the loan you are thinking about getting does not require that you see a reverse mortgage counselor, it is a good idea to meet with one anyway. As outlined in Chapter 13 and 14, a reverse mortgage counselor can help you decide which loan is best for your situation, providing an unbiased opinion after reviewing your financial records and discussing your future plans for yourself and your home.

You can find an updated list of HUD-approved reverse mortgage counselors online at www.hud.gov. The HUD Web site also lists counselors from other states that practice in your state. This can save you time and money if you live far away from the counseling centers in your state, for instance – if you live on the border of another state that has a counseling center nearby. Below is a list of reverse mortgage counselors by state to help you find the nearest counselor in your area.

Alabama

CCCS of Alabama

Auburn University

Auburn, Alabama 36849

Telephone: 800-662-6119

Fax: 334-265-5926

Email: cwalp@budgetwisely.com

2731 Ross Clark Circle, Suite # 7

Decatur, Alabama 35601-6822

Telephone: 334-712-1992

Toll-free: 800-662-6119

Fax: 334-265-5926

Email: cpelham@budgethelp.com

US Army Ft Rucker

Ft Rucker, Alabama 36370

Telephone: 800-662-6119

Fax: 334-265-5926

Email: cpelham@budgethelp.com

777 South Lawrence Street

Suite 101

Montgomery, Alabama 36104-5075

Telephone: 334-265-8545

Toll-free: 800-662-5075

Fax: 334-265-5926

Email: ladams@budgethelp.com

2316 University Blvd.

Tuscaloosa, Alabama 35407

Telephone: 205-752-2598

Fax: 334-265-5926

Email: mdockery@budgetwisely.com

CCCS of Central Alabama

1401 20th Street, South

Suite 100

Birmingham, Alabama 35205

Telephone: 205-251-1572

Toll-Free: 888-260-2227

Fax: 205-313-7205

Email: aclolinger@gway.org

Web site: **www.gway.org**

CCCS of Mobile-Jackson

208 Commerce Street

P.O. Box 1432

Jackson, Alabama 36545

Telephone: 251-246-9898

Toll-free: 888-880-1413

Fax: 251-666-6850

Email: dunaway@cccsmobile.org

Web site: **www.cccsmobile.org**

Human Resource Development Corporation

601 North Saint Andrews Street

P.O. Box 613

Dothan, Alabama 36302

Telephone: 334-678-0084

Toll-free: 877-644-1944

Fax: 334-793-5412

Email: barbaragrubbs@snowhill.com

305 Collier Street

Elba, Alabama 36323

Telephone: 334-897-2667

Toll-free: 877-644-1944

Fax: 334-393-0048

Email: dstrickla_gr@graceba.net

100 George Wallace Drive

P.O. Box 31-1407

Enterprise, Alabama 36331

Telephone: 334-678-0084

Fax: 334-393-0048

Email: barbaragr@graceba.net

312 West Magnolia Street

Geneva, Alabama 36340

Telephone: 334-684-6443

Toll-free: 877-644-1944

Fax: 334-393-0048

Email: junemaloy@snowhill.com

Birmingham Homeownership Center

4117 Second Avenue, South

Birmingham, Alabama 35222

Telephone: 205-591-7500

Fax: 205-591-7566

Email: info@birminghamhome.org

Web site: **www.birminghamhome.org**

Birmingham Urban League, Incorporated

1229 3rd Avenue North

P.O. Box 11269

Birmingham, Alabama 35203

Telephone: 205-326-0162

Fax: 205-521-6951

Email: burbanleague@aol.com

Fair Housing of Northern Alabama

1728 Third Avenue, Suite 4000

Birmingham, Alabama 35203

Telephone: 205-324-0111

Email: Lila1343@aol.com

Jefferson County Committee for Economic Opportunity

300 Eighth Avenue, West

Birmingham, Alabama 35204-3039

Telephone: 205-320-7023

Fax: 205-320-7027

Email: shill@jcceo.org

Jefferson County Housing Authority

3700 Industrial Parkway

Birmingham, Alabama 35217-5316

Telephone: 205-841-7708

Fax: 205-841-6727

Email: daaron@jcha.com

Web site: **www.jcha.com**

Community Action Partnership of North Alabama, Incorporated

1909 Central Parkway, SW

Decatur, Alabama 35601-6822

Telephone: 256-260-3122

Fax: 256-260-3186

Email: sstancil@capna.org

Web site: **www.capna.org**

Community Action Agency of Northwest Alabama, Incorporated

745 Thompson Street

Florence, Alabama 35630-3867

Telephone: 256-766-4330 Ext. 202

Fax: 256-766-4367

Email: caanw@bellsouth.net

Hale Empowerment and Revitalization Organization (HERO)

1120 Main Street

P.O. Box 318

Greensboro, Alabama 36744

Telephone: 334-624-0842

Fax: 334-624-0858

Email: pameladorr1@yahoo.com

WIL-LOW Nonprofit Housing, Incorporated

205 Tuskeena Street

P.O. Box 383

Hayneville, Alabama 36040

Telephone: 334-548-2191

Fax: 334-548-2576

Email: willowa@htcnet.net

Community Action Partnership, Huntsville/Madison & Limestone Counties, Incorporated

3516 Stringfield Road

P.O. Box 3975

Huntsville, Alabama 35810-1758

Telephone: 256-851-9800 Ext. 11

Fax: 256-851-2238

Email: tpitts@caa-htsval.org

Mobile Housing Board

1555-B Eagle Drive

Mobile, Alabama 36605

Telephone: 251-433-1011

Fax: 251-434-2374

Email: hmcdonough@mhb.gov

Web site: **www.mhb.gov**

Legal Services Alabama Incorporated

207 Montgomery Street, Suite 1200

Montgomery, Alabama 36104

Telephone: 334-164-1739

Toll-free: 866-456-4995

Fax: 334-264-1474

Email: klay@alsp.org

Dallas-Selma Community Action And Community Development

713 Jeff Davis Avenue

P.O. Box 988

Selma, Alabama 36702-0988

Telephone: 334-875-2450 Ext. 202

Fax: 334-875-2467

Email: Liheap1@aol.com

Organized Community Action Programs, Incorporated

507 North Three Notch Street

P.O. Box 908

Troy, Alabama 36081-0908

Telephone: 334-566-1712

Fax: 334-566-7417

Email: ocap@troycable.net

Community Service Programs of West Alabama, Incorporated

601 17th Street

Tuscaloosa, Alabama 35401-4807

Telephone: 205-72-5429 Ext. 231

Fax: 205-758-7229

Email: cburton@cspwal.com

Alaska

CCCS of Alaska

208 E 4th Avenue

Anchorage, Alaska 99501-2508

Telephone: 907-279-6501 Ext. 6

Toll-free: 800-478-6501

Fax: 907-478-6083

Email: Scamarata@cccsofak.com

Web site: **www.cccsofak.com**

Arizona

CCCS South West, A Division of MMI

2615 North 4th St., Suite 2

Flagstaff, Arizona 86004-3700

Telephone: 800-308-2227

Fax: 602-493-9481

jeanine.lipka@moneymanagement.org

17235 North 75th Ave., Suite C-125

Glendale, Arizona 85308

Telephone: 800-308-2227

Fax: 623-878-2747

jeanine.lipka@moneymanagement.org

1234 S. Power Rd., Suite 100

Mesa, Arizona 85206-3740

Telephone: 800-308-2227

Fax: 623-878-2747

jeanine.lipka@moneymanagement.org

Phone Center

13430 N. Black Canyon Hwy

Suite 250

Phoenix, Arizona 85029

Telephone: 800-308-2227

1717 East Bell Rd., # 7

Phoenix, Arizona 85308

Telephone: 800-308-2227

jeanine.lipka@moneymanagement.org

722 East Osborn Rd., # B210

Phoenix, Arizona 85014

Telephone: 800-308-2227

jeanine.lipka@moneymanagement.org

1215 Gail Gardner Way, # B

Prescott, Arizona 86305

Telephone: 800-308-2227

Fax: 520-771-0669

jeanine.lipka@moneymanagement.org

950 West Elliot Rd., Ste 122
Tempe, Arizona 85284
Telephone: 800-308-2227
Fax: 520-795-1121
jeanine.lipka@moneymanagement.org

4732 North Oracle Rd, Ste. 217
Tucson, Arizona 85705
Telephone: 800-308-2227
Fax: 520-298-0351
jeanine.lipka@moneymanagement.org

5515 East Grant Rd., Ste. 211
Tucson, Arizona 85712-2253
Telephone: 800-308-2227
Fax: 520-795-1121
jeanine.lipka@moneymanagement.org

2450 South Fourth Ave., # 201
Yuma, Arizona 85364
Telephone: 800-308-2444
Fax: 800-308-2227
jeanine.lipka@moneymanagement.org

Southeastern Arizona Governments Organization

118 Arizona Street
Bisbee, Arizona 85603-1800
Telephone: 520-432-5301
Fax: 520-432-2646
Email: housing@seago.org

Web site: **www.seago.org**

Community Services of Arizona, Incorporated

6704 North 59th Avenue
Glendale, Arizona 85301
Telephone: 623-435-2255 Ext. 100
Toll-free: 800-471-8247
Fax: 523-435-6430
Email: gmickey@csainc.org
Web site: **www.csainc.org**

Acorn Housing

1018 West Roosevelt Street
Phoenix, Arizona 85007-2107
Telephone: 602-253-1111
Fax: 602-258-7143
Email: jvelazquez@acornhousing.org
Web site: **www.acornhousing.org**

Administration of Resources and Choices

1366 East Thomas Road, Suite 108
Phoenix, Arizona 85014
Telephone: 602-241-6169
Toll-free: 888-264-2258
Fax: 602-230-9132
Email: kwhitearc@earthlink.net

P.O. Box 86802
Tucson, Arizona 85754
Telephone: 520-882-9135
Fax: 520-882-9135
Email: kwhitearc@earthlink.net

Neighborhood Housing Services of Phoenix

1405 East McDowell Road # 100

Phoenix, Arizona 85006

Telephone: 605-258-1666

Email: tfrancis@nhsphoenix.org

Web site: **www.nhsphoenix.org**

GreenPath

401 West Baseline, Suite 206

Tempe, Arizona 85283

Telephone: 888-776-6735

Toll-free: 800-550-1961

Email: Sbriggs@greenpath.com

Catholic Community Services of So. Arizona, Inc DBA Pio Decimo Center

848 South Seventh Avenue

Tucson, Arizona 85701-2698

Telephone: 520-624-0551 Ext. 109

Fax: 520-622-4704

Email: jmora@piodecimocenter.org

Tucson Urban League

2305 South Park Avenue

Tucson, Arizona 85713

Telephone: 520-791-9522 Ext. 263

Fax: 520-623-9364

Email: bcrobinsonbc@netscape.net

Old Pueblo Community Foundation

4501 East 15th Street

Tucson, Arizona 85711

Telephone: 520-546-0122 Ext. 204

Fax: 520-777-4512

Email: terrygalligan@helptucson.org

Web site: **www.oldpueblofoundation.org**

Arkansas

Family Service Agency – CCCS

740 S. Salem Road, Suite 104

Conway, Arkansas 72032

Telephone: 501-450-9399

Toll-free: 800-255-2227

Fax: 501-450-3036

Email: wcohns@fsainc.org

Web site: **www.helpingfamilies.org**

7887 S. Phoenix Avenue

Fort Smith, Arkansas 72903

Telephone: 479-484-0311 Ext. 209

Toll-free: 800-255-2227

Fax: 479-484-0317

Email: wcohns@fsainc.org

www.helpingfamilies.org

1401 Malvern Avenue, Suite 100

Hot Springs, Arkansas 71901

Telephone: 501-321-1238

Toll-free: 800-255-2227

Fax: 501-624-5636

Email: wcohns@fsainc.org

628 West Broad, Suite 203

P.O. Box 16615
North Little Rock, Arkansas 72114
Telephone: 501-753-0202
Toll-free: 800-255-2227
Fax: 501-812-4309
Email: wcohns@fsainc.org
www.helpingfamilies.org

211 West 3rd, Suite 215
Pine Bluff, Arkansas 71601
Telephone: 870-536-6003
Toll-free: 800-255-2227
Fax: 870-535-4741
Email: wcohns@fsainc.org

2305 East Parkway
Bank of the Ozarks
Russellville, Arkansas 72802
Telephone: 479-858-6172
Toll-free: 800-255-2227
Fax: 479-750-3036
Email: wcohns@fsainc.org

CCCS of Baton Rouge, A Division of MMI
202 North Washington, Suite 101
El Dorado, Arkansas 71730
Telephone: 800-850-2227
Fax: 877-962-7488
Email: jeanine.lipka@moneymanagement.org

Credit Counseling of Arkansas
1732 Moberly Lane, Suite A

Bentonville, Arkansas 72712
Telephone: 800-889-4916
Fax: 479-521-9200
Email: ccoa@ccoacares.com
Web site: **www.ccoacares.com**

1111 Zion Road
Fayetteville, Arkansas 72703
Telephone: 800-889-4916 Ext. 102
Fax: 479-521-9200
Email: ccoa@ccoacares.com
Web site: **www.ccoacares.com**

Arkansas River Valley Area Council, Inc
613 North 5th Street
P.O. Box 808
Dardanelle, Arkansas 72834-0808
Telephone: 479-229-4861
Fax: 479-229-4863
Email: arvac@arvacinc.org
Web site: **www.arvacinc.org**

Crawford Sebastian Community Development Council
4831 Armour Street
P.O. Box 4069
Fort Smith, Arkansas 72914
Telephone: 479-785-2303 Ext. 124
Fax: 479-785-2341
Email: kphillips@cscdccaa.org
Web site: **www.cscdccaa.org**

Crowley's Ridge Development Council, Incorporated

2401 Fox Meadow Lane

P.O. Box 16720

Jonesboro, Arkansas 72403

Telephone: 870-802-7112

Fax: 870-336-1753

Email: marla@crdcnea.com

Web site: **www.crdcnea.com**

Legal Aid of Arkansas

714 South Main Street

Jonesboro, Arkansas 72401

Telephone: 870-732-6370 Ext. 2202

Email: jwhatley@arlegalaid.org

Web site: **www.arlegalaid.org**

714 South Main Street

Jonesboro, Arkansas 72401

Telephone: 870-972-9224 Ext. 6302

IN Affordable Housing, Incorporated

1200 John Barrow Road, Suite 109

Little Rock, Arkansas 72205

Telephone: 501-221-2203

Fax: 502-221-2279

Email: ihousing@sbcglobal.net

California

Consumer Credit Counseling Service of Orange County

2450 E. Lincoln

Inside EDD Building

Anaheim, California 92806-4272

Telephone: 714-547-2227

Toll-free: 866-784-2227

Fax: 714-245-1690

Email: cccsoc@cccsoc.org

Web site: **www.cccsoc.org**

695 Madison Way

Inside Brea Community Center

Brea, California 92821-5732

Telephone: 714-547-2227

Toll-free: 866-784-2227

Fax: 714-245-1690

Email: cccsoc@cccsoc.org

www.cccsoc.org

2701 S. Harbor Boulevard, E-6

Inside Costa Mesa Federal Credit Union

Costa Mesa, California 92626

Telephone: 714-547-2227

Toll-free: 866-784-2227

Fax: 714-245-1690

Email: cccsoc@cccsoc.org

www.cccsoc.org

1920 Old Tustin Avenue

(P.O. Box 11330, Santa Ana Ca 92711-1330)

Santa Ana, California 92705

Telephone: 714-547-2227

Toll-free: 866-784-2227

Fax: 714-245-1690

Email: cccsoc@cccsoc.org

www.cccsoc.org

CCCS of Kern and Tulare Counties

5300 Lennox Avenue, Suite 200

Bakersfield, California 93309-1662

Telephone: 661-324-9628

Toll-free: 800-272-2482

Fax: 661-324-0750

Email: cccsktc@att.net

Web site: **www.californiacccs.org**

240 Westgate, Suite 241

Watsonville, California 95076

Telephone: 800-540-2227

Fax: 805-383-7722

Web site: **www.gotdebt.org**

Consumer Credit Counselors of the East Bay, A Division of MMI

2140 Shattuck Avenue, # 1208

Berkeley, California 94704

Telephone: 888-889-9347

Toll-free: 800-308-2227

Email: david.michael@
moneymanagement.org

1070 Concord Avenue, Suite 105

Concord, California 94520

Telephone: 800-308-2227

Fax: 510-729-6961

Email: jeanine.lipka@moneymanagement.
org

7677 Oakport St., Suite 210

Oakland, California 94621

Telephone: 800-308-2227

Fax: 510-729-6961

jeanine.lipka@moneymanagement.org

3100 Mowry Avenue # 403A

Fremont, California 94538

Telephone: 888-845-5669

Toll-free: 800-308-2227

david.michael@moneymanagement.org

CCCS of Ventura County

80 N. Wood Road

Suite 308

Camarillo, California 93010-0000

Telephone: 800-383-7770-555

Toll-free: 800-540-2227

Fax: 805-383-7722

Email: joyt@gotdebt.org

Web site: **www.gotdebt.org**

1547 West Grand Avenue

Grover Beach, California 93433

Telephone: 800-540-2227

Fax: 805-383-7722

Web site: **www.gotdebt.org**

1190 South Bascom Avenue, Suite 208

San Jose, California 95128

Telephone: 800-540-2227

Fax: 805-383-7722

www.gotdebt.org

1221 State. St, Suite 4A
Santa Barbara, California 93101
Telephone: 800-540-2227
Fax: 805-383-7722
www.gotdebt.org

CCCS of San Diego, A Division of MMI
730 Broadway (First National Bank)
Chula Vista, California 91911
Telephone: 800-308-2227
jeanine.lipka@moneymanagement.org

1949 Avenida Del Oro
Oceanside, California 92056
Telephone: 800-308-2227
jeanine.lipka@moneymanagement.org

Consumer Credit Counseling Service of San Francisco
2198 Junipero Serra, Suite 300
Daly City, California 94015
Telephone: 415-788-0288
Toll-free: 800-777-7526
Fax: 415-788-0847

2650 Camino del Rio North, # 209
San Diego, California 92108-2907
Telephone: 800-308-2227
jeanine.lipka@moneymanagement.org

595 Market Street, 15th Floor
San Francisco, California 94105
Telephone: 800-777-7526 Ext. 109

Fax: 415-788-7817
Email: rharper@cccsf.org
Web site: **www.housingeducation.org**

85 Brookwood Avenue, Suite 14
Santa Rosa, California 95404
Telephone: 800-777-7526
Fax: 415-788-0739

CCCS of Southern Oregon
1512 S. Oregon
Yreka, California 96097
Telephone: 530-841-1516
Fax: 530-841-1516
Web site: **www.cccsso.org**

Anaheim Housing Authority – Anaheim Housing Counseling Agency
201 South Anaheim Boulevard, Suite 501
Anaheim, California 92805
Telephone: 714-765-4310
Fax: 714-765-4046
Email: gcontreras@anaheim.net
Web site: **www.anaheimhousingcounselingagency.org**

Housing Rights, Inc
1966 San Pablo Avenue
P.O. Box 12895
Berkeley, California 94712
Telephone: 510-548-8776
Toll-free: 800-261-2298
Fax: 510-548-5805

Email: hri@housingrights.com

Web site: **www.housingrights.org**

NIC-HCA Heard

19706 Tajauta Avenue

Carson, California 90746-2568

Telephone: 310-505-6624

Fax: 310-669-9871

Email: heardbd@aol.com

Web site: **www.nidonline.org**

NIC-HCA Reeves

4602 Crenshaw Boulevard

Los Angeles, California 90043-1219

Telephone: 323-299-7900

Fax: 323-299-7472

Email: fsico@sbcglobal.net

www.nidonline.org

NIC-HCA Baker

9670 Empire Road, 2nd Floor

Oakland, California 94603

Telephone: 510-562-0109

Fax: 510-562-0121

Email: joannehavefaith@aol.com

www.nidonline.org

NID-HCA Carlisle

3560 Grand Avenue

Oakland, California 94610

Telephone: 510-268-9792

Fax: 510-268-9794

Email: jcarlisle@nidonline.org

Web site: **www.nidonline.org**

NID-HCA Redmond

3525 Broadway

Sacramento, California 95817

Telephone: 916-456-4495

Fax: 916-736-1010

Email: sandy.l.Redmond@att.net

www.nidonline.org

Community Housing Improvement Program (CHIP)

1001 Willow Street

Chico, California 95928

Telephone: 530-891-4124

Toll-free: 888-423-6333

Fax: 530-891-8547

Email: srodriquez@chiphousing.org

Community Housingworks

1820 South Escondido Boulevard, Suite 101

Escondido, California 92025

Telephone: 619-282-6647 Ext. 314

Fax: 619-640-7119

Email: gdelrio@chworks.org

Web site: **www.chworks.org**

ACORN Housing

4969 East Clinton Avenue, # 108

Fresno, California 93727

Telephone: 559-221-0217

Fax: 559-221-0704

Email: imartinez@acornhousing.org

Web site: **www.acornhousing.org**

3655 South Grand Street, Suite 250

Los Angeles, California 90007

Telephone: 213-748-1345

Fax: 213-747-0736

Email: lnelson@acornhousing.org

www.acornhousing.org

3700 East 12th Street, Suite 2C

Oakland, California 94601

Telephone: 510-436-6532

Toll-free: 877-620-5006

Fax: 510-436-3702

Email: jltrevino@acornhousing.org

www.acornhousing.org

2644 33rd Street

Sacramento, California 95817

Telephone: 916-451-9659

Fax: 916-451-9660

Email: dnavarro@acornhousing.org

www.acornhousing.org

1726 North D Street, Suite A

San Bernadino, California 92405

Telephone: 909-804-4000

Fax: 909-804-4012

Email: lnelson@acornhousing.org

www.acornhousing.org

3554 University Avenue

San Diego, California 92104

Telephone: 619-521-2940

Fax: 619-521-2941

Email: lnelson@acornhousing.org

www.acornhousing.org

395 East Taylor Street, Suite 230

San Jose, California 95112

Telephone: 408-297-3053

Fax: 408-297-3561

Email: jgaleano@acornhousing.org

www.acornhousing.org

ByDesign Financial Solutions – DBA CCCS of Central Valley

4969 East McKinley Avenue, Suite 107

Fresno, California 93727-1968

Telephone: 800-750-2227

Fax: 559-454-1405

Email: cpierce@bydesignsolutions.org

Web site: **www.bydesignsolutions.org**

ByDesign Financial Solutions – DBA CCCS of Los Angeles

412 West Broadway, Suite 212

Glendale, California 91204

Telephone: 323-890-9500

Toll-free: 800-750-2227

Fax: 323-890-9590

Email: rpittman@bydesignsolutions.org

www.bydesignsolutions.org

16800 Devonshire, Suite 301
Granada Hills, California
Telephone: 800-750-2227
Fax: 323-890-9590
Email: rpittman@bydesignsolutions.org
www.bydesignsolutions.org

6001 East Washington Boulevard, Suite 200
Los Angeles, California 90040-2922
Telephone: 800-750-2227
Fax: 323-890-9591
Email: rpittman@bydesignsolutions.org
www.bydesignsolutions.org

1605 East Palmdale Boulevard, Suite E
Palmdale, California 93550
Telephone: 800-750-2227
Fax: 661-265-8508
Email: rpittman@bydesignsolutions.org
www.bydesignsolutions.org

ByDesign Financial Solutions – DBA CCCS of Mid-Counties
3351 M Street, Suite 100
Merced, California 95348
Telephone: 800-750-2227
Fax: 209-723-0149
Email: jthompson@bysdesignsolutions.org
www.bydesignsolutions.org

1101 Standiford Avenue, Suite D-4
Modesto, California 95350

Telephone: 800-750-2227
Fax: 209-522-1294
jthompson@bysdesignsolutions.org
www.bydesignsolutions.org

2291 West March Lane, Suite A-110
Stockton, California 95207
Telephone: 800-750-2227 Ext. 112
Fax: 209-956-1178
jthompson@bysdesignsolutions.org
www.bydesignsolutions.org

ByDesign Financial Solutions, DBA CCCS of Sacramento Valley
4636 Watt Avenue, Second Floor
North Highlands, California 95660
Telephone: 800-750-2227 Ext. 112
Fax: 916-379-0626
Email: ddamskey@bydesignsolutions.org
www.bydesignsolutions.org

1260 Pine Street
Redding, California 96001
Telephone: 800-750-2227 Ext. 112
Fax: 916-379-0626
Email: ddamskey@bydesignsolutions.org
www.bydesignsolutions.org

Eden Council for Hope and Opportunity (ECHO)
770 A Street
Hayward, California 94541-3956
Telephone: 510-581-9380

Fax: 510-537-4793

Email: margie@echofairhousing.org

Web site: **www.echofairhousing.org**

3311 Pacific Avenue

Livermore, California 94704

Telephone: 925-449-7340

Fax: 925-449-0704

Email: mcolbert@att.net

www.echofairhousing.org

1305 Franklin Street, Suite 305

Oakland, California 94612-3213

Telephone: 510-581-9380

Fax: 510-763-3736

Springboard

1555 West Florida Avenue

Hemet, California 92543

Telephone: 800-947-3752

Fax: 951-781-8027

Email: springboard@credit.org

Web site: **www.credit.org**

2181 El Camino Real, Suite 207

Oceanside, California 92054

Telephone: 800-947-3752

Email: springboard@credit.org

www.credit.org

1001 South Palm Canyon, Suite 103

Palm Springs, California 92262

Telephone: 800-947-3752

Fax: 951-781-8027

Email: springboard@credit.org

www.credit.org

4351 Latham Street

Riverside, California 92501

Telephone: 951-781-0114 Ext. 718

Toll-free: 800-947-3752

Fax: 951-328-7718

Email: sbierly@credit.org

www.credit.org

1814 Commerce Center West, Suite B

San Bernardino, California 92408

Telephone: 800-947-3752

Fax: 951-781-8027

Email: springboard@credit.org

www.credit.org

7710 Balboa Avenue, Suite 218-F

San Diego, California 92111

Telephone: 800-947-3752

Fax: 951-781-8027

Email: springboard@credit.org

www.credit.org

Los Angeles Neighborhood Housing Services, Inc

3926 Wilshire Boulevard, Suite 200

Los Angeles, California 90010

Telephone: 213-381-2862 Ext. 112

Toll-free: 888-895-2467

Fax: 213-381-2103

Email: counseling@lanhs.org

Web site: **www.lanhs.org**

West Angeles Community Development Corporation

6028 Crenshaw Boulevard

Los Angeles, California 90043

Telephone: 323-751-3440

Fax: 323-751-7631

Email: phebert@westangelescdc.org

Web site: **www.westangelescdc.org**

National Association of Real Estate Brokers – Investment Division, Inc

3560 Grand Avenue

Oakland, California 94610

Telephone: 510-268-9792

Fax: 510-268-9794

Email: jcarlisle.nid@comcast.net

Web site: **www.nidonline.org**

Avenidas

450 Bryant Street

Palo Alto, California 94301

Telephone: 650-289-5421

Fax: 650-326-3048

Email: jsink@acenidas.org

Web site: **www.avenidas.org**

Project Sentinel

430 Sherman Avenue, Suite 308

Palo Alto, California 94306

Telephone: 650-321-6291

Toll-free: 888-331-3332

Fax: 650-321-4173

Email: projsenpa@aol.com

Web site: **www.housing.org**

1055 Sunnyvale-Saratoga Road # 3

Sunnyvale, California 94087

Telephone: 408-720-9888 Ext. 16

Toll-free: 888-331-3332

Fax: 408-720-0810

Email: mediate4us@projsen.org

www.housing.org

Legal Services of Northern California – Senior Legal Hotline

444 North 3rd Street, Suite 312

Sacramento, California 95811

Telephone: 916-551-2140

Toll-free: 800-222-1753

Fax: 916-551-2197

Web site: **www.seniorlegalhotline.org**

Neighborhood House Association

841 South 41st Street

San Diego, California 92113

Telephone: 619-263-7761 Ext. 139

Fax: 619-263-6398

Email: ebrown@neighborhoodhouse.org

Web site: **www.neighborhoodhouse.org**

San Diego Urban League

720 Gateway Center Drive

San Diego, California 92102

Telephone: 619-263-6258

Fax: 619-263-3660

Email: michael.wilson@sdul.org

Web site: **www.ulsdc.org**

Neighborhood Housing Services Silicon Valley

1156 North Fourth Street

San Jose, California 95112

Telephone: 408-279-2600

Fax: 408-279-4100

Email: emoncrief@nhssv.org

Web site: **www.nhssv.org**

Human Investment Project, Inc

364 South Railroad Avenue

San Mateo, California 94401-4024

Telephone: 650-348-6660 Ext. 303

Fax: 650-348-0284

Email: lfanucchi@hiphousing.org

Orange County Fair Housing Council, Inc

201 South Broadway

Santa Ana, California 92701-5633

Telephone: 714-569-0823 Ext. 212

Toll-free: 800-698-3247

Fax: 714-835-0282

Email: jprayoonvech@fairhousing.org

Web site: **www.fairhousing.org**

Housing Authority of the County of Santa Cruz

2931 Mission Street

Santa Cruz, California 95060

Telephone: 831-454-9455 Ext. 211

Fax: 831-469-3712

Email: housing@hacosantacruz.org

Center for Healthy Aging

2125 Arizona Avenue

Santa Monica, California 90404

Telephone: 310-576-2554

Northern Circle Indian Housing Authority, United Native Housing Development

694 Pinoleville Drive

Ukiah, California 95482

Telephone: 707-468-1336 Ext. 19

Toll-free: 800-521-3191

Fax: 707-468-5615

Email: jlcaffery@pacific.net

Inland Fair Housing Mediation Board

60 East 9th Street, Suite 100

Upland, California 91786

Telephone: 909-984-2254 Ext. 114

Toll-free: 800-321-0911

Email: inmedbd@aol.com

Web site: **www.inmedbd.com**

City of Vacaville Department of Housing and Redevelopment

40 Eldridge Avenue, Suite 2

Vacaville, California 95688-6800

Telephone: 707-449-5691

Fax: 707-449-6242

Email: klawton@cityofvacaville.com

Vallejo Neighborhood Housing Services, Inc
610 Lemon Street
Vallejo, California 94590-7276
Telephone: 707-552-4663 Ext. 13
Fax: 707-643-2143
Email: rwalton@vallejonhs.org
Web site: **www.vallejonhs.org**

Cabrillo Economic Development Corporation
702 County Square Drive
Ventura, California 93003
Telephone: 805-659-6868 Ext. 131
Fax: 805-659-6869
Email: bmgarcia@cabrilloedc.org
Web site: **www.cabrilloedc.org**

Colorado

CCCS of Greater Dallas
1233 Lake Plaza Dr., Suite A
Colorado Springs, Colorado 80906-3555
Telephone: 719-576-0909
Toll-free: 800-798-3328
Fax: 719-576-3756
Email: info@cccs.net
Web site: **www.cccs.net**

200 West 1st Street, Suite 302
Pueblo, Colorado 81003

Telephone: 719-542-6620
Toll-free: 888-218-5741
Fax: 719-542-7057
Email: info@cccs.net
www.cccs.net

5265 N Academy Blvd., Suite 1000
Colorado Springs, Colorado 80918
Telephone: 719-598-2227
Toll-free: 800-249-2227
Fax: 719-598-7850
Email: info@cccs.net
Web site: **www.cccs.net**

CCCS of Greater Denver, A Division of MMI
10065 East Harvard Avenue, Suite 210
Denver, Colorado 80231
Telephone: 303-632-2227
Email: jeanine.lipka@moneymanagement.org

225 N. 5th Street, Suite 820
Grand Junction, Colorado 81501
Telephone: 970-242-2000
jeanine.lipka@moneymanagement.org

7120 East County Line Road
Highlands Ranch, Colorado 80126
Telephone: 303-989-3300
eanine.lipka@moneymanagement.org

355 Union

Lakewood, Colorado 80229
Telephone: 800-308-2227
jeanine.lipka@moneymanagement.org

9101 Harlan Street, Suite 150
Westminster, Colorado 80030
Telephone: 303-426-4442
jeanine.lipka@moneymanagement.org

CCCS of Northern Colorado & SE Wyoming
1247 Riverside Avenue
Fort Collins, Colorado 80524-3258
Telephone: 970-229-0695
Toll-free: 800-424-2227
Fax: 970-229-0721
Email: general@cccsnc.org
Web site: **www.cccsnc.org**

918 13th Street # 2
Greeley, Colorado 80631
Telephone: 970-229-0695
Toll-free: 800-424-2227
Fax: 970-229-0721
Email: general@cccsnc.org
www.cccsnc.org

2919 W. 17th Avenue
Longmont, Colorado 80503
Telephone: 800-424-2227
Fax: 970-229-0721
Email: general@cccsnc.org
www.cccsnc.org

315 E. 7th Street
Loveland, Colorado 80537-4801
Telephone: 970-229-0695
Toll-free: 800-424-2227
Fax: 970-229-0721
Email: general@cccsnc.org
www.cccsnc.org

508 S. 10th Avenue
Sterling, Colorado 80451
Telephone: 800-424-2227
Fax: 970-229-0721
Email: general@cccsnc.org
www.cccsnc.org

City of Aurora Community Development Division
9898 East Colfax Avenue
Aurora, Colorado 80010
Telephone: 303-739-7900
Fax: 303-739-7925
Email: aormsby@auroragov.org
Web site: **www.ci.aurora.co.us**

Boulder County Housing Authority
3482 North Broadway, Sundquist Building
Boulder, Colorado 80304
Telephone: 720-564-2279
Fax: 303-441-1537
Email: chudak@co.boulder.co.us
Web site: **www.co.boulder.co.us/cs/ho**

Upper Arkansas Area Council of Governments

3224 Independence Road

P.O. Box 510

Canon City, Colorado 81212

Telephone: 719-269-7687

Fax: 719-275-2907

Email: housing@uaacog.com

Web site: **www.uaacog.com**

Adams County Housing Authority

7190 Colorado Boulevard, 6th Floor

Commerce City, Colorado 80022-1812

Telephone: 303-227-2072

Fax: 303-227-2098

Email: bbrodie@achaco.com

Web site: **www.adamscountyhousing. com**

Brothers Redevelopment, Inc

2250 Eaton Street, Garden Level

Denver, Colorado 80214-1210

Telephone: 303-202-6340 Ext. 4214

Toll-free: 877-601-4673

Fax: 303-274-1314

Email: zachary@brothersredevelopment. org

Web site: **www.brothersredevelopment. org**

Northeast Denver Housing Center

1735 Gaylord Street

Denver, Colorado 80206-1208

Telephone: 303-377-3334

Fax: 303-377-3327

Email: tsmith111@nedenverhousing.org

Rocky Mountain Mutual Housing Association, Inc

225 East 16th Avenue, Suite 1060

Denver, Colorado 80203

Telephone: 303-388-9613

Fax: 303-322-6880

Email: lewism@rmmha.com

Southwest Improvement Council

1000 South Lowell Boulevard

Denver, Colorado 80219-3339

Telephone: 303-934-8057

Fax: 303-934-0035

Email: lauraswic@hotmail.com

Web site: **www.scic-denver.org**

Housing Solutions for the Southwest

295 Girard Street

Durango, Colorado 81303

Telephone: 970-259-1086 Ext. 15

Fax: 970-259-2037

Email: tmiller@sehousingsolutions.com

Neighbor To Neighbor

1550 Blue Spruce Drive

Fort Collins, Colorado 80524

Telephone: 970-488-2363

Fax: 970-488-2355

Email: wrobinson@n2n.org

Web site: **www.n2n.org**

565 North Cleveland Avenue

Loveland, Colorado 80537-4801

Telephone: 970-663-4163

Fax: 970-663-2860

Email: sgregg@n2n.org

Web site: **www.n2n.org**

Grand Valley Housing Initiatives

1011 North 10th Street

Grand Junction, Colorado 81501

Telephone: 970-245-0388 Ext. 224

Fax: 970-257-8347

Email: HomeOwner@gjha.org

Web site: **www.gvhi.org**

Housing Resources of Western Colorado (HRWC)

524 30 Road, Suite 3

Grand Junction, Colorado 81504

Telephone: 970-241-2871 Ext. 116

Fax: 970-245-4853

Email: jonl@housingresourceswc.org

Web site: **www.housingresourceswc. org**

Catholic Charities of the Diocese of Pueblo, Colorado

729 West 10th Street, Suite 101

Pueblo, Colorado 81003

Telephone: 800-303-4690

Fax: 719-544-4215

Email: jmazur@pueblocharities.org

Web site: **www.pueblocharities.org**

Colorado Rural Housing Development Corporation

3621 West 73rd Avenue, Suite C

Westminster, Colorado 80030

Telephone: 303-428-1448 Ext. 201

Toll-free: 800-566-1252

Fax: 303-428-1989

Email: jpatrick@crhdc.org

Web site: **www.crhdc.org**

Connecticut

CCCS of Southern New England, A Division of MMI

39 Rose Street

Danbury, Connecticut 06810

Telephone: 800-208-2227

225 Pitkin Street, Suite 300

East Hartford, Connecticut 06108

Telephone: 800-845-5669

Fax: 860-291-8483

Email: georgehill@moneymanagement. org

61 Cherry Street

Milford, Connecticut 06460

Telephone: 800-845-5669

Toll-free: 800-308-2227

Fax: 860-291-8483

george.hill@moneymanagement.org

627 Route 32

North Franklin, Connecticut 06254

Telephone: 800-208-2227

Web site: **www.creditcounseling.org**

123 Prospect Street
Stamford, Connecticut 06901
Telephone: 800-208-2227

Acorn Housing
2310 Main Street, 3rd Floor
Bridgeport, Connecticut 06606
Telephone: 203-366-4180
Fax: 203-366-0020
Email: dlatorre@acornhousing.org
Web site: **www.acornhousing.org**

Urban League of Greater Hartford, Inc
140 Woodland Street
Hartford, Connecticut 06105
Telephone: 860-527-0147 Ext. 120
Fax: 860-249-1563
Email: lstevenson@ulgh.org
Web site: **www.ulgh.org**

Neighborhood Housing Services
333 Sherman Avenue
New Haven, Connecticut 06511-3107
Telephone: 203-562-0598 Ext. 14
Fax: 203-772-2876
Email: jpaley.nhs@snet.net
Web site: **www.nhsofnewhaven.org**

139 Prospect Street

Waterbury, Connecticut 06710-2318
Telephone: 203-753-1896 Ext. 15
Fax: 203-757-6496
Email: VLBecker.nhs@sbcglobal.net

Florida

CCCS of Greater Atlanta – Boca Raton
1515 North Federal Highway, Suite 200
Boca Raton, Florida 33434
Telephone: 404-527-7630 Ext. 8823
Toll-free: 866-255-2227
Fax: 404-260-3338
Email: sue.hunt@cccsinc.org
Web site: **www.cccsatl.org**

900 Central Parkway
Stuart, Florida 34997
Telephone: 404-527-7630 Ext. 8823
Toll-free: 866-255-2227
Fax: 404-260-3338
Email: info@cccsinc.org
www.cccsatl.org

700 South Dixie Highway, Suite 103
West Palm Beach, Florida 33401
Telephone: 561-434-2544
Toll-free: 800-330-2227
Fax: 561-434-2540
www.cccsinc.org

CCCS of Central FL and the FL Gulf Coast, Inc

1 East Jefferson Street
(Suntrust Bank)
Brooksville, Florida 34605-3460
Telephone: 800-741-7040
Fax: 407-895-3807
Email: cccscounselor@cccsfl.org
www.cccsfl.org

2127 Del Prado Blvd.
(IronStone Bank)
Cape Coral, Florida 33990
Telephone: 800-741-7040
Fax: 407-895-3807
Email: cccscounselor@cccsfl.org
Web site: **www.cccsfl.org**

4625 East Bay Drive, Suite 205
Clearwater, Florida 33764
Telephone: 800-741-7040
Fax: 407-895-3807
Email: cccscounselor@cccsfl.org
www.cccsfl.org

37837 Meridian Avenue, Suite 200
Dade City, Florida 33525
Telephone: 800-741-7040
Fax: 407-895-3807
Email: cccscounselor@cccsfl.org
www.cccsfl.org

One-Stop Career Center
359 Bill France Blvd

Daytona Beach, Florida 32114
Telephone: 800-741-7040
Fax: 407-895-3807
Email: cccscounselor@cccsfl.org
www.cccsfl.org

840 Deltona Blvd, Suite C
(Justin Square/United Way Center)
Deltona, Florida 32725
Telephone: 800-741-7040
Fax: 407-895-3807
Email: cccscounselor@cccsfl.org
www.cccsfl.org

12811 Kenwood Lane, Suite 111
Fort Meyers, Florida 33907
Telephone: 800-741-7040
Fax: 407-895-3807
Email: cccscounselor@cccsfl.org
www.cccsfl.org

1375 Buena Vista Drive
Lake Buena Vista, Florida 32830
Telephone: 800-741-7040
Fax: 407-895-3807
Email: cccscounselor@cccsfl.org
www.cccsfl.org

900 North 14th Street
Sun Trust Bank Building, 2nd Floor
Leesburg, Florida 34748
Telephone: 800-741-7040

Fax: 407-895-3807
Email: cccscounselor@cccsfl.org
www.cccsfl.org

9 Beth Stacey Blvd, Suite 206
Lehigh Community Services
Lehigh Acres, Florida 33936
Telephone: 800-741-7040
Fax: 407-895-3807
Email: cccscounselor@cccsfl.org
www.cccsfl.org

2480 Vanderbilt Beach Road
Naples, Florida 34109
Telephone: 800-741-7040
Fax: 407-895-3807
Email: cccscounselor@cccsfl.org
www.cccsfl.org

5945 Florida Avenue
New Port Richey, Florida 34652
Telephone: 800-741-7040
Fax: 407-895-3807
Email: cccscounselor@cccsfl.org
www.cccsfl.org

6220 S. Orange Blossom Trail, Suite 115
Building #1
Orlando, Florida 32809
Telephone: 800-741-7040
Fax: 407-895-3807
Email: cccscounselor@cccsfl.org
www.cccsfl.org

3670 Maguire Boulevard, Suite 103
Orlando, Florida 32803
Telephone: 800-741-7040
Fax: 407-895-3807
Email: cccscounselor@cccsfl.org
www.cccsfl.org

1750 17th Street, Unit H
(Schoenbaum Human Service Center)
Sarasota, Florida 34234
Telephone: 800-741-7040
Fax: 407-895-3807
Email: cccscounselor@cccsfl.org
www.cccsfl.org

4040 Commercial Way (US Highway 19)
United Way of Hernando County
Springhill, Florida 34606
Telephone: 800-741-7040
Fax: 407-895-3807
Email: cccscounselor@cccsfl.org
www.cccsfl.org

300 31st Street North, Suite 228-E
St. Petersburg, Florida 33713
Telephone: 800-741-7040
Fax: 407-895-3807
Email: cccscounselor@cccsfl.org
www.cccsfl.org

1311 Executive Center Drive, Suite 206
(Ellis Bldg. Koger Center)

Tallahassee, Florida 32301
Telephone: 800-741-7040
Fax: 407-895-3807
Email: cccscounselor@cccsfl.org
www.cccsfl.org

5421 Beaumont Center Blvd., Suite 600
Tampa, Florida 33634
Telephone: 800-741-7040
Fax: 407-895-3807
Email: cccscounselor@cccsfl.org
www.cccsfl.org

3815 N. Nebraska Avenue
(Tampa Bay Federal Credit Union)
Tampa, Florida 33673
Telephone: 800-741-7040
Fax: 407-895-3807
Email: cccscounselor@cccsfl.org
www.cccsfl.org

13302 N. Palm Drive
USF Federal Credit Union
Tampa, Florida 33612
Telephone: 800-741-7040
Fax: 407-895-3807
Email: cccscounselor@cccsfl.org
www.cccsfl.org

273 South Tamiami Trail
(Fifth Third Bank) Venice Island
Business 41

Venice, Florida 34285
Telephone: 800-741-7040
Fax: 407-895-3807
Email: cccscounselor@cccsfl.org
www.cccsfl.org

CCCS of West FL
212 Wilson Street
Crestview, Florida 32536-0000
Telephone: 850-689-0177
Toll-free: 800-343-3317
Fax: 850-432-5078
Email: lsmith@cccswfl.org
www.cccswfl.org

171 North 9th Street
DeFuniak Springs, Florida 32433
Telephone: 850-892-8666
Toll-free: 800-343-3317
Fax: 850-432-5078
Email: lsmith@cccswfl.org
www.cccswfl.org

6 Hollywood Blvd Suite C
Fort Walton Beach, Florida 32548
Telephone: 850-315-9888
Toll-free: 800-343-3317
Fax: 850-314-9891
Email: apratt@cccawfl.org
www.cccswfl.org

625 Highway 231

Panama City, Florida 32401-0000
Telephone: 850-314-9888
Toll-free: 800-343-3317
Fax: 850-432-5078
Email: lsmith@cccswfl.org
www.cccswfl.org

14 Palafox Place
PO Box 950
Pensacola, Florida 32502
Telephone: 850-434-0268 Ext. 206
Toll-free: 800-343-3317
Fax: 850-432-5078
Email: lrogers@allvista.org
www.cccswfl.org

CCCS of the Midwest
4491 South State Road 7, Suite 201
Davie, Florida 33314
Telephone: 800-355-2227
Fax: 614-552-4800
Email: info@cccservices.com
Web site: **www.cccservices.com/home. asp**

1800 W 49th St, Suite 303
Hialeah, Florida 33012-2900
Telephone: 800-355-2227
Fax: 614-552-4800
Email: info@cccservices.com
Web site: **www.cccservices.com**

3170 N Federal Highway

Lighthouse Point, Florida 33064
Telephone: 800-355-2227
Fax: 614-552-4800
Email: info@cccservices.com
www.cccservices.com/home.asp

1982 N State Road 7, # 441
Margate, Florida 33063
Telephone: 800-355-2227
Fax: 614-552-4800
Email: info@cccservices.com
www.cccservices.com/home.asp

3800 SW 137th Avenue
Miami, Florida 33175
Telephone: 800-355-2227
Fax: 614-552-4800
Email: info@cccservices.com
www.cccservices.com/home.asp

11609 N. Kendall Drive
Miami, Florida 33183
Telephone: 800-355-2227
Fax: 614-552-4800
Email: info@cccservices.com
www.cccservices.com/home.asp

12651S Dixie Hwy, Suite 303
Miami, Florida 33186
Telephone: 800-355-2227
Fax: 614-552-4800
Email: info@cccservices.com
www.cccservices.com/home.asp

11755 Biscayne Blvd Ste 303
North Miami, Florida 33181-3155
Telephone: 800-355-2227
Fax: 614-552-4800
Email: info@cccservices.com
Web site: **www.cccservices.com**

CCCS of Brevard
507 North Harbor City Blvd
Melbourne, Florida 32935
Telephone: 321-259-1070
Fax: 321-259-5202
Email: roy@fccbrevard.com
Web site: **www.cccsbrevard.org**

725 S Deleon Ave
Titusville, Florida 32780-4115
Telephone: 321-636-9210
Fax: 321-259-5202
Email: roy@fccbrevard.com
Web site: **www.cccsbrevard.org**

2046 14th Ave
Vero Beach, Florida 32960-3430
Telephone: 321-259-1070
Fax: 321-259-5202
Email: roy@fccbrevard.com
Web site: **www.cccsbrevard.org**

Catholic Charities
1219 16th Street, West
Bradenton, Florida 34205

Telephone: 941-714-7829
Fax: 941-708-5281
Email: cath.char2@verizon.net
Email: imcath@verizon.net
Web site: **www.catholiccharitiesdov.org**

134 East Church Street, Suite 2
Jacksonville, Florida 32202-3130
Telephone: 904-354-4846 Ext. 240
Fax: 904-354-4718
Email: cmyrick@ccbjax.org
Web site: **www.ccbjax.org**

1213 16th Street North
St. Petersburg, Florida 33705
Telephone: 727-893-1313 Ext. 202
Fax: 727-893-1307
Email: slopez@ccdosp.org
Web site: **www.ccdosp.org**

**Manatee Community Action Agency Inc
F/K/A Manatee Opportunity Council, Inc**
302 Manatee Avenue E, Suite 150
Bradenton, Florida 34208
Telephone: 941-827-2887
Fax: 941-827-3001
Email: ssandhoff@manateecaa.org

**National Foundation For Debt
Management**
14104 58th Street North
Clearwater, Florida 33760
Telephone: 800-334-5153 Ext. 287

Toll-free: 888-301-8167

Fax: 888-294-5487

Email: groe@nfdm.org

Web site: **www.nfdm.org/univ/ homeownership.aspx**

Mid-Florida Housing Partnership, Inc

1834 Mason Avenue

Daytona Beach, Florida 32117

Telephone: 386-274-4441 Ext. 301

Toll-free: 800-644-6125

Fax: 386-274-1415

Email: MFHP@bellsouth.net

Web site: **www.mfhp.org**

Deerfield Beach Housing Authority

533 South Dixie Highway

Deerfield Beach, Florida 33441

Telephone: 954-425-8449

Fax: 954-425-8450

Email: pamedavis@bellsouth.net

Web site: **www.dbhaonline.org**

Consumer Credit Management Services, Inc

315 NE 2nd Avenue

Delray Beach, Florida 33444

Telephone: 561-454-5615

Fax: 561-454-5615

Web site: **www.debt-mgt.org**

Acorn Housing

2700 West Oakland Park Boulevard, Suite 23

Fort Lauderdale, Florida 33311

Telephone: 954-484-3588

Fax: 954-4848-3589

Email: odonate@acornhousing.org

Web site: **www.acornhousing.org**

1380 West Flagler Street, Suite C

Miami, Florida 33135

Telephone: 305-631-9002

Fax: 305-631-9050

Email: jcastigarrabia@acornhousing.org

www.acornhousing.org

120 East Colonial Drive

Orlando, Florida 32801

Telephone: 407-254-5974

Fax: 407-254-0841

Email: Cmorejon@acornhousing.org

www.acornhousing.org

1344 West Cass Street

Tampa, Florida 33606

Telephone: 813-871-2795

Fax: 813-258-1719

Email: odonate@acornhousing.org

www.acornhousing.org

City of Gainesville Housing Division

306 NE 6th Avenue

P.O. Box 490, Station 10-B

Gainesville, Florida 32602-0490

Telephone: 352-334-5026

Fax: 352-334-2272
Email: richardsjs@gainsville.fl.us
Web site: **www.cityofgainesville.org**

Family Foundations of Northeast Florida, Inc
1639 Atlantic Boulevard
Jacksonville, Florida 32207-3346
Telephone: 904-396-4846 Ext. 120
Fax: 904-398-6649
Email: info@familyfoundationsjax.org
Web site: **www.familyfoundationsjax.org**

5000-3 Norwood Avenue
Jacksonville, Florida 32208
Telephone: 904-396-4846 Ext. 128
Fax: 904-398-6649
Email: billt@fcsjax.org
Web site: **www.fcsjax.org**

1409 Kingsley Avenue
Orange Park, Florida 32073-4537
Telephone: 904-396-4846
Toll-free: 888-297-1929
Fax: 904-398-6649
Email: billt@fcsjax.org
Web site: **www.fcsjax.org**

Jacksonville Area Legal Aid, Inc
126 West Adams Street
Jacksonville, Florida 32202-3849
Telephone: 904-356-8371 Ext. 325

Fax: 904-356-8780
Email: michael.figgins@jaxlegalaid.org
Web site: **www.jaxlegalaid.org**

Jacksonville Urban League
903 West Union Street
Jacksonville, Florida 32204-1161
Telephone: 904-356-8336
Fax: 904-356-8369
Email: wandadavis@jaxul.org

CEEDCO Inc
2310 Tall Pines Drive, Suite 220
Largo, Florida 33771
Telephone: 727-499-2201 Ext. 2011
Fax: 727-450-2922
Email: housing@ceedco.org
Web site: **www.ceedco.org**

Broward County Housing Authority
4780 North State Road 7
Main Office
Lauderdale Lakes, Florida 33319
Telephone: 954-739-1114 Ext. 2304
Fax: 954-535-0407
Email: pbrown@bchafl.org
Web site: **www.bchafl.org**

Markon HCA
7414 West Commercial Boulevard
Lauderhill, Florida 33319
Telephone: 954-578-7094

Fax: 954-741-5195

Email: lougreen2@yahoo.com

Al Ansar CDC

5245 NW 7th Avenue

Miami, Florida 33127

Telephone: 305-757-8741

Fax: 305-757-9768

Email: mikalth@comcast.net

Greater Miami Neighborhoods, Inc

300 NW 12th Avenue

Miami, Florida 333128

Telephone: 305-324-5506 Ext. 107

Fax: 305-324-5506

Email: krodriguez@greatermiami.org

Web site: **www.greatermiami.org**

NID-HCA

9425 Sunset Drive, Suite 136

Miami, Florida 33173

Telephone: 786-318-7588

Fax: 305-574-0120

Email: steffyerealtist@msn.com

Web site: **www.nidonline.org**

937 NW 206 Terr

Miami Gardens, Florida 33169

Telephone: 305-999-9594

Fax: 305-999-9570

Email: cassemoniq@aol.com

Web site: **www.nidonline.org**

South Florida Board of Realists

610 NW 193rd Street, Suite 206

Miami, Florida 33169

Telephone: 305-653-3580

Fax: 305-653-8242

Email: Carolyncarroll@bellsouth.net

West Perrine Community Development Corporation

17690 Homestead Avenue

Miami, Florida 33157-5340

Telephone: 305-252-0129 Ext. 118

Fax: 305-235-5809

Email: wpcdc@aol.com

Life and Learning Centers of South Florida, Inc

18800 NW 2nd Avenue # 204

Miami Gardens, Florida 33169

Telephone: 305-690-4391

Toll-free: 866-690-4690

Email: lifeandlearning1@bellsouth.net

Vision to Victory Destination Home

13230 NW 7th Avenue

North Miami, Florida 33168

Telephone: 305-691-3464

Fax: 305-953-8327

Email: hesterlinehall@aol.com

Opa-Locka Community Development Corporation

490 Opa-Locka Boulevard, Suite 20

Opa-Locka, Florida 33054
Telephone: 305-687-3545 Ext. 239
Fax: 305-685-9650
Email: Stephanie@olcdc.org
Web site: **www.olcdc.org**

H.A.N.D.S. Inc
6900 South Orange Blossom Trail, Suite 300
Orlando, Florida 32809
Telephone: 407-477-5686
Fax: 407-447-5692
Email: jill@cflhands.org
Web site: **www.cflhands.org**

Metropolitan Orlando Urban League
2804 Belco Drive
Orlando, Florida 32808
Telephone: 407-841-7654
Fax: 407-841-9114

The Housing Corporation
1620 Tamiami Trail, Suite 103
The City Center
Port Charlotte, Florida 33948
Telephone: 941-255-9454
Fax: 941-624-3253
Email: cdunbar@housingcorpcc.org
Web site: **www.housingcorpcc.org**

Family Counseling Center of Brevard, Inc
220 Coral Sands Drive
Rockledge, Florida 32955-2702

Telephone: 320-259-1070
Fax: 321-259-5202
Email: roy@fccbrevard.com
Web site: **www.cccsbrevard.org**

Golden Rule Housing and Community Development
417 East 2nd Avenue
Sanford, Florida 32771
Telephone: 407-324-9123
Fax: 407-328-7148

The Center for Affordable Housing, Inc
2524 South Park Drive
Sanford, Florida 32773
Telephone: 407-323-3268 Ext. 14
Fax: 407-323-3800
Email: tcfah@bellsouth.net

St. Petersburg Neighborhood Housing Services, Inc
1600 Martin L. King Street South
St. Petersburg, Florida 33701
Telephone: 727-821-6897 Ext. 108
Fax: 727-821-7457
Email: deborah.scanlan@stpetenhs.org
Web site: **www.stpetenhs.org**

Tallahassee Lenders Consortium, Inc
833 East Park Avenue
Tallahassee, Florida 32301
Telephone: 850-222-6609 Ext. 104
Fax: 850-222-6687

Email: llane@tallahasseelenders.org
Web site: **www.tallahasseelenders.org**

Tallahassee Urban League
923 Old Bainbridge Road
Tallahassee, Florida 32303-6042
Telephone: 850-222-6111
Fax: 850-561-8390
Email: curtistaylor@talul.org

Credit Card Management Services, Inc
4611 Okeechobee Boulevard, Suite 114
West Palm Beach, Florida 33417
Telephone: 561-472-8000
Toll-free: 800-920-2262
Fax: 561-844-0406
Email: e4chippa@hotmail.com
Web site: **www.debthelper.com**

Urban League of Palm Beach County, Inc
1700 North Australian Avenue
West Palm Beach, Florida 33407
Telephone: 561-833-1461 Ext. 25
Fax: 561-833-6050
Email: weat6347@bellsouth.net
Web site: **www.ulpbc.org**

Georgia

CCCS of Greater Atlanta – Main Office
100 Edgewood Ave NE Ste 1800
Atlanta, Georgia 30303-3026
Telephone: 404-527-7630

Toll-free: 866-255-2227
Fax: 404-527-7662
Email: info@cccsinc.org
Web site: **www.cccsatl.org**

1 West Court Square, Suite 140
Decatur, Georgia 30030
Telephone: 404-527-7630-8823
Toll-free: 866-255-2227
Fax: 404-260-3338
Email: sue.hunt@cccsinc.org
www.cccsinc.org

2801 Candler Road, Suite 81
Decatur, Georgia 30034
Telephone: 404-527-7630
Toll-free: 866-255-2227
Fax: 404-527-7662
Email: info@cccsinc.org
www.cccsatl.org

4935 Stewart Mill Road, Suite 103
Douglasville, Georgia 30135
Telephone: 404-527-7630 Ext. 8823
Toll-free: 866-255-2227
Fax: 404-260-3338
Email: sue.hunt@cccsinc.org
www.cccsinc.org

140 Carnegie Place, Suite 106
Fayetteville, Georgia 30214
Telephone: 404-527-7630 Ext. 8823

Toll-free: 866-255-2227

Fax: 404-260-3338

Email: sue.hunt@cccsinc.org

www.cccsinc.org

322 Oak Street, Suite 3

Gainesville, Georgia 30501

Telephone: 404-527-7630

Toll-free: 866-255-2227

Fax: 404-260-3338

Email: sue.hunt@cccsinc.org

www.cccsinc.org

1640 Powers Ferry Road

Building 14

Suite 100

Marietta, Georgia 30067

Telephone: 404-527-7630 Ext. 8823

Toll-free: 866-255-2227

Fax: 404-260-3338

Email: sue.hunt@cccsinc.org

www.cccsatl.org

413 Shorter Avenue, Suite 101

Rome, Georgia 30165

Telephone: 404-527-7630 Ext. 8823

Toll-free: 866-255-2227

Fax: 404-260-3338

Email: sue.hunt@cccsinc.org

www.cccsinc.org

CCCS of Augusta, Inc

1341 Druid Park Avenue

Augusta, Georgia 30904

Telephone: 706-736-2090 Ext. 209

Toll-free: 800-736-0033

Fax: 706-736-0637

Email: ksolki@cccsaugusta.org

Web site: **www.cccsaugusta.org**

CCCS of Middle Georgia – Main Office

277 M.L.K. Jr. W Suite 202

Macon, Georgia 31201-0000

Telephone: 478-745-6197

Toll-free: 800-446-7123

Fax: 478-745-6270

Email: s_edwards@cccsmacon.org

Area Committee to Improve Opportunities Now, Inc

594 Oconee Street

Athens, Georgia 30605

Telephone: 706-546-8293

Fax: 706-353-8370

Email: caoschack@aol.com

East Athens Development Corporation

410 McKinley Drive, Suite 101

Athens, Georgia 30601

Telephone: 706-208-0048

Fax: 706-208-0015

Email: wheard0822@aol.com

Web site: **www.eadcinc.com**

Acorn Housing

501 Pulliam Street, Southwest, Suite 405

Atlanta, Georgia 30312

Telephone: 404-525-0033

Fax: 404-525-2655

Email: fakbar@acornhousing.org

Web site: **www.acornhousing.org**

Atlanta Urban League

100 Edgewood Avenue NE, Suite 600

Atlanta, Georgia 30303-3066

Telephone: 404-659-1150 Ext. 6578

Fax: 404-659-5771

Email: skelly@atlul.org

Web site: **www.atlul.org**

Cooperative Resource Center, Inc

191 Edgewood Avenue

Atlanta, Georgia 30303

Telephone: 404-521-0406 Ext. 302

Fax: 404-521-2355

Email: audra@cooperativeresourcecenter.org

Web site: **www.cooperativeresource-center.org**

Dekalb Metro Housing Counseling Center

4151 Memorial Drive, Suite 106D

Decatur, Georgia 30032

Telephone: 404-508-0922 Ext. 101

Fax: 404-508-0967

Email: jbdekalbmetro@bellsouth.net

National African American Relationships Institute

5000 Snapfinger Woods Drive, Suite C315

Decatur, Georgia 30035

Telephone: 770-322-6007

Fax: 770-322-6449

Web site: **www.aarelationshipinstitute.com**

Metro Fair Housing Services, Inc

1514 East Cleveland Avenue, Suite 118

East Point, Georgia 30344

Telephone: 404-765-3985

Fax: 404-765-3986

Email: foscorb@aol.com

D&E Financial Education & Training Institute, Inc (D&E Group)

4532 Jonesboro Road

Forest Park, Georgia 30297

Telephone: 770-961-6900

Toll-free: 800-961-8222

Fax: 770-961-8900

Email: aharris@depower.org

Web site: **www.depower.org**

2260 Lake Harbin Road

Morrow, Georgia 30260

Telephone: 770-961-6900

Email: aharris@depower.org

Economic Opportunity for Savannah Chatham County Area, Inc

618 West Anderson Street

P.O. Box 1353
Savannah, Georgia 31415
Telephone: 912-238-2960 Ext. 115
Fax: 912-238-2974
Email: terryt@eoasga.org
Web site: **www.eoasga.org**

Family Foundations of Northeast Florida, Inc
505 Haines Avenue
Waycross, Georgia 31501-2266
Telephone: 912-284-2261
Toll-free: 888-297-1929
Fax: 912-284-2284
Web site: **www.fcsjax.org**

Homefirst Housing Resource Services, Inc (Formerly) Macon Middle Georgia
682 Cherry Street, Suite 103
Macon, Georgia 31201
Telephone: 478-803-2373
Fax: 478-803-2377
Email: reginald.bell@macon.ga.us
Web site: **www.homefirstga.org**

Hawaii

Legal Aid Society of Hawaii
305 Wailuku Drive
Hilo, Hawaii 96720-2448
Telephone: 800-499-4302
Fax: 808-969-3983

924 Bethel Street
P.O. Box 37375
Honolulu, Hawaii 96813
Telephone: 808-536-4302
Toll-free: 800-499-4302
Fax: 808-527-8088

47-200 Waihee Road, Suite 104
Kaneohe, Hawaii 96744-4947
Telephone: 800-499-4302
Fax: 808-239-3968

1923 Ala Malama Street
Kaunakakai, Hawaii 96748
Telephone: 800-499-4302
Fax: 808-553-5809

4334 Rice Street, # 204A
Lihue, Hawaii 96766
Telephone: 800-499-4302
Fax: 808-246-8824

85-670 Farrington Highway, Suite A
Waianae, Hawaii 96792-2354
Telephone: 800-499-4302
Fax: 808-696-5809

2287 Main Street
Wailuku, Hawaii 96793-1655
Telephone: 800-499-4302
Fax: 808-244-5856

Hale Mahaolu Homeownership/Housing Counseling

200 Hina Avenue

Kahului, Hawaii 96732-1821

Telephone: 808-661-5957

Fax: 808-872-4120

Idaho

Consumer Credit Counseling Services, A Division of MMI

1801 Lincoln Way, Suite 6

Coeur d'Alene, Idaho 83814

Telephone: 866-889-9347

Email: david.michael@moneymangement.org

Idaho Housing and Finance Association

565 West Myrtle

P. O. Box 7899

Boise, Idaho 83702

Telephone: 877-888-3135

Fax: 208-331-4801

Email: susanp@ihfa.org

Web site: **www.ihfa.org**

Neighborhood Housing Services Incorporated

1401 Shoreline Drive

P.O. Box 8223

Boise, Idaho 83707

Telephone: 208-343-4065

Fax: 208-343-4963

Email: canderson@nhsid.org

Web site: **www.nhsid.org**

Community Action Partnership

124 New Sixth Street

Lewiston, Idaho 83501-2133

Telephone: 208-746-3351 Ext. 225

Toll-free: 800-326-4843

Fax: 208-746-5456

Email: p.soule@acommunityactionpartnership.org

Illinois

CCCS of Greater Chicago, A Division of MMI

70 East Lake St., Ste. 1115

Chicago, Illinois 60601

Telephone: 888-527-3328

Fax: 312-338-0907

Email: brian.coyle@moneymanagement.org

1200 Roosevelt Rd., Ste. 121

Glen Ellyn, Illinois 60137

Telephone: 888-527-3328

Fax: 630-932-0537

brian.coyle@moneymanagement.org

1515 North Harlem, Ste. 205

Oak Park, Illinois 60302

Telephone: 888-527-3328

Fax: 708-445-9664

brian.coyle@moneymanagement.org

416 Main St, Suite 920
Peoria, Illinois 61602
Telephone: 888-527-3328
brian.coyle@moneymanagement.org

129 South Phelps Ave., Ste. 811
Rockford, Illinois 61108
Phone: 888-527-3328
Fax: 815-961-1820
brian.coyle@moneymanagement.org

3601 Algonquin Rd., Ste. 230
Rolling Meadows, Illinois 60477
Telephone: 888-527-3328
Fax: 847-398-9404
brian.coyle@moneymanagement.org
Web site: **www.moneymanagement.org**

16860 S. Oak Park Ave., Ste. 203
Tinley Park, Illinois 60477
Telephone: 888-527-3328
Fax: 708-633-8302
brian.coyle@moneymanagement.org

CCCS of Elgin
22 S. Spring Street
Elgin, Illinois 60120
Telephone: 847-695-3680
Toll-free: 888-790-2370
Fax: 847-695-4552
Email: arodriguez@fsaelgin.org
Web site: **www.fsaelgin.org/cccs.htm**

CCCS of McHenry County
4508 Prime Parkway
McHenry, Illinois 60050
Telephone: 815-338-5757
Fax: 815-338-9646

400 Russel Ct
P.O. Box 885
Woodstock, Illinois 60098-2640
Telephone: 815-338-5757
Toll-free: 800-815-2227
Fax: 815-338-9646
Email: vpeschke@illinoiscccs.org
Web site: **www.illinoiscccs.org**

Urban League
210 William Street
P.O. Box 8093
Alton, Illinois 62002-8093
Telephone: 618-463-1906 Ext. 5
Fax: 618-463-9021
Email: cawjan@aol.com

314 South Neil Street
Champaign, Illinois 61820
Telephone: 217-363-3333 Ext. 22
Fax: 217-356-1310
Email: jalgee@urbanleague.net
Web site: **www.urbanleague.net**

4510 South Michigan Avenue
Chicago, Illinois 60653-3898

Telephone: 773-285-1500
Fax: 773-285-0879
Email: mwooten@cul-chicago.org

100 North 11th Street
P.O. Box 3865
Springfield, Illinois 62798
Telephone: 217-789-0830 Ext. 115
Fax: 217-789-9838
Email: hicksgibson@yahoo.com
Web site: **www.springfieldul.org**

Family Counseling Service/CCC of Aurora
70 South River Street, Suite 2
Aurora, Illinois 60506-5178
Telephone: 630-844-3327
Toll-free: 800-349-1451
Fax: 630-844-3084
Email: bderamus@auroracccs.org
Web site: **www.auroracccs.org**

Joseph Corporation of Illinois, Inc
32 South Broadway Avenue
P.O. Box 525
Aurora, Illinois 60507
Telephone: 630-906-9400
Fax: 630-906-9406
Email: charley@josephcorp.org
Web site: **www.josephcorporation.org**

New Song Housing Services
151 East Briarcliff

Bolingbrook, Illinois 60440
Telephone: 630-739-1130
Fax: 630-739-2283

Macoupin County Housing Authority
760 Anderson Street
P.O. Box 226
Carlinville, Illinois 62626
Telephone: 217-854-8606 Ext. 18
Toll-free: 866-363-5142
Fax: 217-854-8749
Email: regina@teamhousingcenter.com
Web site: **www.teamhousingcenter.com**

Central Illinois Debt Management & Credit Education, Inc
201 West Springfield Avenue, Suite 211
Huntington Towers
Champaign, Illinois 61820
Telephone: 309-676-2941 Ext. 22
Toll-free: 888-671-2227
Fax: 309-676-6143
Email: Janice@cidmce.org
Web site: **www.cidmce.org**

407 North Franklin
IETC Building
Danville, Illinois 61832
Telephone: 309-676-2941 Ext. 22
Toll-free: 888-671-2227
Fax: 309-676-6143
Email: Janice@cidmce.org
www.cidmce.org

222 East North Street
Decatur, Illinois 62523
Telephone: 309-676-2941
Toll-free: 888-671-2227
Fax: 309-676-6143
Email: Janice@cidmce.org
www.cidmce.org

180 South Soangetaha Road
Knox Agri-Center Building
U of I Cooperative Extension Service
Galesburg, Illinois 61401
Telephone: 309-676-2941
Toll-free: 888-671-2227
Fax: 309-676-6143
Email: Janice@cidmce.org
www.cidmce.org

719 Main Street
Peoria, Illinois 61602
Telephone: 309-676-2941
Toll-free: 888-671-2227
Fax: 309-676-6143
Email: Janice@cidmce.org
www.cidmce.org

Backbone Road East
Drivers License Facility Building
Options EAP
Princeton, Illinois 61356
Telephone: 309-676-2941 Ext. 22
Toll-free: 888-671-2227

Fax: 309-676-6143
Email: Janice@cidmce.org
www.cidmce.org

Acorn Housing
209 West Jackson, Suite 301
Chicago, Illinois 60606
Telephone: 312-939-1611
Fax: 312-939-4239
Email: dmccree@acornhousing.org
Web site: **www.acornhousing.org**

Chicago Roseland Development Corporation
11015 South Michigan Avenue
Chicago, Illinois 60628-4308
Telephone: 773-264-3500
Fax: 773-264-9634
Email: romelialu@yahoo.com

Chinese American Service League
2141 South Tan Court
Chicago, Illinois 60616
Telephone: 312-791-0418 Ext. 6606
Fax: 312-791-0509
Email: estherw@caslservice.org
Web site: **www.caslservice.org**

Community and Economic Development Association (CEDA)
208 South La Salle Street, Suite 1900
Chicago, Illinois 60604-1104
Telephone: 312-795-8964

Fax: 312-795-1034

Email: bhyshaw@cedaorg.net

Web site: **www.cedaorg.net**

Chicago Heights Community Service Center

1203 West End Avenue

Chicago Heights, Illinois 60411-2746

Telephone: 708-754-4575

Fax: 708-754-4595

Email: kperkins@cedaorg.net

Web site: **www.cedaorg.net**

CEDA Near West

6141 West Roosevelt Road

Cicero, Illinois 60804

Telephone: 708-222-3824

Fax: 708-222-0026

Email: mfavale@cedaorg.net

www.cedaorg.net

Evanston Neighbors at Work

1229 Emerson Street

Evanston, Illinois 60201-3524

Telephone: 847-328-5166

Fax: 847-328-9262

Email: pvance@cedaorg.net

www.cedaorg.net

CEDA Center for Community Action

53 East 154th Street

Harvey, Illinois 60426-3645

Telephone: 708-339-3610

Fax: 708-331-4539

Email: ah**ernandez@cedaorg.net**

www.cedaorg.net

CEDA Northwest Self-Help Center, Inc

1300 W Northwest Hwy

Mount Prospect, Illinois 60056-2217

Telephone: 847-392-2332

Fax: 847-392-2427

Email: rjordan@cedaorg.net

www.cedaorg.net

Southeast CEDA

3518 W 139th Street

Robbins, Illinois 60472-2002

Telephone: 708-371-1247

Fax: 708-371-1247

Email: blucas@cedaorg.net

www.cedaorg.net

Proviso-Leyden Council for Community Action – PLCCA

411 Madison Street

Maywood, Illinois 60153-1939

Telephone: 312-795-8964

Fax: 312-795-1034

Email: bhyshaw@cedaorg.net

www.cedaorg.net

GreenPath, Inc

5306 Avenue of the Cities, Suite A

Moline, Illinois 61265

Telephone: 888-776-6735

Toll-free: 888-860-4167

Web site: **www.greenpath.com**

Menard County Housing Authority

101 W. Sheridan Road

P.O. Box 168

Petersburg, Illinois 62675

Telephone: 217-632-7723 Ext. 226

Fax: 217-632-7255

Email: asmith@menardcha.org

Rockford Area Affordable Housing Coalition

205 North Church Street

Rockford, Illinois 61101-1003

Telephone: 815-962-2011

Fax: 815-962-2650

Email: raahc@raahc.org

Web site: **www.raahc.org**

Community Service Council of Northern Will Co

719 Parkwood Avenue

Romeoville, Illinois 60446-1134

Telephone: 815-886-5000

Fax: 815-886-6700

Email: mweber@thecsc.org

Web site: **www.thecsc.org**

City of Springfield Office of Community Relations

231 South 6th Street, 3rd Floor

Springfield, Illinois 62701

Telephone: 217-789-2270

Fax: 217-789-2268

Email: srobinson@cwlp.com

CEFS

114 East Harrison Street

Sullivan, Illinois 61951

Telephone: 217-728-7721

Toll-free: 800-500-7433

Fax: 217-728-2923

Email: cmeadows@cefsoc.org

Web site: **www.cefsoc.org**

South Route 127, Box 128

Taylor Springs, Illinois 62089

Telephone: 217-532-5971

Toll-free: 8005-289-5289

Fax: 217-532-2367

Email: jjohnson@cefseoc.org

www.cefseoc.org

311 South Main Street

Taylorville, Illinois 62568

Telephone: 217-824-4712 Ext. 14

Fax: 217-824-5018

Email: jrusher@cefseoc.org

www.cefseoc.org

517 West Gallatin Street

P.O. Box 44

Vandalia, Illinois 62471

Telephone: 618-283-2631

Toll-free: 800-283-3213
Fax: 618-283-2715
Email: jwise@cefseoc.org
www.cefseoc.org

Institute for Consumer Credit Education
16335 South Harlem Avenue, Suite # 100
Tinley Park, Illinois 60477
Telephone: 708-633-6355
Toll-free: 800-431-1082
Fax: 708-633-6321
Email: ICCE_60@msn.com

Du Page Homeownership Center, Inc
1333 North Main Street
Wheaton, Illinois 60187-3579
Telephone: 630-260-2500
Fax: 630-260-2505
Email: dru@dhoc.org
Web site: www.dhoc.org

Indiana

Momentive CCCS – Anderson Branch
931 Meridian Plaza, Suite 704
Anderson, Indiana 46016
Telephone: 866-722-9248
Toll-free: 866-722-9248
Fax: 317-266-1315
Email: mortgagehelp@momentive.org
Web site: www.momentive.org

205 N. College, Suite 014

Bloomington, Indiana 47404
Telephone: 866-722-9248
Toll-free: 866-722-9248
Fax: 317-266-1315
Email: mortgagehelp@momentive.org
www.momentive.org

1531 13th Street, Suite 1360
Columbus, Indiana 47201
Telephone: 866-722-9248
Toll-free: 866-722-9248
Fax: 317-266-1315
Email: mortagehelp@momentive.org
www.momentive.org

715 N. First Avenue
Evansville, Indiana 47710
Telephone: 866-722-9248
Toll-free: 866-722-9248
Fax: 812-424-9050
Email: mortgagehelp@momentive.org
www.momentive.org

615 N. Alabama Street, Suite 134
Indianapolis, Indiana 46204-1477
Telephone: 317-266-1300 Ext. 3043
Toll-free: 888-711-7227
Fax: 317-317-3043
Email: kperron@momentive.org
www.momentive.org

2803 N. Oakwood

Muncie, Indiana 47304

Telephone: 866-722-9248

Fax: 317-266-1315

Email: mortagahelp@momentive.org

www.momentive.org

#30 Kenbel Plaza

1400 E. Pugh Drive, Suite 105

Terre Haute, Indiana 47803

Telephone: 866-722-9248

Fax: 317-266-1315

Email: mortgagehelp@momentive.org

www.momentive.org

CCCS of Northeastern Indiana

117 W. 9th Street

Auburn, Indiana 46704

Telephone: 800-432-0420

Fax: 260-432-7415

Email: hashcroft@financialhope.org

4105 W Jefferson Blvd

PO Box 11403

Fort Wayne, Indiana 46858

Telephone: 260-432-8200 Ext. 3307

Toll-free: 800-432-0420

Fax: 260-432-7415

Email: hashcraft@financialhope.org

Web site: **www.financialhope.org**

200 West Market Street

Huntington, Indiana 46750

Telephone: 800-432-0420 Ext. 3307

Toll-free: 800-432-0420

Fax: 260-432-7415

126 Rush Street

Kendallville, Indiana 46755

Telephone: 800-432-0420

Fax: 260-349-0735

850 N. Harrison

Warsaw, Indiana 46580

Telephone: 800-432-0420

Fax: 574-269-3995

Housing Authority of the City of Anderson

528 West 11th Street

Anderson, Indiana 46016-1228

Telephone: 765-641-2620 Ext. 106

Fax: 765-641-2629

Email: aha@ahain.org

Web site: **www.cityofanderson.com/ departments.aspx?id=7**

City of Bloomington

401 North Morton Street

P.O. Box 100

Bloomington, Indiana 47402

Telephone: 812-349-3401

Fax: 812-349-3582

Email: simsd@bloomington.in.gov

Web site: **www.bloomington.in.gov/hand**

Catholic Charities

176 South West Street

Crown Point, Indiana 46307

Telephone: 219-879-9312

Fax: 219-879-9073

Email: mmcpherson@catholic-charities.org

Web site: **www.catholic-charities.org**

Lake County Community Economic Development Dept

2293 North Main Street

Crown Point, Indiana 46307-1885

Telephone: 219-755-3204

Fax: 219-736-5925

Email: hooks@lakecountyin.com

GreenPath, Inc

500 North Nappanee Street, 7A

Elkhart, Indiana 46514

Telephone: 800-550-1961

Toll-free: 888-860-4167

Fax: 574-293-0365

Email: Sbriggs@greenpath.com

Web site: **www.greenpath.com**

416 East Monroe Street, Suite 120

South Bend, Indiana 46601

Telephone: 888-860-4167

www.greenpath.com

HOPE of Evansville, Inc

608 Cherry Street

Evansville, Indiana 47713-1808

Telephone: 812-423-3169

Toll-free: 888-525-4673

Fax: 812-424-2848

Email: office@hopein.com

Web site: **www.hopein.com**

Housing Authority of the City of Fort Wayne

2025 South Anthony Boulevard

P.O. Box 13489

Telephone: 260-449-7800 Ext. 3144

Fax: 260-449-7229

Email: mmorris@fwha.org

Web site: **www.fwha.org**

Housing Authority of the City of Hammond

1402 173rd Street

Hammond, Indiana 46324-2831

Telephone: 219-989-3265 Ext. 310

Fax: 219-989-3275

Email: cdelreal@hammondhousing.org

Web site: **www.hammondhousing.org**

Indianapolis Urban League

777 Indiana Avenue

Indianapolis, Indiana 46202-3135

Telephone: 317-693-7603

Fax: 317-693-7613

Email: mrussell@indplsul.org

Web site: **www.indplsul.org**

Affordable Housing Corporation

812 South Washington Street

Marion, Indiana 46953

Telephone: 765-662-1574 Ext. 104

Toll-free: 866-770-3406

Fax: 765-662-1578

Email: jacquie@ahcgrantcounty.com

Web site: **www.ahcgrantcounty.com**

Muncie Home Ownership and Development Center

409 South Walnut Street

Muncie, Indiana 47305

Telephone: 765-282-6656

Fax: 765-282-8391

Email: munciehomecenter@aol.com

Web site: **www.munciehomecenter.com**

The Housing Partnership – New Albany Branch

311 Hauss Square

New Albany, Indiana 47150

Telephone: 502-585-5451

Fax: 502-585-5568

Email: cmccravy@housingpartnershipinc.org

Housing Development Corporation of St. Joseph County

224 W. Jefferson Boulevard, Suite 100

South Bend, Indiana 46601-1806

Telephone: 574-235-9475

Fax: 574-235-9697

Email: PMEYER@SouthBendIN.gov

Web site: **www.southbendin.gov/living/ community_development/housing_ development_corp.asp**

REAL Services, Inc

1151 South Michigan Street

P.O. Box 1835

South Bend, Indiana 46634

Telephone: 574-284-2644

Email: bzaseck@realservicesinc.com

Housing Opportunities, Inc

2801 Evans Avenue

Valparaiso, Indiana 46383

Telephone: 219-462-3726

Fax: 219-464-9635

Email: caroline.shook@oppent.org

Web site: **www.portercohousing.org**

Generations

1019 North Fourth Street

Vincennes, Indiana 47591

Telephone: 812-888-4279

Iowa

CCCS Of Northeastern Iowa

1608 S Duff Ave Suite 300

Ames, Iowa 50010

Telephone: 515-296-1968

Toll-free: 866-720-9049

Fax: 515-268-4262

Email: ames@cccsia.org

2255 JF Kennedy Rd.
Asbury Square
Dubuque, Iowa 52002
Telephone: 563-582-3885
Toll-free: 866-720-9049
Fax: 563-582-4504
Email: dubuque@cccsia.org

102 North 4th Street
Forest City, Iowa 50436
Telephone: 866-720-9050

1030 Broad Street
Grinnell, Iowa 50158
Telephone: 866-720-9048

30 W. Main Street
Marshalltown, Iowa 50158
Telephone: 641-752-6161
Toll-free: 866-720-9048
Fax: 641-754-6970
Email: marshalltown@cccsia.org
Web site: **www.cccsia.org**

404 S. Monroe Avenue
Mason City, Iowa 50401
Telephone: 641-421-7619
Toll-free: 866-720-9050
Fax: 515-421-7738
Email: masoncitymanager@cccsia.org

6200 Aurora Ave, Suite 504W

Urbandale, Iowa 50322
Telephone: 515-225-2227
Toll-free: 888-388-2227
Fax: 515-457-7317
Email: jhepner@cccsnebr.org
Web site: **www.cccsn.org**

1003 W 4th Street
Waterloo, Iowa 50702-2803
Telephone: 319-234-0661
Toll-free: 800-714-4388
Fax: 319-234-7533
Email: manager@cccsia.org
Web site: **www.cccsia.org**

CCCS of Nebraska
6200 Aurora Ave, Suite 504W
Urbandale, Iowa 50322
Telephone: 515-225-2227
Toll-free: 888-388-2227
Fax: 515-457-7317
Email: jhepner@cccsnebr.org
Web site: **www.cccsn.org**

Iowa State University Financial Counseling Clinic
Palmer HDFS Building # 1331
Ames, Iowa 50011-4380
Telephone: 515-294-8644
Fax: 515-294-9533
Email: dbork@iastate.edu
Web site: **www.hdfs.hs.iastate.edu/ financial**

Family Housing Advisory Services, Inc

10 S. 4th Street

Council Bluffs, Iowa 51503

Telephone: 402-934-7926

Fax: 402-934-7928

Email: Teresa@fhasinc.org

Web site: **www.fhasinc.org**

United Neighbors, Inc

808 Harrison Street

Davenport, Iowa 52803

Telephone: 563-322-7363 Ext. 205

Fax: 563-323-9907

Email: dawnmutumplies@aol.com

Web site: **www.unitedneighbors.com**

Center for Siouxland

715 Douglas Street

Sioux City, Iowa 51101-1208

Telephone: 712-252-1861 Ext. 12

Toll-free: 877-580-5526

Fax: 712-255-1352

Email: jonette.spurlock@
centerforsiouxland.org

Web site: **www.centerforsiouxland.org**

Family Management Credit Counselors, Inc

1409 West 4th Street

Waterloo, Iowa 50702-2907

Telephone: 319-234-6695

Fax: 319-236-6626

Email: rogergold@qwest.net

Web site: **www.fammancredit.com**

Kansas

Consumer Credit Counseling Service, Inc

1521 E. Fulton Terrace

Garden City, Kansas 67846

Telephone: 800-279-2227

Fax: 785-827-8280

Email: jeffw@kscccs.org

Web site: **www.kansascccs.org**

1200 N. Main, Room 414

Hays, Kansas 67601

Telephone: 785-827-6731

Toll-free: 800-279-2227

Fax: 785-827-8280

Email: cccs@salhelp.org

www.kansascccs.org

Quest Building, 1 E 9th Suite 201

Hutchinson, Kansas 67501

Telephone: 800-279-2227

Fax: 785-827-8280

Email: cccs@salhelp.org

www.kansascccs.org

1201 W Walnut St

PO Box 843

Salina, Kansas 67402-0843

Telephone: 785-827-6731

Toll-free: 800-279-2227

Fax: 785-827-8280

Email: jeffw@kscccs.org
www.kansascccs.org

300 W. Douglas Suite 900
Wichita, Kansas 67202
Telephone: 316-265-2000
Fax: 316-265-8507
Email: jeffw@kscccs.org
www.kansascccs.org

Housing and Credit Counseling Incorporated
625 Merchant
Emporia, Kansas 66801
Telephone: 620-342-7788
Toll-free: 800-383-0217
Fax: 785-234-0237
Email: hcci@hcci-ks.org
Web site: www.hcci-ks.org

2518 Ridge Court, Suite 207
Lawrence, Kansas 66046
Telephone: 785-749-4224
Toll-free: 800-383-0217
Fax: 785-234-0237
Email: hcci@hcci-ks.org
www.hcci-ks.org

2601 Anderson Avenue, Suite 200
Manhattan, Kansas 66502
Telephone: 785-539-6666
Toll-free: 800-383-0217
Email: hcci@hcci-ks.org

www.hcci-ks.org

1195 Southwest Buchanan Street, Suite 101
Topeka, Kansas 66604-1183
Telephone: 785-234-0217
Toll-free: 800-383-0217
Fax: 785-234-0237
Email: hcci@hcci-ks.org
www.hcci-ks.org

Northeast Kansas Community Action Program
1260 220th Road
P.O. Box 380
Hiawatha, Kansas 66434-0380
Telephone: 785-742-2222 Ext. 241
Fax: 785-752-2164
Email: delis@nekcap.org

Greater Kansas City Housing Information Center
333 East Poplar, Suite D
Olathe, Kansas 66061
Telephone: 913-829-4584
Fax: 816-931-0722
Email: pgilmore3810@hotmail.com

Urban League of Kansas
1802 East 13th Street, North
Wichita, Kansas 67214-1704
Telephone: 316-262-2463
Fax: 316-262-8841

Email: kandrewsulow@sbcglobal.net

Kentucky

CCCS of the Midwest

617 North Mulberry Ste 24

Elizabethtown, Kentucky 42701

Telephone: 800-355-2227

Fax: 614-552-4800

Email: info@cccservices.com

Web site: **www.cccservices.com/home. asp**

11 Shelby Street

Florence, Kentucky 41042

Telephone: 800-355-2227

Fax: 614-552-4800

Email: info@cccservices.com

www.cccservices.com/home.asp

2265 Harrodsburg Road, Suite 303

Lexington, Kentucky 40504

Telephone: 800-355-2227

Fax: 614-552-4800

Email: info@cccservices.com

www.cccservices.com/home.asp

2100 Gardiner Lane Ste 103A

Louisville, Kentucky 40205

Telephone: 800-355-2227

Fax: 614-552-4800

Email: info@cccservices.com

W**www.cccservices.com/home.asp**

US Bank Bldg

4th Floor

131 Main St.

Pikeville, Kentucky 41501

Telephone: 800-355-2227

Fax: 614-552-4800

Email: info@cccservices.com

www.cccservices.com/home.asp

131 Main St. 4th Floor

Pikeville, Kentucky 41501

Telephone: 800-355-2227

Fax: 614-552-4800

Email: info@cccservices.com

www.cccservices.com/home.asp

REACH, Inc

733 Red Mile Road

Lexington, Kentucky 40504

Telephone: 859-455-8057

Toll-free: 800-985-9271

Fax: 859-455-7436

Email: dturnbull@reachky.com

Web site: **www.reachky.com**

Louisville Urban League

1535 West Broadway

Louisville, Kentucky 40203

Telephone: 502-566-3362

Fax: 502-568-4663

Email: kmitchell@lul.org

Web site: **www.lul.org**

The Housing Partnership, Inc

333 Guthrie Green, Suite 404

Louisville, Kentucky 40202

Telephone: 502-585-5451 Ext. 703

Fax: 502-585-5568

Email: cmccravy@housingpartnershipinc.org

Web site: **www.housingpartnership.org**

Purchase Area Housing Corporation

1002 Medical Drive

P.O. Box 588

Mayfield, Kentucky 42066-0588

Telephone: 270-247-7171

Email: David.Hargrove@purchaseadd.org

Web site: **www.purchaseadd.org**

Brighton Center, Incorporated

741 Central Avenue

Newport, Kentucky 41071

Telephone: 859-491-8303 Ext. 2324

Fax: 859-491-8702

Email: sstiene@brightoncenter.com

Louisiana

CCCS of Baton Rouge, A Division of MMI

1106 MacArthur Dr., Suite 2

Alexandria, Louisiana 71303

Telephone: 800-850-2227

Fax: 877-442-7495

Email: jeanine.lipka@moneymanagement.org

615 Chevelle Court

Baton Rouge, Louisiana 70806

Telephone: 800-850-2227

Fax: 225-926-7912

Email: tommye.white@moneymanagement.org

700 Northgate Rd.

Bossier City, Louisiana 71112

Telephone: 800-850-2227

Fax: 225-926-7912

tommye.white@moneymanagement.org

2430 South Burnside

Gonzales, Louisiana 70737

Telephone: 800-850-2227

Fax: 225-926-7912

Email:Jackie.Boies@moneymanagement.org

120 South Oak St.

Hammond, Louisiana 70403

Telephone: 800-850-2227

Fax: 225-926-7912

tommye.white@moneymanagement.org

117 Liberty Ave.

Lafayette, Louisiana 70508

Telephone: 800-850-2227

Fax: 877-406-5636

tommye.white@moneymanagement.org

2021 Oak Park Blvd.

Lake Charles, Louisiana 70601

Telephone: 800-850-2227

Fax: 877-924-9061

tommye.white@moneymanagement.org

2912 Evangeline

Monroe, Louisiana 71201

Telephone: 800-850-2227

Fax: 877-924-9061

tommye.white@moneymanagement.org

Web site: **www.moneymangement.org**

8575 Business Park Dr.

Shreveport, Louisiana 71105

Telephone: 800-850-2227

Fax: 877-795-0803

tommye.white@moneymanagement.org

CCCS of Greater New Orleans

401 Whitney Ave, Ste 101

Gretna, Louisiana 70056-2658

Telephone: 504-366-8952

Toll-free: 800-454-8023

Fax: 504-367-5360

Email: cccsno@cccsno.org

Web site: **www.cccsno.org**

1340 W Tunnel Blvd, Ste 500

Houma, Louisiana 70360-2801

Telephone: 985-876-2225

Toll-free: 888-876-2240

Fax: 985-876-2182

Email: cccsno@cccsno.org

Web site: **www.cccsno.org**

4051 Veterans Blvd., Suite 226

Metairie, Louisiana 70001

Telephone: 504-454-2300

Toll-free: 800-454-8615

Fax: 504-457-3004

Email: cccsno@cccsno.org

Web site: **www.cccsno.org**

1215 Prytania St. - Suite 424

New Orleans, Louisiana 70130-5858

Telephone: 504-529-2396

Toll-free: 800-880-2221

Fax: 504-598-6366

Email: cccsno@cccsno.org

www.cccsno.org

1338 Gause Blvd, Ste 202

Slidell, Louisiana 70458-3040

Telephone: 985-641-4158

Toll-free: 888-641-4159

Fax: 985-641-4159

Email: cccsno@cccsno.org

www.cccsno.org

Cenla Community Action Committee, Incorporated

1335 Jackson Street

Alexandria, Louisiana 71301-6930

Telephone: 318-487-5860

Fax: 318-484-2176

Email: msjoanlee@yahoo.com

Jefferson Community Action Program
4008 U.S. Highway 90
Avondale, Louisiana 70092
Telephone: 504-349-5414
Fax: 504-349-5417
Email: nferrier@jeffparish.net

1221 Elmwood Park Boulevard, Suite 402
Jefferson, Louisiana 70123
Telephone: 504-736-6900
Fax: 504-736-7093
Email: Estucke@jeffparish.net
Web site: **www.jeffparish.net**

1121 Causeway Boulevard
Jefferson, Louisiana 70121-1925
Telephone: 504-838-4277
Fax: 504-838-1179
Email: Mpeck@jeffparish.net
Web site: **www.jeffparish.net**

Saint Mary Community Action Agency, Inc
1407 Barrow Street
P.O. Box 271
Franklin, Louisiana 70538-3514
Telephone: 337-828-5703 Ext. 17
Toll-free: 800-368-1851
Fax: 337-828-5754
Email: Jeffery_Beverly@hotmail.com

Southeast Louisiana Legal Services
1200 Derek Drive, Suite 100

Hammond, Louisiana 70404
Telephone: 985-345-2130
Toll-free: 800-349-0886
Fax: 985-345-2686
Email: blenard@slls.org
Web site: **www.slls.org**

4051 Westbank Expressway
Marrero, Louisiana 70072
Telephone: 504-340-1381
Toll-free: 800-624-4771
Fax: 504-348-0175
Email: mamoreau@nolac.org
Web site: **www.slls.org**

People's Organization for Social Equality, Inc
625 Veteran's Boulevard
Kenner, Louisiana 70062
Telephone: 504-468-2063
Fax: 504-468-3469
Email: posehome@bellsouth.net

Cajun Area Agency on Aging, Inc
110 Toledo Drive
Lafayette, Louisiana 70506
Telephone: 337-572-8940

Lafayette Consolidated Government Neighborhood Counseling Services
111 Shirley Picard Drive
Lafayette, Louisiana 70501
Telephone: 337-291-5452

APPENDIX: REVERSE MORTGAGE COUNSELORS

Fax: 337-291-5459

Email: smoore@lafayettegov.net

Web site: **www.lafayettegov.net**

Saint Martin, Iberia, Lafayette Community Action Agency

501 Saint John Street

P.O. Box 3343

Lafayette, Louisiana 70501-5709

Telephone: 334-234-3272 Ext. 203

Fax: 337-234-3274

Email: ijb@smilecaa.org

Web site: **www.smilecaa.org**

Acorn Housing

1024 Elysian Fields Avenue

New Orleans, Louisiana 70117-8402

Telephone: 504-301-3064

Fax: 504-218-7176

Email: cleffall@acornhousing.org

Web site: **www.acornhousing.org**

Desire Community Housing Corporation

4298 Elysian Fields Avenue, Suite B

New Orleans, Louisiana 70122

Telephone: 504-905-1425

Email: wthomasceo@aol.com

Neighborhood Housing Services of New Orleans

4700 Freret Street

New Orleans, Louisiana 70115

Telephone: 504-899-5900 Ext. 105

Fax: 504-899-6190

Email: laurenanderson@nhsnola.org

Web site: **www.nhsnola.org**

Caddo Community Action Agency

4055 Saint Vincent Avenue

Shreveport, Louisiana 71108-2542

Telephone: 318-861-4808

Fax: 318-861-4958

Email: matti@shreve.net

Queensborough Neighborhood Association, Incorporated

2756 Greenwood Road

Shreveport, Louisiana 71109

Telephone: 318-635-8100

Toll-free: 877-636-8100

Fax: 318-631-5921

Email: queensbo@bellsouth.net

Web site: **www.qna.bravehost.com**

Maine

CCCS of Maine, A Division of MMI

250 Center Street Suite 205

Auburn, Maine 04210

Telephone: 800-873-2227

Fax: 207-784-7320

Email: brian.coyle@moneymanagement. org

157 Park Street Suite 34

Bangor, Maine 04401

Telephone: 800-873-2227

Fax: 207-942-2910

brian.coyle@moneymanagement.org

Park 111, 407 Alfred Road Suite 202

Biddeford, Maine 04005

Telephone: 800-873-2227

Fax. 207-284-5744

brian.coyle@moneymanagement.org

114 Maine Street Suite 9B

Brunswick, Maine 04011

Telephone: 800-873-2227

Fax: 207-729-8469

brian.coyle@moneymanagement.org

103 Water Street Room 205

Hallowell, Maine 04347

Telephone: 800-873-2227

Fax: 207-623-6027

brian.coyle@moneymanagement.org

111 Wescott Road

PO Box 2560

South Portland, Maine 04106

Telephone: 800-873-2227

Fax: 207-773-1824

brian.coyle@moneymanagement.org

Central Maine Area Agency on Aging AKA Senior Spectrum

One Weston Court

P.O. Box 2589

Augusta, Maine 04338-2589

Telephone: 800-639-1553

Fax: 207-622-7857

Email: tsimon@seniorspectrum.com

Web site: **www.seniorspectrum.com**

Penquis Community Action Program

262 Harlow Street

P.O. Box 1162

Bangor, Maine 04402-1162

Telephone: 207-973-3500

Toll-free: 888-424-0151

Fax: 207-973-3699

Email: kwashburn@penguis.org

Web site: **www.penguis.org**

People's Regional Opportunity Program

510 Cumberland Avenue

Portland, Maine 04101

Telephone: 207-772-1163

Fax: 207-772-1191

Email: SUM@propeople.org

Web site: **www.propeople.org**

York County Community Action Agency

6 Spruce Street

P.O. Box 72

Sanford, Maine 04073

Telephone: 207-324-5762 Ext. 2960

Fax: 207-490-5025

Email: chrisl@yccac.org

Web site: **www.yccac.org**

Community Concepts, Inc

17-19 Market Square

P.O. Box 278

South Paris, Maine 04281

Telephone: 207-743-7716

Fax: 207-743-6513

Email:dtrenoweth@community-concepts.
org

Web site: **www.community-concepts.
org**

Coastal Enterprises, Incorporated

41 Water Street

P.O. Box 268

Wiscasset, Maine 04578-0268

Telephone: 207-882-7552 Ext. 186

Toll-free: 877-340-2649

Fax: 207-882-4455

Email: jml@ceimaine.org

Web site: **www.ceimaine.org**

Maryland

CCCS of Greater Washington, A Division of MMI

Suite 404

1003 W. 7th Street

Fredrick, Maryland 21701

Telephone: 301-695-0369

Toll-free: 800-747-4222

Fax: 301-695-4878

Email: lori.johnson@moneymanagement.
org

Web site: **www.creditcounselingnetwork.org**

Suite 112B

920 W. Washington Street

Hagerstown, Maryland 21740

Telephone: 301-416-8284

Toll-free: 800-747-4222

Fax: 301-791-1641

Email: lori.johnson@moneymanagement.
org

www.creditcounselingnetwork.org

15847 Crabbs Branch Way

Rockville, Maryland 20855-2635

Telephone: 800-747-4222

Toll-free: 800-747-4222

Fax: 301-948-7498

Web site: **www.moneymanagement.org**

8613 Piney Branch Road

Silver Spring, Maryland 20901

Telephone: 800-747-4222

Email: lori.johnson@moneymanagement.
org

www.creditcounselingnetwork.org

8605 Cameron Street Ste M2

Silver Spring, Maryland 20910

Telephone: 800-747-4222

Fax: 877-405-0596

Email: lori.johnson@moneymanagement.
org

www.creditcounselingnetwork.org

Anne Arundel County Economic Opportunity Comm.
251 West Street
P.O. Box 1951
Annapolis, Maryland 21404
Telephone: 410-626-1900 Ext. 1018
Fax: 410-267-9143
Email: kspencer@aaceoc.com
Web site: **www.aaceoc.org**

Acorn Housing
16 West 25th Street
Baltimore, Maryland 21218
Telephone: 410-243-9790
Fax: 410-243-9794
Email: llee@acornhousing.org
Web site: **www.acornhousing.org**

Community Assistance Network
7701 Dunmanway
Baltimore, Maryland 21222-5437
Telephone: 410-285-4674
Fax: 410-288-1740
Email: pjohnson@canconnects.org
Web site: **www.canconnects.org**

Druid Heights Community Development Corp
2140 McCulloh Street
Baltimore, Maryland 21217-3529
Telephone: 410-523-1350 Ext. 10
Fax: 410-523-1374
Email: klittle@druidheights.com

Web site: **www.druidheights.com**

Govans Economic Management Senate, Inc
3921 Old York Road
Baltimore, Maryland 21218
Telephone: 410-433-3400
Fax: 410-433-7140
Email: gemscdc5@aol.com

Greater Baltimore Urban League
512 Orchard Street
Baltimore, Maryland 21201-1947
Telephone: 410-523-8150
Fax: 410-523-4022
Email: nrollins@bul.org

Southeast Community Development Corporation
3700 Eastern Avenue
Baltimore, Maryland 21224
Telephone; 410-342-3234 Ext. 25
Fax: 410-342-1719
Email: luisa@southeastcdc.org
Web site: **www.southeastcdc.org**

St. Ambrose Housing Aid Center, Inc
321 East 25th Street
Baltimore, Maryland 21218-5303
Telephone: 410-366-8362 Ext. 216
Fax: 410-366-8795
Email: lisae@stambros.org
Web site: **www.stanbros.org**

The Development Corporation of Northwest Baltimore

3521 West Belvedere Avenue

Baltimore, Maryland 21215-5802

Telephone: 410-578-7190 Ext. 14

Fax: 410-578-7193

Email: fvrobinson@thedevelopmentcorporation.org

Harford County Housing Agency

15 South Main Street, Suite 106

Bel Air, Maryland 21014

Telephone: 410-638-3045 Ext. 3047

Fax: 410-893-9816

Email: wlbhola@harfordcountymd.gov

Web site: **www.harfordcountymd.gov**

United Communities Against Poverty

1400 Doewood Lane

P.O. Box 13156

Capital Heights, Maryland 20731-0356

Telephone: 301-322-5700

Fax: 301-322-3881

Email: mail@ucappgc.org

Web site: **www.ucappgc.org**

Howard County Office on Aging

6751 Columbia Gateway Dr.

Columbia, Maryland 21046

Telephone: 410-313-6410

St. Stephens Economic Development

7320 Roosevelt Boulevard

Elkridge, Maryland 21075

Telephone: 410-540-9188

Fax: 410-540-9180

Email: jeally2001@yahoo.com

Cecil County Housing Agency

200 Chesapeake Boulevard, Suite 1800

Elkton, Maryland 21921

Telephone: 410-996-8215

Fax: 410-996-5256

Email: btoth@ccgov.org

Frederick Community Action Agency

100 South Market Street

Frederick, Maryland 21701-5527

Telephone: 301-600-1506

Fax: 301-662-9079

Email: mspurrier@cityoffrederick.com

Web site: **www.cityoffrederick.com/departments/CAA/Agency.htm**

Housing Commission of Anne Arundel County

7477 Baltimore-Annapolis Boulevard

P.O. Box 817

Glen Burnie, Maryland 21060-2817

Telephone: 410-222-6200 Ext. 123

Fax: 410-222-6214

Email: laloyd@hcaac.org

Maryland Rural Development Corporation

101 Cedar Avenue

P.O. Box 739

Greensboro, Maryland 21639-0739

Telephone: 410-479-3566 Ext. 14

Fax: 410-479-3710

Email: gjx@mrdc.net

Web site: **www.mrdc.net**

Washington County Community Action Council

101 Summit Avenue

Hagerstown, Maryland 21740

Telephone: 301-797-4161 Ext. 124

Fax: 301-791-9062

Email: djordan@wccac.org

Web site: **www.wccac.org**

Southern Maryland Tri-County Community Action

8383 Leonardtown Road

P.O. Box 280

Hughesville, Maryland 20637

Telephone: 301-274-4474 Ext. 253

Fax: 301-274-0423

Email: swynice@smtccac.org

Web site: **www.smtccac.org**

Housing Initiatives Partnership, Inc

6525 Belcrest Road, Suite 555

Hyattsville, Maryland 20782

Telephone: 301-699-3835

Email: mharrington@hiphomes.org

Garrett County Community Action Committee, Inc

104 East Center Street

Oakland, Maryland 21550-1328

Telephone: 301-334-9431 Ext. 149

Toll-free: 888-877-8403

Email: csharon@garrettcac.org

Web site: **www.garrettcac.org**

Salisbury Neighborhood Housing Service, Inc

513 Camden Avenue

Salisbury, Maryland 21801

Telephone: 410-543-4626 Ext. 201

Fax: 410-543-9204

Email: cherylm@salisburynhs.org

Web site: **www.salisburynhs.org**

Shore Up!, Inc

520 Snow Hill Road

Salisbury, Maryland 21804-6031

Telephone: 410-749-1142

Fax: 410-742-9191

Email: tchase@shoreup.org

Web site: **www.shoreup.org**

National Foundation for Credit Counseling, Inc

801 Roeder Road, Suite 900

Silver Spring, Maryland 20910-3372

Telephone: 800-388-2227

Toll-free: 866-845-2227

Fax: 301-589-8256

Web site: **www.nfcc.org**

Roots of Mankind Corporation
4273 Branch Avenue, Suite 205
Temple Hills, Maryland 20748
Telephone: 301-899-6800
Toll-free: 866-490-6800
Fax: 301-899-8444
Email: whitmireck@romkind.org
Web site: **www.romkind.org**

Massachusetts

CCCS of Southern New England, A Division of MMI
409 Main Street, Room 105
Amherst, Massachusetts 01002
Telephone: 800-308-2227

100 Cummings Center, Suite 311H
Beverly, Massachusetts 01915
Telephone: 800-208-2227

8 Winter Street
Boston, Massachusetts 02108
Telephone: 800-308-2227

40 Central Street
Lowell, Massachusetts 01852
Telephone: 800-208-2227

888 Purchase Street, Suite 319
New Bedford, Massachusetts 02740
Telephone: 800-208-2227

34 Depot Street, Suite 202

Pittsfield, Massachusetts 01202
Telephone: 800-208-2227

247 North Main Street, Suite 200
Randolph, Massachusetts 02368
Telephone: 800-208-2227

59 Interstate Drive, Ste. 10
West Springfield, Massachusetts 01089
Telephone: 800-208-2227

800 West Cummings Park, Suite 1075
Woburn, Massachusetts 01801
Telephone: 800-208-2227

74 Elm Street
Worcester, Massachusetts 01609
Telephone: 800-208-2227

Homeowner Options for Massachusetts Elders
150 Grossman Drive, 4th Floor
Braintree, Massachusetts 02184
Telephone: 781-848-5200
Toll-free: 800-583-5337
Fax: 781-848-5222
Email: maselders@verizon.net
Web site: **www.home-ma.org**

Acorn Housing
196 Adams Street
Dorchester, Massachusetts 02122-1338
Telephone: 617-436-6161

Fax: 617-822-1647

Email: tnaylor@acornhousing.org

Web site: **www.acornhousing.org**

1655 Main Street # 505

Springfield, Massachusetts 01103

Telephone: 413-736-7713

Fax: 413-736-0942

Email: tnaylor@acornhousing.org

Web site: **www.acornhousing.org**

Catholic Social Services

1600 Bay Street

P.O. Box M, South Station

Fall River, Massachusetts 02724

Telephone: 508-674-4681 Ext. 124

Fax: 508-675-2224

Email: c_Hernandez@cssdioc.org

Web site: **www.cssdioc.org**

59 Rockland Street

New Bedford, Massachusetts 02740-4751

Telephone: 508-674-4681 Ext. 131

Fax: 508-675-2224

Email: mlv@cssdioc.org

Web site: **www.cssdioc.org**

Housing Assistance Corp

460 West Main Street

Hyannis, Massachusetts 02601

Telephone: 508-771-5400 Ext. 289

Fax: 508-775-7434

Email: ncrockan@haconcape.org

Web site: **www.haconcapecod.org**

Legal Services for Cape, Plymouth, and Islands, Inc

460 West Main Street

Hyannis, Massachusetts 02601-3653

Telephone: 508-775-7020 Ext. 106

Toll-free: 800-742-4107

Fax: 508-709-3955

Email: ryox@lscpi.org

Web site: **www.lscpi.org**

Plymouth Redevelopment Authority

11 Lincoln Street

Plymouth, Massachusetts 02360

Telephone: 508-747-1620 Ext. 146

Fax: 508-830-4116

Email: redevelopment@townhall.
plymouth.ma.us

Web site: **www.plymouthdevelopment.
org**

Neighborhood Housing Services of the South Shore

422 Washington Street

Quincy, Massachusetts 02169

Telephone: 617-770-2227 Ext. 26

Fax: 617-770-2249

Email: n.grenier@neighborhoodhousing.
org

Web site: **www.neighborhoodhousing.
org**

Quincy Community Action Programs, Inc

1509 Hancock Street

Quincy, Massachusetts 02169-5200
Telephone: 617-479-8181 Ext. 166
Fax: 617-479-7228
Email: nsullivan@qcap.org
Web site: **www.qcap.org**

Urban Edge Housing Corp
1542 Columbus Avenue, Suite 2
Roxbury, Massachusetts 02119
Telephone: 617-989-9316
Fax: 617-427-8931
Email: eosorio@urbanedge.org
Web site: **www.urbanedge.org**

HAP, Inc
322 Main Street
Springfield, Massachusetts 01105
Telephone: 413-785-1251
Toll-free: 800-332-9667
Fax: 413-731-8723
Email: dbroaden@haphousing.org
Web site: **www.hhhp.org**

Springfield Neighborhood Housing Services
111 Wilbraham Road
Springfield, Massachusetts 01109
Telephone: 413-739-4737 Ext. 212
Fax: 413-739-8070
Email: rucks@springfieldnhs.org
Web site: **www.springfieldnhs.org**

Community Service Network, Inc

52 Broadway
Stoneham, Massachusetts 02180-1003
Telephone: 781-438-5981
Fax: 781-438-6037
Email: sheilaberbeck@csninc.org
Web site: **www.csninc.org**

Michigan

GreenPath, Inc
315 East Eisenhower, Suite 206
Ann Arbor, Michigan 48108
Telephone: 888-860-4167
Web site: **www.greenpath.com**

131 East Columbia Avenue, Suite 213
Battle Creek, Michigan 49015-3761
Telephone: 888-860-4167
www.greenpath.com

2525 Telegraph Road, Suite 306
Bloomfield Hills, Michigan 48302-0289
Telephone: 248-332-5273
Fax: 248-332-5537

211 North First Street, Suite 300
Brighton, Michigan 48116-1297
Telephone: 888-860-4167

3011 West Grand Boulevard, Suite 1507
Detroit, Michigan 48202
Telephone: 888-860-4167
Web site: **www.greenpath.com**

17200 East 10 Mile Road, Suite 155
Eastpointe, Michigan 48021
Telephone: 888-860-4167
www.greenpath.com

38505 Country Club Drive, Suite 210
Farmington Hills, Michigan 48331
Telephone: 888-860-4167
Fax: 248-553-8970
www.greenpath.com

2222 South Linden Road, Suite I
Flint, Michigan 48532
Telephone: 888-860-4167
www.greenpath.com

3051 Commerce Drive, Suite 3
Fort Gratiot, Michigan 48059-3820
Telephone: 888-860-4167
www.greenpath.com

810 South Otsego, Suite 105
Gaylord, Michigan 49735-1780
Telephone: 888-860-4167
www.greenpath.com

1241 East Beltline, Suite 110
Grand Rapids, Michigan 49505
Telephone: 888-860-4167

www.greenpath.com
675 East 16th Street, Suite 220

Holland, Michigan, 49423-3752
Telephone: 616-394-9003
Fax: 616-394-4308
www.greenpath.com

Plaza Central
415 Stephenson Avenue
Iron Mountain, Michigan 49801
Telephone: 906-774-7565
Fax: 906-774-0461
www.greenpath.com

629 West Cloverland Drive, Suite 9
Ironwood, Michigan 49938
Telephone: 888-860-4167
www.greenpath.com

211 West Ganson
Jackson, Michigan 49201-1241
Telephone: 888-860-4167
www.greenpath.com

2450 44th Street SE, Suite 204
Kentwood, Michigan 49512-9081
Telephone: 616-281-0013
Fax: 616-281-0293
www.greenpath.com

612 South Creyts Road, Suite C
Lansing, Michigan 48917-9201
Telephone: 888-860-4167
www.greenpath.com

712 Chippewa Square, Suite 102
Marquette, Michigan 49855-4827
Telephone: 888-860-4167
www.greenpath.com

25 South Monroe Street, Suite 312
Monroe, Michigan 48161-2230
Telephone: 888-860-4167
www.greenpath.com

800 Ellis Road, Suite 540
Muskegon, Michigan 49441
Telephone: 888-860-4167
www.greenpath.com

7127 South Westnedge Avenue, Suite 5C
Portage, Michigan 49081
Telephone: 888-860-4167
www.greenpath.com

4600 Fashion Square Boulevard, Suite 110
Saginaw, Michigan 48604-2616
Telephone: 888-860-4167
www.greenpath.com

20300 Civic Center Drive, Suite 305
Southfield, Michigan 48034
Telephone: 888-860-4167
www.greenpath.com

8750 South Telegraph Road, Suite 100
Taylor, Michigan 48180

Telephone: 888-860-4167
www.greenpath.com

10850 East Traverse Highway, Suite 1104
Traverse City, Michigan 49684
Telephone: 888-860-4167
www.greenpath.com

5700 Crooks Road, Suite 202
Troy, Michigan 48098
Telephone: 888-860-4167
www.greenpath.com

11111 Hall Road, Suite 422
Utica, Michigan 48317
Telephone: 888-860-4167
www.greenpath.com

38545 Ford Road, Suite 202
Westland, Michigan 48185-7901
Telephone: 888-860-4167
www.greenpath.com

ACCESS
23300 Greenfield Road, Suite 102
Oak Park, Michigan 48237
Telephone: 866-648-8114
Toll-free: 800-546-3247

Southwest Michigan Community Action Agency
185 East Main Street, Suite 200
Benton Harbor, Michigan 49022

Telephone: 269-925-9077

Toll-free: 800-334-7670

Fax: 269-925-9271

Email: jpeterson@smcaa.com

Web site: **www.smcaa.com**

Northwest Michigan Human Services Agency, Inc

1640 Marty Paul Street

Cadillac, Michigan 49601-9608

Telephone: 231-775-9781

Toll-free: 800-947-3780

Fax: 231-775-1448

441 Bay Street

Petoskey, Michigan 49770-2408

Telephone: 616-347-9070

Toll-free: 800-443-9070

Fax: 616-347-3664

Michigan State University Extension Services

Verkuilen Building

21885 Dunham Road, Suite 12

Clinton Twp, Michigan 48036

Telephone: 586-469-5180

Fax: 586-469-6948

Bethel Housing Counseling Agency

5050 St. Antoine Street

Detroit, Michigan 48202

Telephone: 313-833-9912

Fax: 313-833-5312

Email: bqolfi42898@sbcglobal.net

Detroit Non-Profit Housing Corporation

8904 Woodward Avenue, Suite 279

Considine Center

Detroit, Michigan 48202

Telephone: 313-972-1111

Fax: 313-972-1125

Email: detroitnon@aol.com

Mission of Peace

9000 Woodward Avenue

Detroit, Michigan 48202

Telephone: 313-872-2900

Fax: 810-341-8471

Email: mopc@aol.com

Web site: **www.missionofpeace.com**

877 East 5th Avenue

Flint, Michigan 48503

Telephone: 810-232-0104 Ext. 113

Fax: 810-235-6878

Email: mopc@aol.com

Web site: **www.missionofpeace.com**

Phoenix Housing & Counseling Non-Profit, Inc

1640 Porter Street

Detroit, Michigan 48216-1936

Telephone: 313-964-4207

Fax: 313-964-3861

Email: phoenixhousing@sbcglobal.net

Greater East Side Community Association

2804 North Franklin Avenue

Flint, Michigan 48506

Telephone: 810-233-0507

Fax: 810-233-7322

Email: katefields@aol.com

Metro Housing Partnership, Inc

Mott Foundation Building

503 South Saginaw Street, Suite 804

Flint, Michigan 48502

Telephone: 810-767-4622 Suite 24

Fax: 810-767-4664

Email: acrews@flint.org

Web site: **www.metrohousing.org**

Home Repair Services of Kent County, Inc

1100 South Division Avenue

Grand Rapids, Michigan 49507

Telephone: 616-241-2601

Fax: 616-241-5151

Email: djacobs@homerepairservices.org

Web site: **www.homerepairservices.org**

Inner City Christian Federation

920 Cherry SE

Grand Rapids, Michigan 49506

Telephone: 616-336-9333 Ext. 303

Fax: 616-336-9323

Email: sortiz@iccf.org

Web site: **www.iccf.org**

Kalamazoo Neighborhood Housing Services, Inc

802 South Westnedge Avenue

Kalamazoo, Michigan 49008

Telephone: 269-385-2916

Fax: 269-385-9912

Email: tim@knhs.org

Web site: **www.knhs.org**

Oakland County Housing Counseling

250 Elizabeth Lake Road, Suite 1900

Pontiac, Michigan 48341-0414

Telephone: 248-858-5402

Toll-free: 888-350-0900

Fax: 248-858-5311

Email: williamska@oakgov.com

Web site: **www.oakgov.com/chi/housing_counsel**

Saginaw County Community Action Committee, Inc

2824 Perkins Street

Saginaw, Michigan 48601-1505

Telephone: 989-753-7741

Fax: 989-753-2439

Email: liwilliams@saginawcac.org

Northwest Michigan Human Services Agency, Inc

3963 Three Mile Road

Traverse City, Michigan 49686-9164

Telephone: 231-947-3780

Toll-free: 800-947-3780

Fax: 231-947-4935

Email: kemerson@mnhsa.org

Minnesota

CCCS of the Village Family Service Center

460 Northside Drive #5

Alexandria, Minnesota 56308

Telephone: 800-450-4019

Fax: 701-451-5057

Email: moneyhelp@thevillagefamily.org

Web site: **www.helpwithmoney.org**

200 S 6th Street

Brianerd, Minnesota 56401

Telephone: 800-450-4019

Fax: 701-451-5057

Email: moneyhelp@thevillagefamily.org

www.helpwithmoney.org

7000 57th Avenue North, Suite 105

Crystal Minnesota 55428

Telephone: 800-450-4019

Fax: 763-536-8044

Email: moneyhelp@thevillagefamily.org

www.helpwithmoney.org

715 N. 11th Street, Suite 108D

Moorhead, Minnesota 56560

Telephone: 701-235-3328

Toll-free: 800-450-4019

Fax: 701-451-5057

Email: moneyhelp@thevillagefamily.org

www.helpwithmoney.org

St. Stephen State Bank

3950 3rd St N Ste 102

St. Cloud, Minnesota 56301

Telephone: 800-450-4019

Fax: 320-253-0541

Email: moneyhelp@thevillagefamily.org

www.helpwithmoney.org

Lutheran Social Services/ CCCS of Duluth

East Brianerd Mall

716 E Street

Brianerd, Minnesota 56401

Telephone: 888-577-2227

Fax: 218-726-1251

Email: cccs@lssmn.org

Web site: **www.lssmn.org/debt**

424 West Superior Street

PO Box 306

Duluth, Minnesota 55802-0306

Telephone: 888-577-2227

Fax: 218-726-1251

Email: cccs@lssmn.org

Web site: **www.lssmn.org/debt**

302 Grant Avenue

Eveleth, Minnesota 55734

Telephone: 888-577-2227

Fax: 218-726-1251

Email: cccs@lssmn.org

www.lssmn.org/debt
33 10th Avenue S, Suite 150
Hopkins, Minnesota 55343
Telephone: 888-577-2227
Fax: 218-726-1251
Email: cccs@lssmn.org
www.lssmn.org/debt

710 South 2nd Street
Mankato, Minnesota 56001
Telephone: 888-577-2227
Fax: 218-726-1251
Email: cccs@lssmn.org
www.lssmn.org/debt

2414 Park Avenue
Minneapolis, Minnesota 55404
Telephone: 888-577-2227
Fax: 218-726-1251
Email: cccs@lssmn.org
www.lssmn.org/debt

590 Park Street, Suite 310
St. Paul, Minnesota 55103
Telephone: 888-577-2227
Fax: 218-726-1251
Email: cccs@lssmn.org
www.lssmn.org/debt

333 Litchfield Avenue SW
Willmar, Minnesota 56201
Telephone: 888-577-2227
Fax: 218-726-1251

Email: cccs@lssmn.org
www.lssmn.org/debt

Anoka County Community Action Program, Inc

1201 89th Avenue, Suite 345
Blaine, Minnesota 55434-3373
Telephone: 763-783-4880
Fax: 763-783-4700
Email: jan.backlin@accap.org
Web site: **www.accap.org**

Community Action Partnership of Suburban Hennepin

33 10th Avenue South, Suite 150
Hopkins, Minnesota 55343-1303
Telephone: 952-933-9639
Fax: 952-933-8016
Email: mharris@capsh.org
Web site: **www.capsh.org**

Reverse Mortgage Counselors, Incorporated

3333 Fourth Street North
Minneapolis, Minnesota 55412
Telephone: 612-865-6434
Toll-free: 888-690-7829
Fax: 651-644-3282
Email: eande@comcast.net
Web site: **www.reversemortgagecoun-selors.us**

1885 University Avenue West, Suite 211
St. Paul, Minnesota 55104

Telephone: 651-690-3141
Toll-free: 888-690-7829
Fax: 651-644-3282
Email: housingsense@msn.com
www.reversemortgagecounselors.us

Jewish Family and Children's Services
13100 Wayzata Boulevard, Suite 400
Minnetonka, Minnesota 55305
Telephone: 952-542-4812

Catholic Charities Diocese of St. Cloud
157 Roosevelt Road # 200
Saint Cloud, Minnesota 56301
Telephone: 800-830-8254 Ext. 2660
Fax: 320-253-7464
Email: mbulson@gw.stcdio.org
Web site: www.ccstcloud.org

Acorn Housing, St. Paul and Minneapolis
Security Building
757 Raymond Avenue, Suite 200
St. Paul, Minnesota 55114
Telephone: 651-203-0008
Fax: 651-203-1046
Email: amilton@acornhousing.org
Web site: www.acornhousing.org

Mississippi

CCCS of Greater New Orleans, Inc
2318 Pass Road, Suite 2
Biloxi, Mississippi 39531

Telephone: 228-388-9408
Toll-free: 888-287-6676
Fax: 228-388-1273
Email: cccsno@cccsno.org
Web site: www.cccsno.org

6158 Highway 49 East
Hattiesburg, Mississippi 39401
Telephone: 601-544-2227
Toll-free: 800-413-2227
Fax: 601-544-2230
Email: cccsno@cccsno.org
www.cccsno.org

1018 N. Gloster, Suite H
Tupelo, Mississippi 38804
Telephone: 662-680-9750
Toll-free: 800-915-2227
Fax: 662-680-9751
Email: cccsno@cccsno.org
www.cccsno.org

Catholic Charities
200 North Congress Street, Suite 100
Jackson, Mississippi 39202
Telephone: 601-442-0107
Fax: 601-960-8493
Email: Martha.mitternight@catholiccha-
ritiesjac

200 North Congress Street, Suite 100
Natchez, Mississippi 39120
Telephone: 601-442-0107

Fax: 601-960-8493

Email: evelyn.peters@catholiccharities-jackson

Mississippi Faith Based Coalition for Community Renewal, Inc

1770 Ellis Avenue, Suite 200

Jackson, Mississippi 39212

Telephone: 601-346-7503

Fax: 601-346-5950

Web site: **www.msfaithbasedcoalition.org**

Mississippi Housing Partnership, Inc

1217 North West Street

P.O. Box 22987

Jackson, Mississippi 39202

Telephone: 601-969-1895

Fax: 601-969-5300

Email: uthompson1@comcast.net

Urban League of Greater Jackson, Inc

2310 Highway 80 West

Building 1, Suite E

Jackson, Mississippi 39204

Telephone: 601-714-4600

Fax: 601-714-4040

Email: willie.cole@gmail.com

Multi-County Community Service Agency

2900 St. Paul Street

Meridian, Mississippi 39301

Telephone: 601-484-3969

Toll-free: 800-898-0659

Fax: 601-484-3963

Email: mbigelow@multi-county.org

Sacred Heart Southern Missions Housing Corporation

P.O. Box 365

Walls, Mississippi 38680-0365

Telephone: 662-342-3350

Fax: 662-781-0886

Email: taddcox@shsm.org

Missouri

CCCS of the Midwest

1900 N Providence, Ste 309

Columbia, Missouri 65202

Telephone: 800-355-2227

Fax: 614-552-4800

Email: info@cccservices.com

Web site: **www.cccservices.com/home.asp**

3737 S. Elizabeth St., Suite 103

Independence, Missouri 64057-1785

Telephone: 800-355-2227

Fax: 913-642-5643

Email: info@cccservices.com

www.cccservices.com/home.asp

9300 Troost

Kansas City, Missouri 64131

Telephone: 800-355-2227

Fax: 614-552-4800

Email: info@cccservices.com
www.cccservices.com/home.asp

3115 Ashland Ave Ste 200
St Joseph, Missouri 64506
Telephone: 800-355-2227
Fax: 614-552-4800
Email: info@cccservices.com
www.cccservices.com/home.asp

CCCS of Springfield

3130 Wisconsin, Suite 4
Joplin, Missouri 64804
Telephone: 800-346-4930
Toll-free: 800-882-0808
Email: susan@cccs-swmo.org
www.cccsoftheozarks.org

1410 E. Kearney, Suite F
Springfield, Missouri 65803
Telephone: 800-346-4930
Toll-free: 800-882-0808
Email: mike@cccs-swmo.org
www.cccsoftheozarks.org

1515 S Glenstone
Springfield, Missouri 65804
Telephone: 800-346-4930
Toll-free: 800-882-0808
Email: tonya@cccsoftheozarks.org
www.cccsoftheozarks.org

1522 Porter Wagner Boulevard, Suite 1
West Plains, Missouri 65775
Telephone: 800-346-4930
Email: kathyv@cccs-swmo.org
www.cccs-swmo.org

West Central Missouri Community Action Agency

106 West 4th Street
P.O. Box 125
Appleton City, Missouri 64724
Telephone: 660-476-2185 Ext. 1500
Fax: 660-476-0175
Email: kmiller@wcmcaa.org

Acorn Housing

6301 Rockhill Road, Suite 201
Kansas City, Missouri 64131
Telephone: 816-444-0804
Fax: 816-444-5582
Email: cblatt@acornhousing.org
Web site: **www.acornhousing.org**

4304 Manchester Avenue
St. Louis, Missouri 63110-2138
Telephone: 314-531-6204
Fax: 314-531-4942
Email: amilton@acornhousing.org
www.acornhousing.org

Catholic Charities

1112 Broadway
Kansas City, Missouri 64105

Telephone: 816-221-4377

Toll-free: 800-875-4377

Fax: 816-232-2607

Email: dmaples@ccharities.com

Web site: **www.catholiccharities-kcsj. org**

426 South Jefferson, Suite 202

Springfield, Missouri 65806

Telephone: 417-865-0050

Toll-free: 866-604-9494

Fax: 417-865-0070

Email: dmaples@ccharities.com

www.catholiccharities-kcsj.org

1302 Faraon Street

St. Joseph, Missouri 64501

Telephone: 816-232-2885

Email: tcollister@ccharities.org

Greater Kansas City Housing Information Center

6285 Paseo Boulevard

Kansas City, Missouri 64110

Telephone: 816-931-0443

Fax: 816-931-0722

Email: pgilmore3810@hotmail.com

Legal Aid of Western Missouri

1125 Grand Boulevard, Suite 2000

Kansas City, Missouri 64106

Telephone: 816-474-6750 Ext. 206

Fax: 816-474-9751

Email: jlevin@lawmo.org

920 Southwest Boulevard

Kansas City, Missouri 64108

Telephone: 816-474-9868

Fax: 816-474-7575

Email: yhernandez@lawmo.org

106 South Seventh Street

St. Joseph, Missouri 64502

Telephone: 816-364-2325

Toll-free: 800-892-2101

Fax: 816-364-2647

Email: jsoper@lawmo.org

Housing Options Provided for the Elderly

4265 Shaw Boulevard

St. Louis, Missouri 63110-3526

Telephone: 314-776-0155

Toll-free: 888-776-0155

Fax: 314-776-0852

Email: zbuz@hotmail.com

Justine Peterson Housing and Reinvestment Corporation

1023 North Grand Boulevard

St. Louis, Missouri 63106

Telephone: 314-664-5051

Fax: 314-664-5364

Email: sflanigan@justinepeterson.org

Web site: **www.justinepeterson.org**

Redemption Center CDC

4454 Manchester Avenue

St. Louis, Missouri 63110

Telephone: 314-533-3344

Fax: 314-537-5592

Email: redeem_outmin@yahoo.com

Montana

CCCS of Montana

307 E. Park

Anaconda, Montana 59711

Telephone: 406-723-5176

Toll-free: 877-275-2227

Email: crobbins@cccsmt.org

1620 Alderson #27

P.O. Box 20815

Billings, Montana 59102

Telephone: 406-656-4370

Toll-free: 877-275-2227

Fax: 406-656-2925

Email: mikeh@cccsmt.org

Web site: **www.cccsmt.org**

220 W. Lamme Suite 1D

Bozeman, Montana 57915

Telephone: 406-582-9273

Toll-free: 877-275-2227

Fax: 406-582-9128

Email: beverlyj@cccsmt.org

www.cccsmt.org

730 N. Montana

Dillon, Montana 59725

Telephone: 406-723-5176

Toll-free: 877-275-2227

Email: crobbins@cccsmt.org

2022 Central Avenue

Great Falls, Montana 59401

Telephone: 406-761-8721

Toll-free: 877-275-2227

Fax: 406-761-8622

Email: timr@cccsmt.org

Web site: **www.cccsmt.org**

1728 2nd Street W, Suite B

Havre, Montana 59501

Telephone: 406-761-8721

Toll-free: 877-275-2227

Fax: 406-761-8622

Email: timr@cccsmt.org

1275 Maple Ave, Suite E

P.O. Box 5163

Helena, Montana 59601

Telephone: 406-443-1774

Toll-free: 877-275-2227

Fax: 406-499-0602

Email: angelah@cccsmt.org

690 N. Meridan, Suite 206

Kalispell, Montana 59901

Telephone: 406-257-4069

Toll-free: 877-275-2227

Fax: 406-755-1484

Email: megank@cccsmt.org

2110 South Reserve

P.O. Box 4642

Missoula, Montana 59801

Telephone: 406-543-1188

Toll-free: 877-275-2227

Fax: 406-549-2696

Email: terric@cccsmt.org

District 7 Human Resources Development Council

7 North 31st Street

P.O. Box 2016

Billings, Montana 59103

Telephone: 406-247-4741

Toll-free: 800-433-1411

Fax: 406-869-2585

Email: ckramer@hrdc7.org

Web site: **www.hrdc7.org**

Yellowstone County Council on Aging, Inc

1309 16th Street West

Billings, Montana 59102

Telephone: 406-259-5212

Email: yccoabm@imt.net

Neighborhood Housing Services Inc of Great Falls

509 First Avenue, South

Great Falls, Montana 59401

Telephone: klee@nhsgf.org

Web site: **www.nwmt.org**

Homeword

127 North Higgins Avenue, #307

Missoula, Montana 59802

Telephone: 406-532-4663 Ext. 18

Fax: 406-541-0239

Email: betsy@homeword.org

Web site: **www.homeword.org**

Nebraska

CCCS of Nebraska

2121 North Webb Road, Suite 307

Grand Island, Nebraska 68803

Telephone: 308-381-4551

Toll-free: 800-950-3328

Fax: 308-381-1434

Email: tauberts@aol.com

Web site: **www.cccsn.org**

1001 S. 70th Street, Suite 200

Lincoln, Nebraska 68505

Telephone: 402-484-7200

Toll-free: 877-494-2227

Fax: 402-484-7332

Email: tauberts@aol.com

www.cccsn.org

700 1/2 Benjamin Country Club Plaza

Norfolk, Nebraska 68701

Telephone: 402-371-4656

Toll-free: 877-494-2227

Fax: 402-371-7462

Email: nfmgr@cableone.net

www.cccsn.org

509 E. 4th Street, Suite F1
North Platte, Nebraska 69103
Telephone: 877-494-2227
Email: tauberts@aol.com
www.cccsn.org

8805 Indian Hills Drive, Suite 105
Omaha, Nebraska 68114
Telephone: 402-333-8609 Ext. 320
Toll-free: 877-494-2227
Fax: 402-333-8443
Email: tauberts@aol.com
www.cccsn.org

11225 Davenport
Omaha, Nebraska 68154
Telephone: 877-494-2227
Fax: 402-333-8440
Email: higinsmb@aol.com
www.cccsn.org

11330 Q Street, Suite 219
Omaha, Nebraska 68137
Telephone: 877-494-2227
Fax: 402-333-8440
Email: tauberts@aol.com
www.cccsn.org

124 S. 24th Street
Suite 200
Omaha, Nebraska 68102

Telephone: 877-494-2227
Fax: 402-333-8440
Email: tauberts@aol.com
www.cccsn.org

21 E. 20th Street
Scottsbluff, Nebraska 69361
Telephone: 308-532-9760
Toll-free: 877-494-2227
Fax: 800-808-2227
Email: tauberts@aol.com
www.cccsn.org

High Plains Community Development Corporation

130 East 2nd Street
Chadron, Nebraska 69337-2329
Telephone: 308-432-4346 Ext. 5
Toll-free: 866-432-4346
Fax: 308-432-4655
Email: margueritem@gpcom.net
Web site: www.highplainscdc.com

Lincoln Action Program, Inc

210 O Street
Lincoln, Nebraska 68508
Telephone: 402-471-4515
Fax: 402-471-4844
Email: shinrichs@lincoln-action.org
Web site: www.lincoln-action.org

Credit Advisors Foundation

1818 South 72nd Street

Omaha, Nebraska 68124
Telephone: 402-393-1234
Toll-free: 800-942-9027
Fax: 402-393-7660
Web site: **www.creditadvisors.org**

Family Housing Advisory Services, Inc
2401 Lake Street
Omaha, Nebraska 68111
Telephone: 402-934-7926 Ext. 6386
Toll-free: 888-573-0495
Fax: 402-934-7928
Email: Teresa@fhasinc.org
Web site: **www.fhasinc.org**

3605 Q Street
Omaha, Nebraska 68107
Telephone: 402-546-1013
Fax: 402-734-8887
Email: Teresa@fhasinc.org
Web site: **www.fhasinc.org**

Nevada

CCCS of Southern Nevada
841 E 2ND
Carson City, Nevada 89701
Telephone: 800-451-4505
Email: ccanv@aol.com
Web site: **www.cccsnevada.org**

2920 N. Green Valley Parkway
Henderson, Nevada 89014

Telephone: 702-364-0344
Fax: 702-364-5836
Email: cccs@cccsnevada.org
www.cccsnevada.org

2650 S. Jones Blvd
Las Vegas, Nevada 89146-0000
Telephone: 702-364-0344
Toll-free: 800-451-4505
Fax: 702-364-1382
Email: cccs@cccsnevada.org
www.cccsnevada.org

Nellis Air Force Base, NV
Las Vegas, Nevada 89119
Telephone: 702-364-0344
Toll-free: 800-451-4505
Email: 702-364-5836
Email: cccs@cccsnevada.org
www.cccsnevada.org

3100 Mill Street, Ste.111
Reno, Nevada 89502
Telephone: 775-337-6363
Toll-free: 800-451-4505
Fax: 775-337-6679
Email: ccanv@aol.com
www.cccsnevada.org

Acorn Housing
953 E. Sahara Avenue, # 226
Las Vegas, Nevada 89104

Telephone: 702-384-3022

Fax: 702-384-4520

Email: llopez@acornhousing.org

Web site: **www.acornhousing.org**

Washoe County Department of Senior Services – Senior Law Project

1155 East Ninth Street

Rono, Nevada 00512-2027

Telephone: 775-328-2592

Fax: 775-328-6193

Email: slawproj@washoecounty.us

Web site: **www.washoecounty.us/ seniorsrv/legal.htm**

New Hampshire

CCCS of New Hampshire & Vermont

64 Main Street

Keene, New Hampshire 03431

Telephone: 800-327-6778

Web site: **www.cccsnh-vt.org**

CCCS of Maine, A Division of MMI

100 Borthwick Av

Northeast Credit Union

Portsmouth, New Hampshire 03802-1240

Telephone: 800-873-2227

Toll-free: 877-664-3328

New Hampshire Housing Finance Authority

32 Constitution Drive

Bedford, New Hampshire 03110

Telephone: 603-472-8623

Toll-free: 800-649-0470

Fax: 603-472-2663

Email: cboland@nhhfa.org

Web site: **www.nhhfa.org**

New Jersey

CCCS of South Jersey, Division of MMI

312 E. White Horse Pike, Ste. 102

Absecon, New Jersey 08201

Telephone: 800-873-2227

Fax: 609-344-5267

Email: brian.coyle@moneymanagement. org

The Berkeley Ctr., 160 Route 9

Bayville, New Jersey 08721

Telephone: 800-873-2227

Fax: 609-569-1752

brian.coyle@moneymanagement.org

3073 English Creek Ave., Ste. 3

Egg Harbor Township, New Jersey 08234

Telephone: 800-873-2227

Fax: 609-652-2226

brian.coyle@moneymanagement.org

106 Apple St., Suite 105

Tinton Falls, New Jersey 07724

Telephone: 800-873-2227

brian.coyle@moneymanagement.org

Plaza Office Center, #6, 5581 Route 42

Turnersville, New Jersey 08012
Telephone: 800-873-2227
Fax: 856-935-3675
brian.coyle@moneymanagement.org

CCCS of New Jersey

185 Ridgedale Avenue
Cedar Knolls, New Jersey 07927
Telephone: 973-267-4324
Toll-free: 888-726-3260
Fax: 973-267-0484
Email: smarabotto@cccsnj.org
Web site: www.cccsnj.org

484 Bloomfield Avenue
Montclair, New Jersey 07042
Telephone: 888-726-3260
www.cccsnj.org

30 Clinton Street
Newark, New Jersey 07102
Telephone: 888-726-3260
www.cccsnj.org

148 Prospect Avenue
Ridgewood, New Jersey 07450
Telephone: 888-726-3260
www.cccsnj.org

100 West Main St.
Somerville, New Jersey 08876
Telephone: 888-726-3260

www.cccsnj.org

CCCS of the Delaware Valley

One Cherry Hill Suite 215
Cherry Hill, New Jersey 08002
Telephone: 215-563-5665 Ext. 2
Toll-free: 800-989-2227
Fax: 215-563-7020
Email: customerservice@cccsdv.org
Web site: http://www.cccsdv.org

CCCS of Central Jersey, A Division of Family Guidance Center

1931 Nottingham Way
Hamilton, New Jersey 08619
Telephone: 609-586-2574
Toll-free: 888-379-0604
Fax: 609-586-4759
Email: cccs@erols.com
Web site: www.cccscentralnj.com

The Alliance for Affordable Homeownership, Education & Development

DBA – All Ahead
C/O Good Hope Baptist Church
1306 Washington Avenue
Asbury Park, New Jersey 07712
Telephone: 732-774-1717
Toll-free: 866-584-3134
Fax: 732-223-5513
Email: Jennifer@allahead.org
Web site: www.allahead.org

2517 Highway 35, Building B, Suite 303
Manasquan, New Jersey 08736
Telephone: 866-587-4511
Fax: 732-223-5513
Web site: **www.allahead.org**

Atlantic Human Resources
1 South New York Avenue, Suite 303
Atlantic City, New Jersey 08401-8012
Telephone: 609-348-4131 Ext. 214
Fax: 609-345-5750
Email: mrjegsr@atlhmrcs.com

Jersey Counseling and Housing Development
29 South Black Horse Pike
Blackwood, New Jersey 08012-2952
Telephone: 856-227-3683
Fax: 856-228-0662
Email: Jerseycou@aol.com

1840 South Broadway
Camden, New Jersey 08104-1334
Telephone: 856-541-1000
Fax: 856-541-8836
Email: Jerseycou@aol.com

Tri-County Community Action Agency
110 Cohansey Street
Bridgeton, New Jersey 08302
Telephone: 856-451-6330 Ext. 259
Fax: 856-453-9481
Email: clebron@tricountycaa.org

Web site: **www.tricountycaa.org**

New Jersey Citizen Action
One Port Center
Two Riverside Drive, Suite 632
Camden, New Jersey 08103
Telephone: 800-656-9637
Fax: 973-643-8100
Email: application@njcitizen.org
Web site: **www.njcitizenaction.org**

85 Raritan Avenue, Suite 100
Highland Park, New Jersey 08904
Telephone: 800-656-9637
Fax: 973-643-8100
Email: application@njcitizen.org
www.njcitizenaction.org

744 Broad Street, Suite 2080
Newark, New Jersey 07102
Telephone: 973-643-8800 Ext. 14
Toll-free: 800-656-9637
Fax: 973-643-8100
Email: Phyllis@njcitizenaction.org
www.njcitizenaction.org

128 Market Street
Passaic, New Jersey 07055
Telephone: 800-656-9637
Fax: 973-643-8100
Email: application@njcitizen.org
www.njcitizenaction.org

83 Irons Street
P.O. Box 5386
Toms River, New Jersey 08754
Telephone: 800-656-9637
Fax: 973-643-8100
Email: application@njcitizen.org
www.njcitizenaction.org

118 West State Street
Trenton, New Jersey 08608
Telephone: 800-656-9637
Fax: 973-643-8100
Email: application@njcitizen.org
Web site: **www.njcitizenaction.org**

Tri-City Peoples Corporation
55 Washington Street
East Orange, New Jersey 07017
Telephone: 973-676-5506
Toll-free: 800-201-4095
Fax: 973-675-4493
Email: tcaldwell@tri-citypeoples.org
Web site: **www.tri-citypeoples.org**

675 South 19th Street
Newark, New Jersey 07103
Telephone: 973-676-5506
Toll-free: 800-860-0566
Fax: 973-675-4493
Email: tcaldwell@tri-citypeoples.org
www.tri-citypeoples.org

Urban League
288 North Broad Street
Elizabeth, New Jersey 07208-3789
Telephone: 908-351-7200
Fax: 908-351-9906
Email: ulunioncty@aol.com

106 West Palisade Avenue
Englewood, New Jersey 07631-2619
Telephone: 201-568-4989
Fax: 201-568-4989
Email: ulbc@verizon.net
Web site: **www.urbanleaguebc.org**

300 Madison Avenue, Suite A
P.O. Box 9179
Morristown, New Jersey 07960
Telephone: 973-539-2121
Fax: 973-998-6520
Web site: **www.ulmcnj.org**

Garden State Consumer Credit Counseling, Inc/NovaDebt
225 Willowbrook Road
Freehold, New Jersey 07728
Telephone: 866-472-4557
Fax: 732-409-6284
Email: education@novadebt.org
Web site: **www.novadebt.org**

Monmouth County Board of Chosen Freeholders

Monmouth County Division of Social Services

P.O. Box 3000

Freehold, New Jersey 07728

Telephone: 732-431-6028

Fax: 732-431-6267

Email: mdifedel@oel.state.nj.us

County of Bergen, Department of Human Services, Division of Senior Services

One Bergen County Plaza, 2nd Floor

Hackensack, New Jersey 07601-7076

Telephone: 201-336-7425

Fax: 201-336-7436

Email: fpower@co.bergen.nj.us

Web site: **www.co.bergen.nj.us/bcdhs**

Senior Citizens United Community Services of Camden County, Inc

146 Black Horse Pike

Mount Ephraim, New Jersey 08059-2007

Telephone: 856-456-1121

Fax: 856-456-1076

Email: rmonou@scucs.org

Web site: **www.community.nj.com/cc/ scucs**

Puerto Rican Action Board, Inc (Housing Coalition Unit)

90 Jersey Avenue

P.O. Box 240

New Brunswick, New Jersey 08903-0240

Telephone: 732-249-9700 Ext. 123

Fax: 932-249-4121

Email: clawrence@prab.org

Web site: **www.prab.org**

Acorn Housing

972 Broad Street, 8th Floor

Newark, New Jersey 07102

Telephone: 973-792-1222

Fax: 973-792-1225

Email: jltrevino@acornhousing.org

Web site: **www.acornhousing.org**

Episcopal Community Development, Inc

31 Mulberry Street

Newark, New Jersey 07102

Telephone: 973-430-9975

Fax: 973-622-3503

Email: phawkins@dioceseofnewark.org

Web site: **www.ecdonline.org**

Paterson Task Force for Community Action, Inc

9 Colt Street

Paterson, New Jersey 07505

Telephone: 973-279-2333 Ext. 25

Fax: 973-279-2334

Email: paterson.taskforce@verizon.net

North West New Jersey Community Action Program

350 Marshall Street

Phillipsburg, New Jersey 08865

Telephone: 908-454-7000 Ext. 160

Toll-free: 888-454-4778

Fax: 908-454-3768

Email: korpj@norwescap.org

Web site: **www.norwescap.org**

Somerset County Coalition on Affordable Housing

600 First Avenue, Suite 3

Raritan, New Jersey 08869

Telephone: 908-704-8901

Fax: 908-704-9235

Email: sccoah@bellatlantic.net

Web site: **www.sccoah.org**

Ocean Community Economic Action Now, Inc (O.C.E.A.N.)

40 Washington Street

Toms River, New Jersey 08753

Telephone: 732-244-2351

Fax: 732-557-4120

Email: pford@oceaninc.org

Web site: **www.oceaninc.org**

American Credit Alliance, Inc

26 South Warren Street

Trenton, New Jersey 08608-2108

Telephone: 609-393-5400

Toll-free: 800-332-8648

Fax: 215-428-6746

Email: housing@501plan.org

Web site: **www.acahomecounseling.com**

New Mexico

CCCS South West, A Division of MMI

5200 Eubank Blvd. NE

Albuquerque, New Mexico 87111

Telephone: 800-308-2227

Fax: 505-325-5191

Email: jeanine.lipka@moneymanagement.org

2727 San Pedro NE, Ste. 117

Albuquerque, New Mexico 87110

Telephone: 800-308-2227

Fax: 505-890-2639

jeanine.lipka@moneymanagement.org

3761 NM Highway 528

Albuquerque, New Mexico 87114

Telephone: 800-308-2227

Fax: 505-332-5526

eanine.lipka@moneymanagement.org

3001 Northridge Dr., Ste. A

Farmington, New Mexico 87401

Telephone: 800-308-2227

Fax: 505-984-8798

jeanine.lipka@moneymanagement.org

1065 South Main St., Ste. B-12

Las Cruces, New Mexico 88005

Telephone: 800-308-2227

Fax: 610-821-8932

jeanine.lipka@moneymanagement.org

228 St. Francis Dr., Ste. C-2

Santa Fe, New Mexico 87501-2453

Telephone: 800-308-2227

Fax: 505-272-1975

jeanine.lipka@moneymanagement.org

CCCS of Greater Dallas – Clovis

1800 Sheffield Suite B

Clovis, New Mexico 88101

Telephone: 575-763-2227

Toll-free: 800-538-2227

Fax: 575-769-3245

Email: info@cccs.net

Web site: **www.cccs.net**

Acorn Housing

411 Bellamah NW

Albuquerque, New Mexico 87102

Telephone: 505-244-1086

Fax: 505-244-1088

Email: llopez@acornhousing.org

Web site: **www.acornhousing.org**

Santa Fe Community Housing Trust

500 West San Francisco

Santa Fe, New Mexico 87501

Telephone: 505-989-3960

Fax: 505-982-3690

Email: nelliemartinez@qwest.net

New York

Consumer Credit Counseling Services – A Division of MMI

888 Grand Concourse, Suite 1K

Bronx, New York 10451

Telephone: 800-308-2227

Toll-free: 800-346-2227

26 Court Street, #1801

Brooklyn, New York 11242

Telephone: 866-889-9347

Email: brian.coyle@moneymanagement.org

Web site: **www.moneymanagement.org**

88-32 Sutphin Blvd

Jamaica, New York 11435

Telephone: 800-308-2227

Toll-free: 800-346-2227

brian.coyle@moneymanagement.org

www.moneymanagement.org

11 Penn Plaza, Suite 5148

New York City, New York 10001

Telephone: 800-308-2227

Toll-free: 800-346-2227

brian.coyle@moneymanagement.org

www.moneymanagement.org

CCCS of Central New York

2 Computer Drive West

Albany, New York 12205-1622

Telephone: 518-482-2227

Toll-free: 800-479-6026

Fax: 518-482-2296

Email: counseling@cccscny.org

Web site: **www.CreditHelpNY.org**

The Metro Center, 49 Court Street

Binghamton, New York 13901

Telephone: 607-723-2671

Toll-free: 800-479-6026

Fax: 607-723-3007

Email: counseling@cccscny.org

www.CreditHelpNY.org

500 S Salina Street, Suite 600

Syracuse, New York 13202-3394

Telephone: 315-474-6026

Toll-free: 800-479-6026

Fax: 315-479-8421

Email: counseling@cccscny.org

Web site: **www.CreditHelpNY.org**

289 Genesee Street

Utica, New York 13501-3804

Telephone: 315-797-5366

Toll-free: 800-479-6026

Fax: 315-797-9410

Email: counseling@cccscny.org

www.CreditHelpNY.org

215 Washington Street

Watertown, New York 13601

Telephone: 315-782-2227

Toll-free: 800-479-6026

Fax: 315-482-0203

Email: counseling@cccscny.org

www.CreditHelpNY.org

CCCS of Buffalo, Inc

40 Gardenville Parkway, Suite 300

West Seneca, New York 14224

Telephone: 800-926-9685

Toll-free: 800-926-9685

Fax: 716-712-2079

Email: cccs@cccsbuff.org

Web site: **www.cccsbuff.org**

Catholic Charities

United Tenants of Albany

23 Clinton Avenue, Albany New York 12207

Telephone: 518-436-8997

Fax: 518-436-0320

Email: utalb@verizon.net

Web site: **www.unitedtenantsalbany.org**

40 North Main Avenue

Albany, New York 12203

Telephone: 518-436-8997

Fax: 518-436-0320

Email: utalb@verizon.net

www.unitedtenantsalbany.org

215 East Church Street

Elmira, New York 14901-2743

Telephone: 604-734-9784 Ext. 132

Fax: 607-734-6588

Email: jgalvin@dor.org

Economic Opportunity Council

Amityville/Copiague/Farmingdale

ACE Family Development Center
48 Cedar Road
Amityville, New York 11701
Telephone: 631-289-2124 Ext. 112
Toll-free: 800-300-4362
Fax: 631-289-2178
Email: aharmon@eoc-suffolk.com
Web site: **www.eoc-suffolk.com**

COBRA Office
357 Broadway, Suite 4
Amityville, New York 11701
Telephone: 631-289-2124 Ext. 112
Toll-free: 800-300-4362
Fax: 631-289-2178
Email: aharmon@eoc-suffolk.com
Web site: **www.eoc-suffolk.com**

E.O.C. of Suffolk Counseling Center
25 Fourth Avenue
Bay Shore, New York 11706
Telephone: 631-289-2124 Ext. 112
Toll-free: 800-300-4362
Fax: 631-289-2178
Email: aharmon@eoc-suffolk.com
www.eoc-suffolk.com

Greenport Family Development Center
421 First Street, Suite 1
Greenport, New York 11944
Telephone: 631-289-2124 Ext. 112
Toll-free: 800-300-4362

Fax: 631-289-2178
Email: aharmon@eoc-suffolk.com
www.eoc-suffolk.com

475 East Main Street, Suite 206
Patchogue, New York 11772
Telephone: 631-289-2124 Ext. 112
Toll-free: 800-300-4362
Fax: 631-289-2178
Email: aharmon@eoc-suffolk.com
www.eoc-suffolk.com

Riverhead Family Development Center
733 East Main Street
Riverhead, New York 11901
Telephone: 631-289-2124 Ext. 112
Toll-free: 800-300-4362
Fax: 631-289-2178
Email: aharmon@eoc-suffolk.com
Web site: **www.eoc-suffolk.com**

Cornell Cooperative Extension
50 West High Street
Ballston Spa, New York 1202-1979
Telephone: 518-885-8995 Ext. 219
Toll-free: 800-443-0107
Fax: 518-885-9078
Email: jmb69@cornell.edu
Web site: **www.ccesaratoga.org**

Bellport, Hagerman, East Patchogue Alliance, Inc
1492 Montauk Highway

P.O. Box 121

Bellport, New York 11713

Telephone: 631-286-9236

Fax: 631-286-3948

Email: bhepalliance@aol.com

Web site: **www.bhepalliance.com**

Tri-County Housing Council

143 Hibbard Road

P.O. Box 451

Big Flats, New York 14814

Telephone: 607-562-2477

Fax: 607-562-3856

Email: info@tricountyhousing.org

Web site: **www.tricountyhousing.org**

Metro-Interfaith Services, Incorporated

21 New Street

Binghamton, New York 13903

Telephone: 607-723-0723

Fax: 607-722-8912

Email: metrolauri@aol.com

Web site: **www.metrointerfaith.org**

Bishop Sheen Ecumenical Housing Foundation

P.O. Box 460

Bloomfield, New York 14469

Telephone: 585-657-4114

Fax: 585-657-4167

Email: sheen2@rochester.rr.com

Web site: **www.sheenhousing.org**

935 East Avenue, Suite 300

Rochester, New York 14607-2216

Telephone: 585-461-4263

Fax: 585-461-5177

Email: sheen@rochester.rr.com

Web site: **www.sheenhousing.org**

Long Island Housing Services, Incorporated

640 Johnson Avenue, Suite 8

Bohemia, New York 11716-2624

Telephone: 631-467-5111

Toll-free: 800-660-6920

Fax: 631-467-5131

Email: info@LIFairhousing.org

Web site: **www.LIFairhousing.org**

GreenPath, Inc

2050 Eastchester Road, Suite 203

Bronx, New York 11801

Telephone: 888-860-4167

Web site: **www.greenpath.com**

700 Veterans Memorial Highway, Suite 305

Hauppauge, New York 11788

Telephone: 888-860-4167

www.greenpath.com

380 North Broadway, Suite 304

Jericho, New York 11753

Telephone: 888-860-4167

www.greenpath.com

80-02 Kew Gardens Road, Suite 710
Kew Gardens, New York 11415
Telephone: 888-860-4167
www.greenpath.com

120 Broadway, Suite 220
New York, New York 10271
Telephone: 888-860-4167
www.greenpath.com

250 West 34th Street, Suite 2108
New York, New York 10119
Telephone: 888-860-4167
www.greenpath.com

Neighborhood Housing Services
1178 East Gun Hill Road
Bronx, New York 10469
Telephone: 718-881-1180
Fax: 718-881-1190
Email: infonorthbronx@nhsnyc.org
Web site: **www.nhsnyc.org**

Concourse Plaza
200 East 61st Street
Bronx, New York 10452
Telephone: 718-992-5979
Fax: 718-992-6056
Email: infosouthbronx@hnsnyc.org
www.nhsnyc.org

1012 Gates Avenue
Brooklyn, New York 11221
Telephone: 718-919-2100
Fax: 718-919-2725
Email: infobedstuy@nhsnyc.org
www.nhsnyc.org

2806 Church Avenue
Brooklyn, New York 11226
Telephone: 718-469-4679
Fax: 718-469-4743
Email: inforeastflatbush@nhsnyc.org
www.nhsnyc.org

115 West Clinton Street
Ithaca, New York 14850
Telephone: 607-277-4500
Fax: 607-277-4536
Email: pmazzarella@ithacanhs.org
Web site: **www.ithacanhs.org**

89-70 162nd Street
Jamaica, New York 11432
Telephone: 718-291-7400
Fax: 718-298-6505
Email: infojamaica@nhsnyc.org
Web site: **www.nhsjamaica.org**

307 West 36th Street, 12th Floor
New York, New York 10018-6495
Telephone: 212-519-2500
Fax: 212-727-8171

Email: hud@nhsnyc.org

Web site: **www.nhsnyc.org**

306 West 37th Street, 12th Floor

New York, New York 10018

Telephone: 718-732-8100

Fax: 718-230-0032

Email: infohoc@nhsnyc.org

Web site: **www.nhsnyc.org**

1205 Castleton Avenue

Staten Island, New York 10310

Telephone: 718-442-8080

Fax: 718-442-8245

Email: infostatenisland@nhsnyc.org

Web site: **www.nhsofstatenisland.org**

60-20 Woodside Avenue

Woodside, New York 11377

Telephone: 718-457-1017

Fax: 718-457-1247

Email: infoig@nhsnyc.org

Web site: **www.nhsnorthernqueens.org**

New York City Commission on Human Rights

1932 Arthur Avenue, Suite 203A

Bronx, New York 10457

Telephone: 718-579-6900

Fax: 718-579-6995

Email: oasencio@cchr.nyc.gov

Web site: **www.nyc.gov/cchr**

275 Livingston Street, 2nd Floor

Brooklyn, New York 11217

Telephone: 718-722-3130

Fax: 718-722-3140

Email: dslaughter@cchr.nyc.gov

www.nyc.gov/cchr

136-56 39th Avenue, Room 305

Flushing, New York 11354

Telephone: 718-886-6162

Fax: 718-463-3452

Email: kbracken@cchr.nyc.org

www.nyc.org

40 Rector Street, 10th Floor

New York, New York 10006

Telephone: 718-886-6162

Fax: 718-463-3452

Email: iparsee@cchr.nyc.org

www.nyc.gov

Acorn Housing

2-4 Nevins Street, 2nd Floor

Brooklyn, New York 11217

Telephone: 718-246-8080

Fax: 718-246-7939

Email: jmiller@acornhousing.org

Web site: **www.acornhousing.com**

Brooklyn Neighborhood Improvement Association

1482 Saint Johns Place, Suite 1F

Brooklyn, New York 11213-3929

Telephone: 718-773-4116 Ext. 11

Fax: 718-221-1711

Email: andreapm51@aol.com

Cypress Hills Local Development Corporation

625 Jamaica Avenue

Brooklyn, New York 11208-1203

Telephone: 718-647-8100

Email: renea@cypresshills.org

Web site: **www.cypresshills.org**

Neighbors Helping Neighbors, Inc

443 39th Street, Suite 202

Brooklyn, New York 11232

Telephone: 718-686-7946 Ext. 11

Fax: 718-686-7948

Email: j.Fitzgerald@nhnhome.org

Web site: **www.nhnhome.org**

Belmont Shelter Corporation

1195 Main Street

Buffalo, New York 14209-2196

Telephone: 716-884-7791 Ext. 118

Toll-free: 800-836-0335

Fax: 716-884-8026

Email: kobrien@belmontshelter.org

Web site: **www.belmontshelter.org**

Buffalo Urban League

15 East Genesee Street

Buffalo, New York 14203-1405

Telephone: 716-854-7625 Ext. 207

Fax: 716-854-8960

Email: lmerritt@buffalourban.org

Orange County Rural Development Advisory Corporation

3136 Route 207, Professional Building

P. O. Box 149

Montgomery, New York 12549

Telephone: 845-291-7300

Fax: 845-291-7322

Email: ocrdac@frontiernet.net

Putnam County Housing Corporation

11 Seminary Hill Road

Carmel, New York 10512

Telephone: 845-225-8493 Ext. 212

Fax: 845-225-8532

Email: puthousing@aol.com

Web site: **www.putnamhousing.com**

Albany County Rural Housing Alliance, Inc

P.O. Box 83

10 Cayuga Plaza

Cohoes, New York 12047

Telephone: 518-235-3920

Fax: 518-235-3920

Email: sgalvin@acrha.org

Web site: **www.acrha.org**

Faith Plaza, Route 9West

P.O. Box 58

Ravena, New York 12143
Telephone: 518-756-3656
Fax: 518-756-3656
Email: lbachner@acrha.org
Web site: **www.acrha.org**

24 Martin Road
P.O. Box 407
Voorheesville, New York 12186
Telephone: 518-765-2425
Fax: 518-765-9014
Email: jeisgruber@acrha.org
Web site: **www.acrha.org**

Cortland Housing Assistance Council, Incorporated
159 Main Street
Cortland, New York 13045
Telephone: 604-753-8271 Ext. 15
Fax: 607-756-6267
Email: info@cortlandhousing.org
Web site: **www.cortlandhousing.org**

Chautauqua Opportunities, Incorporated
17 West Courtney Street
Dunkirk, New York 14048-2754
Telephone: 716-661-9430
Fax: 716-661-9436
Email: chautopp@cecomet.net
Web site: **www.chautauquaopportunities.com**

610 West 3rd Street

Jamestown, New York 14701-4705
Telephone: 716-661-9430
Fax: 716-661-9436
Email: dfricke@chautopp.org
www.chautauquaopportunities.com

Victory Housing Development Fund
1415 Montauk Highway
East Patchogue, New York 11772
Telephone: 631-286-5525
Fax: 631-286-0325
Email: fransuk@optonline.net

Housing Assistance Program of Essex County
103 Hand Avenue
P.O. Box 157
Elizabethtown, New York 12932-0157
Telephone: 518-873-6888
Fax: 518-873-9102
Email: info@hapec.org
Web site: **www.hapec.org**

Margert Community Corporation
325 Beach 37th Street
Far Rockaway, New York 11691-1510
Telephone: 718-471-3724
Fax: 718-471-5342
Email: jgb@nyct.net
Web site: **www.magert.org**

Asian Americans for Equality
133-04 39th Avenue

Flushing, New York 11354

Telephone: 718-961-0888

Fax: 718-961-0988

Email: flora@aafecdf.org

Web site: **www.aafe.org**

111 Division Street

New York, New York 10002

Telephone: 212-964-2288

Fax: 212-964-6003

Email: siukwanc2000@yahoo.com

Web site: **www.aafecdf.org**

108-110 Norfolk Street

New York, New York 10002

Telephone: 212-979-8381 Ext. 107

Fax: 212-979-8386

Email: chriskui@aafe.org

Web site: **www.aafe.org**

Housing Help, Incorporated

91-101 Broadway, Suite 6

Greenlawn, New York 11740

Telephone: 631-754-0373

Fax: 631-754-0821

Email: Susan.Lagville@verizon.net

Web site: **www.housinghelp.net**

North Fork Housing Alliance, Incorporated

110 South Street

Greenport, New York 11944-1619

Telephone: 631-477-1070

Fax: 631-477-1769

Email: NFHA@aol.com

Delaware Opportunities, Incorporated

35430 State Highway 10

Hamden, New York 13782

Telephone: 607-746-1600 Ext. 601

Fax: 607-746-1648

Long Island Housing Partnership, Incorporated

180 Oser Avenue, Suite 800

Hauppauge, New York 11788-3709

Telephone: 631-435-4710 Ext. 2

Fax: 631-435-4751

Email: dweir@lihp.org

Web site: **www.lihp.org**

C/O Nassau County OHIA

100 County Seat Drive

Mineola, New York 11501

Telephone: 631-435-4710 Ext. 2

Fax: 631-435-4751

Email: dweir@lihp.org

Web site: **www.lihp.org**

Housing Opportunities for Growth, Advancement, and Revitalization, Inc

49 West Broad Street

P.O. Box 577

Haverstraw, New York 10927

Telephone: 845-429-1100

Fax: 845-429-0193

Email: HOGARINC@aol.com

County of Nassau Economic Development

Office of Housing & Intergovernmental Affairs
40 Main Street, Suite B
Hempstead, New York 11550
Telephone: 516-572-0815 Ext. 226
Fax: 516-572-2789
Email: classandro@nassaucountyny.gov
Web site: www.nassaucountyny.gov

Family and Children's Association

336 Fulton Avenue
Hempstead, New York 11550
Telephone: 516-292-1300 Ext. 2282
Fax: 516-538-2548
Email: dzaiff@familyandchildrens.org
Web site: www.familyandchildrens.org

100 East Old Country Road
Mineola, New York 11501-4614
Telephone: 516-292-1300 Ext. 2282
Fax: 516-538-2548
Email: dzaiff@familyandchildrens.org
www.familyandchildrens.org

Housing Resources of Columbia County, Incorporated

757 Columbia Street
Hudson, New York 12534-2509
Telephone: 518-822-0707

Fax: 518-822-0367
Email: Kevin@housingresources.org
Web site: www.housingresources.org

Tompkins County Office for the Aging

320 North Tioga Street
Ithaca, New York 14850-4206
Telephone: 607-274-5492
Fax: 607-274-5495
Email: dstoyell@tompkins-co.org
Web site: www.tompkins-co.org/cofa

Jamaica Housing Improvement, Incorporated

161-10 Jamaica Avenue, Suite 601
Jamaica, New York 11432-6149
Telephone: 718-658-5050
Fax: 718-658-5065
Email: jhi_morris@yahoo.com

Rural Ulster Preservation Company

289 Fair Street
Kingston, New York 12401
Telephone: 845-331-2140 Ext. 207
Fax: 845-331-6217
Email: kleahy@rupco.org
Web site: www.rupco.org

Community Action in Self Help, Incorporated

48 Water Street
Lyons, New York 14489-1244
Telephone: 345-946-6992

Fax: 315-946-3314

Email: cashhc@rochester.rr.com

Web site: **www.cashinc.org**

Chautauqua Home Rehabilitation and Improvement Corporation (CHRIC)

2 Academy Street

Mayville, New York 14757

Telephone: 716-753-4650

Fax: 716-753-4508

Email: john_murphy@chric.org

Web site: **www.chric.org**

Rural Sullivan Housing Corporation

6 Pelton Street

P.O. Box 1497

Monticello, New York 12701-1128

Telephone: 845-794-0348

Fax: 845-794-3042

Email: ruralsullivanhousing@hvc.rr.com

Westchester Residential Opportunities, Incorporated

144 North 5th Avenue

Mt. Vernon, New York 10550

Telephone: 914-668-4424

Fax: 914-668-9515

Email: vacquah@wroinc.org

Web site: **www.wroinc.org**

Harlem Congregations for Community Improvement

2854 Frederick Douglass Boulevard

New York, New York 10039

Telephone: 212-283-1377

Fax: 212-281-4885

Email: lmcewen@hcci.org

Web site: **www.hcci.org**

New York Mortgage Coalition

50 Broad Street, Suite 1125

New York, New York 10004-2376

Telephone: 212-742-0762 Ext. 2

Fax: 212-474-1114

Email: cecilia.f@anhd.org

Web site: **www.anhd.org**

West Harlem Group Assistance, Incorporated

500 West 134th Street

New York, New York 10031

Telephone: 212-862-1399 Ext. 26

Fax: 212-862-3281

Email: chylton@whgainc.org

Web site: **www.whgainc.org**

1652 Amsterdam Avenue

New York, New York 10031

Telephone: 212-862-1399 Ext. 26

Fax: 212-862-3281

Email: chylton@whgainc.org

Web site: **www.whgainc.org**

Center City Neighborhood Development Corporation

1824 Main Street

Niagara Falls, New York 14305

Telephone: 716-282-3738

Fax: 716-282-9607

Email: centercity@pce.net

Web site: **www.centercitynf.org**

Opportunities for Chenango, Incorporated

44 West Main Street

P.O. Box 470

Norwich, New York 13815-1613

Telephone: 607-336-2101 Ext. 116

Toll-free: 866-456-3051

Fax: 607-336-3089

Email: kglasbergen@ofcinc.org

Web site: **www.ofcinc.org**

Oswego Housing Development Council, Incorporated

2971 County Route 26

P.O. Box 147

Parish, New York 13131

Telephone: 315-625-4520

Toll-free: 866-706-2679

Fax: 315-625-7347

Email: rgillen@ohdcinc.org

The Family Resource Center of Peekskill, Incorporated (FRC)

156-2 North Division Street

Peekskill, New York 10566

Telephone: 914-739-0411

Fax: 914-739-6421

Email: vmcfrc@aol.com

Dutchess County Office for the Aging

27 High Street

Poughkeepsie, New York 12601

Telephone: 845-486-2555

Toll-free: 866-486-2555

Fax: 845-486-2571

Email: emiccio@co.dutchess.ny.us

Web site: **www.dutchessny.gov**

Housing Council In Monroe County, Incorporated

75 College Avenue, Suite 412

Rochester, New York 14607

Telephone: 585-546-3700

Fax: 585-546-2946

Email: info@thehousingcouncil.org

Web site: **www.thehousingcouncil.org**

Neighborworks Rochester

570 South Avenue

Rochester, New York 14620-1345

Telephone: 585-325-4170 Ext. 316

Fax: 585-325-2587

Email: evandusen@nwrochester.org

Web site: **www.nhsrochester.org**

Better Neighborhoods, Incorporated

986 Albany Street

Schenectady, New York 12307

Telephone: 518-372-6469

Fax: 518-372-6460

Email: eaugust@better-neighborhoods.org

Web site: **www.better-neighborhoods.org**

Western Catskills Community Revitalization Council, Incorporated

125 Main Street, Box A

Stamford, New York 12167

Telephone: 607-652-8029

Fax: 607-652-2825

Email: dperr@westerncatskills.org

Web site: **www.westerncatskills.org**

Northfield Community Local Development Corporation

160 Heberton Avenue

Staten Island, New York 10302

Telephone: 718-442-7351 Ext. 23

Fax: 718-981-3441

Email: northfieldldc_davidanderson@yahoo.com

Home Headquarters, Incorporated

124 East Jefferson Street

Syracuse, New York 13202

Telephone: 315-474-1939 Ext. 228

Fax: 315-474-0637

Email: sharono@homehq.org

Web site: **www.homehq.org**

Troy Rehabilitation and Improvement Program

251 River Street

Troy, New York 12180-2834

Telephone: 518-690-0020

Fax: 518-690-0025

Email: bobbi@triponline.org

415 River Street

Troy, New York 12180

Telephone: 518-690-0020

Fax: 518-690-0025

Email: bobbi@triponline.org

UNHS Neighborworks Homeownership Center

1611 Genesee Street

Utica, New York 13501-4731

Telephone: 315-724-4197 Ext. 226

Fax: 315-724-1415

Email: jforte@unhs.org

Web site: **www.thehomeownershipcenter.org**

Westchester Residential Opportunities, Incorporated

470 Mamaroneck Avenue, Suite 410

White Plains, New York 10605-1830

Telephone: 914-428-4507

Fax: 914-428-9455

Email: housinghelp.wroinc.org

Web site: **www.wroinc.org**

Wyandanch Community Development Corporation

59 Cumberbach Street

Wyandanch, New York 11798-3326

Telephone: 631-253-0139

Fax: 631-643-9128

Email: wyandanchcdc@optonline.org

North Carolina

Consumer Credit Counseling Service

952 Copperfield Boulevard

Concord, North Carolina 28025-2954

Telephone: 704-786-7918

Fax: 704-786-7709

Email: gjennings@ufsclt.org

CCCS of Greater Greensboro

513-C White Oak St.

Asheboro, North Carolina 27203

Telephone: 336-373-8882

Toll-free: 888-755-2227

Fax: 336-387-9167

Email: debtdoc@familyservice-piedmont.org

Web site: **www.familyservice-piedmont.org/default.htm**

236 N. Mebane St.

Burlington, North Carolina 27217

Telephone: 336-373-8882

Toll-free: 888-755-2227

Fax: 336-387-9167

debtdoc@familyservice-piedmont.org

www.familyservice-piedmont.org/default.htm

315 E. Washington Street

Greensboro, North Carolina 27401

Telephone: 336-373-8882

Toll-free: 888-755-2227

Fax: 336-387-9167

debtdoc@familyservice-piedmont.org

www.familyservice-piedmont.org/default.htm

17 Hwy 70 SE

Hickory, North Carolina 28602

Telephone: 888-755-2227

Fax: 336-387-9167

debtdoc@familyservice-piedmont.org

www.familyservice-piedmont.org/default.htm

1401 Long Street

High Point, North Carolina 27262

Telephone: 336-889-6108

Toll-free: 888-755-2227

Fax: 336-387-9167

debtdoc@familyservice-piedmont.org

www.familyservice-piedmont.org/default.htm

1303 Greensboro St. Ext.

Lexington, North Carolina 27292

Telephone: 336-373-8882

Toll-free: 888-755-2227

Fax: 336-387-9167

debtdoc@familyservice-piedmont.org

www.familyservice-piedmont.org/default.htm

301 E. Meeting Street
Morganton, North Carolina 28655
Telephone: 336-373-8882
Toll-free: 888-755-2227
Fax: 336-387-9167
debtdoc@familyservice-piedmont.org
www.familyservice-piedmont.org/ default.htm

525 NC-65
Wentworth, North Carolina 27320
Telephone: 336-373-8882
Toll-free: 888-755-2227
Fax: 336-387-9167
debtdoc@familyservice-piedmont.org
www.familyservice-piedmont.org/ default.htm

Consumer Credit Counseling Service of WNC, Inc
50 S French Broad Ave Ste 227
Asheville, North Carolina 28801-3217
Telephone: 828-255-5166 Ext. 123
Toll-free: 800-737-5485
Fax: 828-255-5129
Email: celestec@cccsofwnc.org
Web site: **www.cccsofwnc.org**

CCCS of United Family Services
601 E. 5th Street, Suite 400
Charlotte, North Carolina 28202
Telephone: 704-367-2770
Fax: 704-362-3137

Email: bhamlett@ufsclt.org
Web site: **www.unitedfamilyservices.org**

952 Copperfield Blvd.
Concord, North Carolina 28025
Telephone: 704-367-2770
Fax: 704-373-1604
Email: bhamlett@ufsclt.org
www.unitedfamilyservices.org

9601 Holly Point Drive Ste 200
Huntersville, North Carolina 28078
Telephone: 704-332-9034
Fax: 704-655-0234
Email: bhamlett@ufsclt.org
www.unitedfamilyservices.org

105- AE. Jefferson Street
Monroe, North Carolina 28112
Telephone: 704-367-2770
Fax: 704-373-1604
Email: bhamlett@ufsclt.org
www.unitedfamilyservices.org

153 N. Main Street
Mooresville, North Carolina 28115
Telephone: 704-367-2770
Fax: 704-373-1604
Email: bhamlett@ufsclt.org
www.unitedfamilyservices.org

CCCS of Durham

315 East Chapel Hill Street
Durham, North Carolina 27701-3221
Telephone: 919-688-3381 Ext.·223
Toll-free: 888-562-3732
Fax: 919-680-2281
Email: glyndola@yahoo.com

201 West Main Street, Suite 202G
Durham, North Carolina 27701
Telephone: 919-821-0790
Toll-free: 800-283-6904
Fax: 919-821-1893
Email: lbarber@tfsnc.org
Web site: **www.tfsnc.org**

CCCS of Gaston County
214 E. Franklin Blvd.
Gastonia, North Carolina 28052
Telephone: 704-862-0702
Toll-free: 888-213-8853
Fax: 704-862-0239
Email: ccgaston@quik.com

206 E. Main Street
Lincolnton, North Carolina 28092
Telephone: 704-864-7704
Toll-free: 888-213-8853
Fax: 704-864-7704
Email: ccgaston@quik.com

201 W. Marion Street
Shelby, North Carolina 28150

Telephone: 704-481-9419
Toll-free: 888-213-8853
Fax: 704-487-1720
Email: ccgaston@quik.com

CCCS of Forsyth County, Inc
626 Central School Road
Jefferson, North Carolina 28640
Telephone: 336-837-0648
Toll-free: 888-474-8015
Email: kathy.banks@cccsforsyth.org

431 Bodenhamer Street
Kernersville, North Carolina 27284
Telephone: 336-837-0648
Toll-free: 888-474-8015
Email: kathy.banks@cccsforsyth.org

773 Sanford Avenue
Mocksville, North Carolina 27028
Telephone: 336-837-0648
Email: kathy.banks@cccsforsyth.org

8064 North Point Boulevard, Suite 204
Winston Salem, North Carolina 27106
Telephone: 336-896-1191
Fax: 336-896-0481
Email: kathy.banks@cccsforsyth.org
Web site: **www.cccsforsyth.org**

CCCS of Raleigh
401 Hillsborough Street

Raleigh, North Carolina 27603

Telephone: 919-821-0790

Toll-free: 800-283-6904

Fax: 919-821-1893

Email: lbarber@tfsnc.org

Web site: **www.tfsnc.org**

CCCS of the Carolina Foothills, Inc

200 Ohio St

PO Box 6

Spindale, North Carolina 28160-0006

Telephone: 828-286-7062

Toll-free: 800-567-7062

Fax: 828-286-7064

Email: ncarpenter@cccsofcf.org

Affordable Housing Coalition

34 Wall Street, Suite 607

Asheville, North Carolina 28801

Telephone: 828-259-9216 Ext. 111

Fax: 828-259-9469

Email: philipper@ahcabc.org

331 West Main Street, Suite 408

Durham, North Carolina 27701-3232

Telephone: 919-683-1185 Ext. 24

Fax: 919-688-0082

Email: rich@dahc.org

Web site: **www.dahc.org**

Northwestern Regional Housing Authority

869 Highway 105 Ext, Suite 10

P.O. Box 2510

Boone, North Carolina 28607-2510

Telephone: 828-264-6683

Fax: 828-264-0160

Email: efowler@nwrha.com

Northeastern Community Development Corporation

154 Highway 158 East

P.O. Box 367

Camden, North Carolina 27921-0367

Telephone: 252-338-5466 Ext. 22

Email: mgarcia@northeasterncdc.org

Web site: **www.northeasterncdc.org**

Community Action Program, Incorporated

103 Saunders Street

P.O. Box 937

Carthage, North Carolina 28327-0937

Telephone: 910-947-5675 Ext. 26

Fax: 910-947-5514

Email: nezziesmith@nc.rr.com

122 Railroad Street

P.O. Box 389

Ellerbe, North Carolina 28338-0389

Telephone: 910-652-6167

Fax: 910-947-5514

Email: nezziesmith@nc.rr.com

316 Green Street

P.O. Box 2009 (Zip for P.O. Box - 29302)

Fayetteville, North Carolina 28302

Telephone: 910-323-3192 Ext. 33

Fax: 910-323-4621

Email: p.tyson@mindspring.com

678 North Spence Avenue

Goldsboro, North Carolina 27534

Telephone: 919-751-3868

Fax: 919-751-0382

Email: p.tyson@mindspring.com

217 South Main Street, Suite B

Troy, North Carolina 27371-3200

Telephone: 910-576-9071

Fax: 910-947-5514

Email: nezziesmith@nc.rr.com

207 Park Road

P.O. Box 65

Wadesboro, North Carolina 28170-0065

Telephone: 704-694-5161

Fax: 704-694-4787

Email: nezziesmith@nc.rr.com

Alliance Credit Counseling

13777 Ballantyne Corporate Place, Suite 100

Charlotte, North Carolina 28277

Telephone: 704-943-2044

Toll-free: 866-303-3328

Fax: 704-943-2058

Email: housing@knowdebt.org

Web site: **www.knowdebt.org**

Durham Regional Financial Center

DBA Durham Regional Community Development

315 East Chapel Hill Street, Suite 304

Durham, North Carolina 27701

Telephone: 919-688-3381 Ext. 222

Toll-free: 866-388-7427

Fax: 919-680-2281

Email: glyndola@yahoo.com

Web site: **www.drfcenter.com**

Victorious Community Development Corporation

2116 Page Road, Research Triangle Park

Durham, North Carolina 27703

Telephone: 919-954-7500 Ext. 103

Fax: 919-957-7502

Email: yvette@victoriouspraise.org

Elizabeth City State University

1704 Weeksville Road

Elizabeth City, North Carolina 27909

Telephone: 252-335-3250

Fax: 252-335-3735

Email: maautry@mail.ecsu.edu

River City Community Development Corporation

501 East Main Street

Elizabeth City, North Carolina 27909

Telephone: 252-331-2925

Fax: 252-331-1425

Email: ljarvismackey@rivercitycdc.org

Web site: **www.rivercitycdc.org**

Kingdom Community Development Corporation
308 Green Street, Suite 202, Box 13
Fayetteville, North Carolina 28301
Telephone: 910-484-2722
Fax: 910-484-5630
Email: kingdom.cdc@worldnet.att.net
Web site: **www.kingdomcdc.org**

Progressive Action & Restoration Incorporated
401 West First Street, Suite B
Greenville, North Carolina 27834
Telephone: 252-329-8141 Ext. 1
Fax: 252-329-0575
Email: dawjac52@aol.com

Western Piedmont Council of Governments
736 4th Street Southwest
P.O. Box 9026
Hickory, North Carolina 28602
Telephone: 828-322-9191 Ext. 220
Fax: 828-322-5991
Email: doug.taylor@wpcog.org
Web site: **www.wpcog.org**

Prosperity Unlimited, Incorporated
1660 Garnet Street
Kannapolis, North Carolina 28083
Telephone: 704-933-7405 Ext. 1002

Fax: 704-938-7431
Email: lmack@prodigy.net
Web site: **www.prosperitycdc.org**

Davidson County Community Action Incorporated
15 East Second Avenue
P.O. Box 389
Lexington, North Carolina 27293-0389
Telephone: 336-249-0234
Fax: 336-249-2078
Email: dcca@lexcominc.net

Monroe-Union Community Development Corporation
349 East Franklin Street
P.O. Box 887
Monroe, North Carolina 28112
Telephone: 704-283-8804
Fax: 704-292-1037
Email: gmuccdc@carolina.rr.com
Web site: **www.muccdc.org**

Olive Hill Community Economic Development Corporation
420 C West Fleming Drive
P.O. Box 4008
Morganton, North Carolina 28680-4008
Telephone: 828-439-8893
Fax: 828-439-8894
Email: ohcedc@conninc.com
Web site: **www.ohcedc.org**

Twin Rivers Opportunities, Incorporated
318 Craven Street

P.O. Box 1482

New Bern, North Carolina 28563

Telephone: 252-637-3599

Fax: 252-637-0507

Email: tro_section8@earthlink.net

New Life CDC
103 East Waterstreet Street

Plymouth, North Carolina 27962

Telephone: 252-791-0095

Fax: 252-793-9407

Email: lmcnair@earthlink.net

Resources for Seniors
1110 Navaho Drive, Suite 400

Raleigh, North Carolina 27609-7318

Telephone: 919-713-1537

Fax: 919-872-9574

Email: christenas@rfsnc.org

Web site: **www.resourcesforseniors. com**

Choanoke Area Development Association
120 Sessoms Drive

Rich Square, North Carolina 27869

Telephone: 252-539-4155

Fax: 252-539-2048

Email: ssurface@nc-cada.org

Web site: **www.nc-cada.org**

Johnston-Lee-Harnett Community Action, Incorporated
1102 Massey Street

P.O. Drawer 711

Smithfield, North Carolina 27577-0711

Email: jlhca@earthlink.net

Web site: **www.jlhca.org**

Statesville Housing Authority
110 West Allison Street

Statesville, North Carolina 28677

Telephone: 704-872-9811 Ext. 209

Fax: 704-878-8780

Email: trathbone@sha-online.org

Web site: **www.sha.org**

Mid-East Commission- Area Agency on Aging
1385 John Small Avenue

P.O. Box 1787

Washington, North Carolina 27889-1787

Telephone: 252-974-1835

Fax: 252-948-1884

Email: cdavis@mideastcom.org

Wilmington Housing Finance and Development, Inc
3508 Frog Pond Place

P.O. Box 547

Wilmington, North Carolina 28403

Telephone: 910-793-7709

Fax: 910-763-7705

Cape Fear Regional CDC
508 Compton Street
P.O. Box 2765
Wilmington, North Carolina 28401
Telephone: 910-762-7555
Fax: 910-762-7565
Email: info@cfrcdc.org
Web site: **www.cfrcdc.org**

Wilson Community Improvement Association, Inc
504 East Green Street
Wilson, North Carolina 27893
Telephone: 252-243-4855
Fax: 252-243-2945
Email: blackstonwcia@earthlink.net

North Dakota

CCCS of the Village Family Service Center
411 North 4th Street Ste 10
Bismarck, North Dakota 58501
Telephone: 800-450-4019
Fax: 701-255-7647
Email: moneyhelp@thevillagefamily.org
Web site: **www.helpwithmoney.org**

1201 25th Street South
Fargo, North Dakota 58103
Telephone: 701-235-3328
Toll-free: 800-450-4019
Fax: 701-451-5057

Email: moneyhelp@thevillagefamily.org
www.helpwithmoney.org

1726 S Washington, Suite 33A
Grand Forks, North Dakota 58201
Telephone: 701-746-4584
Toll-free: 800-450-4019
Fax: 701- 746-1239
Email: moneyhelp@thevillagefamily.org
www.helpwithmoney.org

300 2nd Ave NE, Suite 217
Jamestown, North Dakota 58402
Toll-free: 800-450-4019
Fax: 701- 451-5057
Email: moneyhelp@thevillagefamily.org
www.helpwithmoney.org

20 1ST ST, SW STE 250
Minot, North Dakota 58701
Telephone: 701- 852-3328
Toll-free: 800-450-4019
Fax: 701- 838-2521
Email: moneyhelp@thevillagefamily.org
www.helpwithmoney.org

Community Action Program
2105 Lee Avenue
Bismarck, North Dakota 58504-6798
Telephone: 701-258-2240
Fax: 701-258-2245
Email: katief@cap7.com

Web site: **www.cap7.com**

North Dakota Housing Finance Agency
1500 East Capitol Avenue
P.O. Box 1535
Bismarck, North Dakota 58502-1535
Telephone: 701-328-8080
Toll-free: 800-292-8621
Fax: 701-328-8090
Email: maanders@ndhfa.org
Web site: **www.ndhfa.org**

Community Action Partnership
202 East Villard
Dickinson, North Dakota 58601-5247
Telephone: 701-227-0131 Ext. 1019
Toll-free: 800-359-2243
Fax: 701-227-4750

2020 8th Avenue SE
Minot, North Dakota 58701
Telephone: 701-839-7221 Ext. 12
Toll-free: 800-726-8645
Fax: 701-839-1747
Email: denise@capminotregion.org
Web site: **www.capminotregion.org**

Southeastern North Dakota Community Action Agency
3233 South University Drive
Fargo, North Dakota 58104-6221
Telephone: 701-232-2452 Ext. 17
Toll-free: 800-726-7960

Fax: 701-298-3115
Email: denisem@sendcaa.org
Web site: **www.sendcaa.org**

Ohio

CCCS of the Midwest
2569 Romig Road
Akron, Ohio 44220
Telephone: 800-355-2227
Fax: 614-552-4800
Email: info@cccservices.com
Web site: **www.cccservices.com/home.asp**

1147 Cincinnati Batavia Pike
Batavia, Ohio 45103
Telephone: 800-355-2227
Fax: 614-552-4800
Email: info@cccservices.com
www.cccservices.com/home.asp

21403 Chagrin Blvd., Suite 106
Beachwood, Ohio 44122
Telephone: 800-355-2227
Fax: 614-552-4800
Email: info@cccservices.com
www.cccservices.com/home.asp

8261 Market Street, Suite K
Boardman, Ohio 44512
Telephone: 800-355-2227
Fax: 614-552-4800

Email: info@cccservices.com
www.cccservices.com/home.asp

110 Central Plaza South
Canton, Ohio 44702
Telephone: 800-355-2227
Fax: 614-552-4800
Email: info@cccservices.com
www.cccservices.com/home.asp

35 S. Paint Street
Chillicothe, Ohio 45601
Telephone: 800-355-2227
Fax: 614-552-4800
Email: info@cccservices.com
www.cccservices.com/home.asp

9545 Kenwood Road, Suite 204
Cincinnati, Ohio 45242
Telephone: 800-355-2227
Fax: 614-552-4800
Email: info@cccservices.com
www.cccservices.com/home.asp

2800 Euclid Avenue, Suite 101
Cleveland, Ohio 44115
Telephone: 800-355-2227
Fax: 614-552-4800
Email: info@cccservices.com
www.cccservices.com/home.asp

10317 Lorain Avenue

Cleveland, Ohio 44111
Telephone: 800-355-2227
Fax: 614-552-4800
Email: info@cccservices.com
www.cccservices.com/home.asp

4401 Lorain Avenue
Cleveland, Ohio 44113
Telephone: 800-355-2227
Fax: 614-552-4800
Email: info@cccservices.com
www.cccservices.com/home.asp

2490 Lee Blvd, Suite 310
Cleveland Heights, Ohio 44118-1255
Telephone: 800-355-2227
Fax: 614-552-4800
Email: info@cccservices.com
www.cccservices.com/home.asp

4500 East Broad Street
Columbus, Ohio 43213
Telephone: 800-355-2227
Fax: 614-552-4800
Email: info@cccservices.com
www.cccservices.com/home.asp

314 N. Wilson Road
Columbus, Ohio 43204
Telephone: 800-355-2227
Fax: 614-552-4800
Email: info@cccservices.com
www.cccservices.com/home.asp

401 Broad Street, Suite 205
Elyria, Ohio 44035
Telephone: 800-355-2227
Fax: 614-552-4800
Email: info@cccservices.com
www.cccservices.com/home.asp

315 N. Columbus Street
Lancaster, Ohio 43130
Telephone: 800-355-2227
Fax: 614-552-4800
Email: info@cccservices.com
www.cccservices.com/home.asp

One Marion Avenue, Suite 307
Mansfield, Ohio 44903-7907
Telephone: 800-355-2227
Fax: 614-552-4800
Email: info@cccservices.com
www.cccservices.com/home.asp

704 N. Court Street
Medina, Ohio 44256
Telephone: 800-355-2227
Fax: 614-552-4800
Email: info@cccservices.com
www.cccservices.com/home.asp

7519 Mentor Avenue Rm. A104
Mentor, Ohio 44060
Telephone: 800-355-2227
Fax: 614-552-4800

Email: info@cccservices.com
www.cccservices.com/home.asp

4556 Montgomery Road
Norwood, Ohio 45212
Telephone: 800-355-2227
Fax: 614-552-4800
Email: info@cccservices.com
www.cccservices.com/home.asp

5339 Ridge Rd Ste 201
Parma, Ohio 44129-1467
Telephone: 800-355-2227
Fax: 614-552-4800
Email: info@cccservices.com
www.cccservices.com/home.asp

524 W. Perkins Avenue
Sandusky, Ohio 44870
Telephone: 800-355-2227
Fax: 614-552-4800
Email: info@cccservices.com
www.cccservices.com/home.asp

457 S. Reynolds Road
Toledo, Ohio 43615
Telephone: 800-355-2227
Fax: 614-552-4800
Email: info@cccservices.com
www.cccservices.com/home.asp

3465 Massillon Road

Uniontown, Ohio 44685
Telephone: 800-355-2227
Fax: 614-552-4800
Email: info@cccservices.com
www.cccservices.com/home.asp

554 N. Park Avenue NE
Warren, Ohio 44481
Telephone: 800-355-2227
Fax: 614-552-4800
Email: info@cccservices.com
www.cccservices.com/home.asp

CCCS of the Mid Ohio Valley
9030 Hocking Hill
The Plains, Ohio 45780
Telephone: 304-485-3141 Ext. 26
Toll-free: 866-481-4752
Fax: 304-485-3286
Email: cccspksbg@wirefire.com
Web site: **www.wvcccs.org**

Fair Housing Contact Service
441 Wolf Ledges Parkway, Suite 200
Akron, Ohio 44311
Telephone: 330-376-6191
Toll-free: 877-376-6191
Fax: 330-376-8391
Email: tskipper@fairhousingakron.org
Web site: **www.fairhousingakron.org**

NID-HCA

2950 West Market Street, Suite M
Akron, Ohio 44333
Telephone: 330-761-2294
Fax: 330-864-1983
Email: sbmccray@yahoo.com
Web site: **www.nidonline.org**

2490 Lee Boulevard, Suite # 218
Cleveland Heights, Ohio 44118
Telephone: 216-932-6624
Fax: 216-932-4555
Email: jenvalentine1@msn.com
www.nidonline.org

Catholic Charities
4200 Park Avenue, 3rd Floor
Ashtabula, Ohio 44004
Telephone: 440-992-2121
Toll-free: 888-881-7559
Fax: 440-992-5974
Email: lynnz@doyccac.org
Web site: **www.catholiccharitiesashtabula.org**

2401 Belmont Avenue
Youngstown, Ohio 44505
Telephone: 330-744-3320
Fax: 330-744-3677

Community Housing Solutions
12114 Larchmere Boulevard
Cleveland, Ohio 44120
Telephone: 216-231-5815

Fax: 216-231-5845

Email: jayb@commhousingsolutions.org

Web site: **www.commhousingsolutions. org**

1967 West 45th Street

Cleveland, Ohio 44102-3449

Telephone: 216-651-0077

Fax: 216-651-0072

Email: jayb@commhousingsolutions.org

www.commhousingsolutions.org

Neighborhood Housing Services of Greater Cleveland

5700 Broadway Avenue

Cleveland, Ohio 44127

Telephone: 216-458-4663 Ext. 12

Fax: 216-458-4672

Email: ltisler@nhscleveland.org

Web site: **www.nhscleveland.org**

The Housing Advocates, Inc

3214 Prospect Avenue

Cleveland, Ohio 44115

Telephone: 216-431-7400

Email: kramere@aol.com

Columbus Housing Partnership, Inc

562 East Main Street

Columbus, Ohio 43215-5312

Telephone: 614-221-8889 Ext. 126

Fax: 614-221-8591

Email: Rhilbert@chpcolumbus.org

Web site: **www.chpcolumbus.org**

Dayton Urban Ministry Center

3665 Otterbein Avenue

Dayton, Ohio 45406

Telephone: 937-278-1167

Fax: 937-278-9231

Email: klj@daytonumc.com

Community Action Commission of Belmont County

153-½ West Main Street

Saint Clairsville, Ohio 43950

Telephone: 740-695-0293 Ext. 234

Fax: 740-699-2578

Email: gobloy@cacbelmont.org

Web site: **www.cacbelmont.org**

Jefferson County Community Action Council

114 North Fourth Street

P.O. Box 130

Steubenville, Ohio 43952

Telephone: 740-282-0971 Ext. 133

Fax: 740-282-8361

Email: rgildow_cac@hotmail.com

Children's & Family Service AKA Family Service Agency

535 Marmion Avenue

Youngstown, Ohio 44502-2323

Telephone: 330-782-5664 Ext. 138

Fax: 330-782-1614

Email: dlazor@familyserviceagency.com

Web site: **www.familyserviceagency. com**

Oklahoma

CCCS of Greater Dallas

333 W. Main, Suite 150

Ardmore, Oklahoma 73402

Telephone: 580-226-5885

Toll-free: 800-944-3826

Fax: 580-224-9196

Email: info@cccs.net

Web site: **www.cccs.net**

CCCS of Oklahoma

117 SW 5th St. Ste 408

Bartlesville, Oklahoma 74003

Telephone: 918-336-7619

Toll-free: 800-324-5611

Fax: 918-336-2722

Email: cccsok@aol.com

Web site: **www.cccsofok.org**

317 South Main St.

Broken Arrow, Oklahoma 74012

Telephone: 918-259-0164

Toll-free: 800-324-5611

Fax: 918-258-6237

Email: dneibling@cccsofok.org

www.cccsofok.org

104 South Missouri, Suite 205

Claremore, Oklahoma 74017

Telephone: 918-343-3313

Toll-free: 800-324-5611

Fax: 918-343-2712

Email: dneibling@cccsofok.org

www.cccsofok.org

100 North 5th, Suite B

McAlester, Oklahoma 74501

Telephone: 918-744-5611

Toll-free: 800-324-5611

www.cccsofok.org

323 W. Broadway Street, Suite 404

Muskogee, Oklahoma 74401

Telephone: 918-683-2778

Toll-free: 800-324-5611

Fax: 918-683-5571

Email: dneibling@cccsofok.org

www.cccsofok.org

19 North Main

Sapulpa, Oklahoma 74066

Telephone: 918- 224-8412

Toll-free: 800-324-5611

Fax: 918- 224-8759

Email: dneibling@cccsofok.org

www.cccsofok.org

Hwy 62 South

Tahlequah, Oklahoma 74464

Telephone: 800-324-5611

Toll-free: 888-697-9697

Email: dneibling@cccsofok.org

www.cccsofok.org

4646 S Harvard Ave

PO Box 4450

Tulsa, Oklahoma 74159-0450

Telephone: 918-744-5611

Toll-free: 800-324-5611

Fax: 918- 744-0232

Email: dneibling@cccsofok.org

www.cccsofok.org

CCCS of Central Oklahoma

3230 N. Rockwell Avenue

Bethany, Oklahoma 73008

Telephone: 405-789-2227

Toll-free: 800-364-2227

Fax: 405-789-5052

Email: lhoover@cccsok.org

www.cccsok.org

317 West Cherokee, Suite A

Enid, Oklahoma 73701

Telephone: 405-789-2227

Toll-free: 800-364-2227

Fax: 405-789-5052

Email: lhoover@cccsok.org

www.cccsok.org

Ft. Sill Credit Union

5202 SW Lee Blvd.

Lawton, Oklahoma 73505

Telephone: 405-384-3473

Toll-free: 800-364-2227

Fax: 405-789-5052

Email: lhoover@cccsok.org

www.cccsok.org

Western Tower Building

5350 South Western Suite 103

Oklahoma City, Oklahoma 73109

Telephone: 405-789-2227

Toll-free: 800-364-2227

Fax: 405-789-5052

Email: lhoover@cccsok.org

www.cccsok.org

Expressways Building

2525 NW Expressway, Suite #660

Oklahoma City, Oklahoma 73112

Toll-free: 800-364-2227

Fax: 405-789-5052

Email: lhoover@cccsok.org

www.cccsok.org

First National Bank

130 E. MacArthur

Shawnee, Oklahoma 74801

Toll-free: 800-364-2227

Fax: 405-789-5052

Email: lhoover@cccsok.org

www.cccsok.org

The Murphy Building
118 W. 8th Ave.
Stillwater, Oklahoma 74074
Toll-free: 800-364-2227
Fax: 405-789-5052
Email: lhoover@cccsok.org
www.cccsok.org

Building 420
Tinker AFB, Oklahoma 73145
Telephone: 405-789-2227
Toll-free: 800-364-2227
Fax: 405-789-5052
Email: lhoover@cccsok.org
www.cccsok.org

Community Action Agency
122 North Cleveland
Cushing, Oklahoma 74023
Telephone: 405-477-0832
Toll-free: 800-256-5940
Fax: 405-701-1536
Email: gcorson@cocaa.org
www.cocaa.org

109 Oklahoma
Guthrie, Oklahoma 73044
Telephone: 405-282-4332
Toll-free: 800-256-5940
Fax: 405-275-9442
Email: gcorson@cocaa.org
www.cocaa.org

807 Jim Thorpe Boulevard
Prague, Oklahoma 74864
Telephone: 405-587-4591
Toll-free: 800-256-5940
Fax: 405-275-9441
Email: gcorson@cocaa.org
www.cocaa.org

209 North 4th Street
Hugo, Oklahoma 74743
Telephone: 580-326-3351
Fax: 580-326-2305
Email: breynolds@littledixie.org
Web site: www.littledixie.org

319 Southwest 25th Street
Oklahoma City, Oklahoma 73109
Telephone: 405-232-0199 Ext. 3200
Fax: 405-232-9074
Email: spdirector@caaofokc.org
Web site: www.caaofokc.org

Community Development Support Association
2615 East Randolph
Enid, Oklahoma 73701-4670
Telephone: 580-242-6131
Fax: 580-235-3554
Email: cdsahousing@sbcglobal.net

Housing Authority of the City of Lawton
609 Southwest F Avenue
Lawton, Oklahoma 73501

Telephone: 580-353-7392

Fax: 580-353-6111

Email: rlove@lawtonhousing.org

Web site: **www.lawtonhousing.org**

Housing Authority of the City of Muskogee

220 North 40th Street

Muskogee, Oklahoma 74401

Telephone: 918-687-6301 Ext. 17

Fax: 918-687-3249

Email: foster@mhastaff.org

Web site: **www.mhastaff.org**

Neighborhood Housing Services of Oklahoma City

1320 Classen Drive, Suite 200

Oklahoma City, Oklahoma 73103

Telephone: 405-231-4663

Fax: 405-231-5137

Email: rolandc@nhsokc.org

Web site: **www.nhsokc.org**

Deep Fork Community Action Foundation

223 West 6th Street

P.O. Box 670

Okmulgee, Oklahoma 74447-0670

Telephone: 918-756-2826

Fax: 918-756-7030

Email: deepforkca@aol.com

Web site: **www.deepforkcommunityaction.netfirms.com**

Housing Authority of the City of Shawnee

601 West 7th Street

P.O. Box 3427

Telephone: 405-275-6330 Ext. 314

Fax: 405-273-9344

Email: lgreenland-sha@hotmail.com

Web site: **www.shawneeok.org**

Stillwater Housing Authority

807 South Lowry

Stillwater, Oklahoma 74074

Telephone: 405-372-4906 Ext. 18

Fax: 405-372-1416

Email: glen_stillwater_ha@sbcglobal.net

Web site: **www.pages.sbcglobal.net/ stillwater_ha.net**

Housing Partners of Tulsa, Incorporated

415 East Independence

P.O. Box 6369

Tulsa, Oklahoma 74106

Telephone: 918-581-5711

Fax: 918-585-5609

Email: lori.russell@tulsahousing.org

Web site: **www.tulsahousing.org**

Oregon

CCCS of Mid-Oregon, A Division of MMI

1010 NW 14th Street

Bend, Oregon 97701

Telephone: 888-845-5669

Email: david.michael@

moneymanagement.org

1200 High St., Ste. 150, Suite 150
Eugene, Oregon 97401
Telephone: 800-308-2227
Fax: 541-342-5467
Email: trish.potts@moneymanagement.org

CCCS of the Tri-Cities
240 E. Gladys, Suite 3
Hermiston, Oregon 97838
Telephone: 541-667-8738
Fax: 541-667-8740
Email: hercccs@bmi.net

CCCS of Southern Oregon
820 Crater Lake Ave., Suite 202
Medford, Oregon 97504-6581
Telephone: 541-779-2273
Fax: 541-779-6412
Email: cadel@cccsso.org
Web site: **www.cccsso.org**

Open Door Counseling Center
34420 Southwest Tualatin Valley Highway
Hillsboro, Oregon 97123-5470
Telephone: 503-640-6689
Toll-free: 866-640-6689
Fax: 503-640-9374
Email: vfuller@opendoorcc.net
Web site: **www.opendoorcc.net**

Access Incorporated
3630 Aviation Way
P.O. Box 4666
Medford, Oregon 97501
Telephone: 541-779-6691
Fax: 541-779-8886
Email: cdyer@access-inc.org
Web site: **www.access-inc.org**

Acorn Housing
5102 Southeast Powell Boulevard
Portland, Oregon 97206
Telephone: 503-788-9989
Fax: 503-788-0242
Email: ksheehan@acornhousing.org
Web site: **www.acornhousing.org**

Neighbor Impact FKA Central Oregon Community Action Agency Network (COCAAN)
2303 Southwest First Street
Redmond, Oregon 97756
Telephone: 541-548-2380 Ext. 101
Fax: 541-923-2527
Email: corkys@neighborimpact.org
Web site: **www.neighborimpact.org**

Umpqua Community Action Network
2448 West Harvard Boulevard
Roseburg, Oregon 97470
Telephone: 541-672-3421
Fax: 541-672-1983
Email: anna.bateman@ucancap.org

Web site: **www.ucancap.org**

Pennsylvania

CCCS of Western Pennsylvania

917A Logan Blvd.

Royal/Remax Plaza

Altoona, Pennsylvania 16602

Telephone: 888-511-2227

Email: mloftus@advantagecccs.org

Web site: **www.cccspa.org**

524 Franklin Avenue

Beaver, Pennsylvania 15001

Telephone: 888-511-2227

Email: mloftus@advantagecccs.org

Web site: **www.cccspa.org**

112 Hollywood Drive, Suite 101

Butler, Pennsylvania 16001

Telephone: 888-511-2227

Email: mloftus@advantagecccs.org

www.cccspa.org

4402 Peach Street

Erie, Pennsylvania 16509

Telephone: 888-511-2227

Email: mloftus@advantagecccs.org

www.cccspa.org

One Northgate Square

Greensburg, Pennsylvania 05601

Telephone: 888-511-2227

Email: mloftus@advantagecccs.org

www.cccspa.org

118 S. Broad Street

Grove City, Pennsylvania 16127

Telephone: 888-511-2227

Fax: 614-552-4800

Email: info@cccservices.com

Web site: **www.cccservices.com/home.asp**

2000 Linglestown Road

Harrisburg, Pennsylvania 17110

Telephone: 888-511-2227

Fax: 717-540-4670

Email: mloftus@advantagecccs.org

www.cccspa.org

2403 Sidney Street

River Park Commons

Pittsburgh, Pennsylvania 15203

Telephone: 412-390-1314

Toll-free: 888-511-2227

Fax: 412-390-1335

Email: mloftus@advantagecccs.org

www.cccspa.org

CCCS of Northeastern Pennsylvania

702 Sawmill Road

Bloomsburg, Pennsylvania 17815

Telephone: 800-922-9537

www.cccsnepa.org

81 S. Church Street
Hazleton, Pennsylvania 18201
Telephone: 800-922-9537
www.cccsnepa.org

232 Sunrise Avenue, Rte. 191
Honesdale, Pennsylvania 18431
Telephone: 800-922-9537
www.cccsnepa.org

401 Laurel St
Pittston, Pennsylvania 18640-3557
Telephone: 570-602-2227
Toll-free: 800-922-9537
Fax: 570-602-2238
Email: cselner@cccsnepa.org
www.cccsnepa.org

202 W. Hamilton Ave.
State College, Pennsylvania 16801
Telephone: 814-238-3668
Toll-free: 800-922-9537
Fax: 814-238-3669
Email: cccsnepa@ceinetworks.com
www.cccsnepa.org

411 Main Street, Suite 102
Stroudsburg, Pennsylvania 18360
Telephone: 570-420-8980
Toll-free: 800-922-9537
Fax: 570-420-8981
Email: cccsnepa@ceinetworks.com

www.cccsnepa.org

217 S. Center Street
Sunbury, Pennsylvania 17801
Telephone: 800-922-9537
www.cccsnepa.org

77 E. Market Street, 7th floor
Wilkes Barre, Pennsylvania 18701
Telephone: 570- 821-0837
Toll-free: 800-922-9537
Fax: 570- 821-1785
Email: cccsofpa@epix.net
www.cccsnepa.org

201 Basin Street, Suite 600
Williamsport, Pennsylvania 17701
Telephone: 570- 323-6627
Toll-free: 800-922-9537
Fax: 570- 323-6626
Email: cccsofpa6@epix.net
www.cccsnepa.org

CCCS of the Delaware Valley
1777 Sentry Parkway West
Blue Bell, Pennsylvania 19422
Telephone: 800-989-2227
Fax: 215-563-7020
Email: customerservice@cccsdv.org

www.cccsdv.org
1230 New Rogers Rd., Ste F1

Bristol, Pennsylvania 19007
Telephone: 215-563-5665
Toll-free: 800-989-2227
Fax: 215-563-7020
Email: customerservice@cccsdv.org
www.cccsdv.org

261 Old York Road
Pavilion, Suite 401
Jenkintown, Pennsylvania 19046
Toll-free: 800-989-2227
Fax: 215-563-7020
Email: customerservice@cccsdv.org
www.cccsdv.org

280 N. Providence Road
Media, Pennsylvania 19063
Telephone: 215-563-5665
Toll-free: 800-989-2227
Fax: 215-563-7020
Email: customerservice@cccsdv.org
www.cccsdv.org

1515 Market St, Suite 1325
Philadelphia, Pennsylvania 19101
Telephone: 215-563-5665
Toll-free: 800-989-2227
Fax: 215-563-7020
Email: customerservice@cccsdv.org
www.cccsdv.org

7340 Jackson Street

Philadelphia, Pennsylvania 19136
Toll-free: 800-989-2227
Fax: 215-563-7020
Email: customerservice@cccsdv.org
www.cccsdv.org

790 E. Market Street, Suite 170
West Chester, Pennsylvania 19382
Toll-free: 800-989-2227
Fax: 215-563-7020
Email: customerservice@cccsdv.org
www.cccsdv.org

CCCS of Lehigh Valley, A Division of MMI

306 Spring Garden St.
Easton, Pennsylvania 18042
Telephone: 800-220-2733
Fax: 610-821-8932
Email: brian.coyle@moneymanagement.
org

1954 East High Street
Pottstown, Pennsylvania 19464
Telephone: 800-220-2733
Fax: 610-821-8932
brian.coyle@moneymanagement.org

245 W. Broad St.
Quakertown, Pennsylvania 18951
Telephone: 800-220-2733
Fax: 610-821-8932
brian.coyle@moneymanagement.org

3671 Cresent Court East
Whitehall, Pennsylvania 18052
Telephone: 800-220-2733
Fax: 610-821-8932
brian.coyle@moneymanagement.org

833 N. Park Rd., Ste. 103
Wyomissing, Pennsylvania 19610
Telephone: 800-220-2733
Fax: 610-821-8932
brian.coyle@moneymanagement.org

CCCS of the Midwest
118 S. Broad Street
Grove City, Pennsylvania 16127
Telephone: 800-355-2227
Fax: 614-552-4800
Email: info@cccservices.com
Web site: **www.cccservices.com/home. asp**

Saint Martin Center, Inc
1701 Parade Street
Erie, Pennsylvania 16503-1994
Telephone: 814-452-6113 Ext. 110
Fax: 814-461-9483
Email: cheryl1027@aol.com
Web site: **www.stmartincenter.org**

Urban League
601 Indiana Avenue
Farrell, Pennsylvania 16121-1759
Telephone: 721-981-5310

Email: hsgsvul@neohio.twbc.com

One Smithfield Street, Third Floor
Pittsburgh, Pennsylvania 15222-2222
Telephone: 412-227-4163
Fax: 412-471-6199
Email: dwilliams@ulpgh.org
Web site: **www.ulpgh.org**

Mon Valley Initiative
303-305 East 8th Avenue
Homestead, Pennsylvania 15120-1517
Telephone: 412-464-4000 Ext. 4011
Fax: 412-464-1750
Email: smasick@monvalleyinitiative.com
Web site: **www.monvalleyinitiative.com**

Community Action Program, Incorporated
827 Water Street
P.O. Box 187
Indiana, Pennsylvania 15701-1755
Telephone: 721-465-2657
Fax: 724-465-5118
Email: rfoster@iccap.net

247 North 5th Street
Reading, Pennsylvania 19601-3303
Telephone: 610-375-7866
Fax: 610-375-7830
Email: gmiller@bcapberks.org

150 West Beau Street, Suite 304

Washington, Pennsylvania 15301

Telephone: 724-225-9550 Ext. 403

Toll-free: 877-814-0788

Fax: 724-228-9966

Email: cferris@caswg.org

Web site: **www.caswg.org**

Tabor Community Services, Incorporated

308 East King Street

Lancaster, Pennsylvania 17608-1676

Telephone: 717-397-5182 Ext. 120

Fax: 717-399-4127

Email: kmmcdivitt@tabornet.org

Web site: **www.tabornet.org**

Center for Family Services, Incorporated

213 West Center Street

Meadville, Pennsylvania 16335-3406

Telephone: 814-337-8450

Fax: 814-337-8457

Email: cfsinc@alltel.net

Web site: **www.thecenter-nwpa.org**

TREHAB

10 Public Avenue

P.O. Box 366

Montrose, Pennsylvania 18801-0366

Telephone: 570-278-5227

Toll-free: 800-982-4045

Fax: 570-278-1889

Email: dphelps@trehab.org

Web site: **www.trehab.org**

American Credit Alliance

2 South Delmorr Avenue

Morrisville, Pennsylvania 19067

Telephone: 215-295-7195

Toll-free: 800-332-8648

Fax: 215-428-6746

Email: housing@501plan.org

Web site: **www.acahomecounseling. com**

Lawrence County Social Services, Incorporated

241 West Grant Street

P.O. Box 189

New Castle, Pennsylvania 16103-0189

Telephone: 724-658-7258

Toll-free: 800-252-5104

Fax: 724-658-7664

Email: dhennon@lawcss.org

Web site: **www.lccap.org**

Acorn Housing

846 North Broad Street, First Floor

Philadelphia, Pennsylvania 19130

Telephone: 215-765-1221

Fax: 215-765-0045

Email: rravelo@acornhousing.org

Web site: **www.acornhousing.org**

Northwest Counseling Service

5001 North Broad Street

Philadelphia, Pennsylvania 19141-2217

Telephone: 215-324-7500

Fax: 215-324-0524

Email: nwcs@erols.com

Web site: **www.nwcsonline.com**

Philadelphia Council for Community Advancement

One Penn Center

1617 JFK Boulevard, Suite 1550

Philadelphia, Pennsylvania 19103-2736

Telephone: 215-567-7803 Ext. 2126

Toll-free: 800-930-4663

Fax: 215-963-9941

Email: mail@philipcca.org

Web site: **www.pccahousing.org**

Garfield Jubilee Association, Incorporated

5138 Penn Avenue

Pittsburgh, Pennsylvania 15224-1616

Telephone: 412-665-5204

Fax: 412-665-5205

Email: chico81637@aol.com

Web site: **www.garfieldjubilee.org**

Three Rivers Center for Independent Living

900 Rebecca Avenue

Pittsburgh, Pennsylvania 15221-2938

Telephone: 412-371-7700 Ext. 118

Toll-free: 800-633-4588

Fax: 412-371-9430

Email: rmcwilliams@trcil.org

Web site: **www.trcil.org**

Schuykill Community Action

206 North Second Street

Pottsville, Pennsylvania 17901

Telephone: 570-622-1995

Fax: 570-622-0429

Email: info@schuykillcommunityaction. com

Web site: **www.schuykillcommunityac-tion.com**

Catholic Social Services

516 Fig Street

Scranton, Pennsylvania 18505

Telephone: 570-558-3019

Fax: 570-207-4551

Email: mcoyle@cssscranton.org

Web site: **www.dioceseofscranton.org**

United Neighborhood Centers of Northeastern Pennsylvania

425 Alder Street

Scranton, Pennsylvania 18505

Telephone: 570-343-8835 Ext. 108

Fax: 570-342-3972

Email: ldurkin@uncnepa.org

Web site: **www.unitedneighborhoodcen-ters.org**

Fayette County Community Action Agency

140 North Beeson Avenue

Uniontown, Pennsylvania 15401

Telephone: 724-430-3013

Toll-free: 800-427-4636

Fax: 724-437-4418

Email: jstark@fccaa.org

Web site: **www.fccaa.org**

Southwestern Pennsylvania Legal Services, Incorporated

48 East Main Street

Uniontown, Pennsylvania 15301

Telephone: 800-846-0871

Toll-free: 888-855-3873

Fax: 724-250-1078

Email: legalservices@splas.org

Web site: **www.splas@pulsenet.com**

63 South Washington Street

Waynesburg, Pennsylvania 15370

Telephone: 800-846-0871

Toll-free: 888-885-3873

Fax: 724-250-1078

Email: legalservices@splas.org

www.splas@pulsenet.com

Commission on Economic Opportunity of Luzerne

165 Amber Lane

P.O. Box 1127

Wilkes Barre, Pennsylvania 18703-1127

Telephone: 570-826-0510 Ext. 216

Toll-free: 800-822-0359

Fax: 570-829-1665

Email: ceo@sunlink.net

Web site: **www.ceopeoplehelping-people.org**

Housing Alliance of York

35 South Duke Street

York, Pennsylvania 17401-1106

Telephone: 717-854-1541 Ext. 123

Toll-free: 800-864-4909

Fax: 717-845-7934

Email: leighsnydersmith@aol.com

Web site: **www.housingallianceofyork.com**

Puerto Rico

CCCS of Puerto Rico

Edif JMJ Cabrera Hnos

Arecibo, Puerto Rico 00612

Telephone: 787-816-0210

Toll-free: 800-717-2227

Fax: 787-816-0202

Email: info@ccspr.org

Web site: **www.cccspr.org**

Bayamon Shopping Center, Oficina 206

Bayamon, Puerto Rico 00961

Telephone: 787-269-4100

Toll-free: 800-717-2227

Fax: 787-269-4153

Email: info@ccspr.org

www.cccspr.org

1A Calle Nazario

Esq. Dr. Goyco y Padial

Caguas, Puerto Rico 00725

Telephone: 787-703-0506

Toll-free: 800-717-2227
Fax: 787-703-0580
Email: info@ccspr.org
www.cccspr.org

Urb. Villa Fontana 3D-S5, Ave. Fragoso
Carolina, Puerto Rico 00983
Telephone: 787-750-7664
Toll-free: 800-717-2227
Fax: 787-769-1360
Email: info@ccspr.org
www.cccspr.org

25 Calle Mendez Vigo (oeste)
Mayaguez, Puerto Rico 00608
Telephone: 787-265-0480
Toll-free: 800-717-2227
Fax: 787-265-0560
Email: info@ccspr.org
www.cccspr.org

1369 Calle Salud
Ponce, Puerto Rico 00731
Telephone: 787-844-4550
Toll-free: 800-717-2227
Fax: 787-844-4540
Email: info@ccspr.org
www.cccspr.org

1603 Ave. Ponce de Leon
Cobian's Plaza, GM-9
Santurce, Puerto Rico 00909
Telephone: 787-722-8835

Toll-free: 800-717-2227
Fax: 787-722-6979
Email: info@ccspr.org
www.cccspr.org

Ceibo Housing and Economic Development Center

Ave Lauro Pinero 252
P.O. Box 203
Ceibo, Puerto Rico 00735-0203
Telephone: 787-885-3020
Fax: 787-885-0716
Email: cdec@libertypr.net

Ponce Neighborhood Housing Services, Incorporated

57 Mendez Vigo Street
P.O. Box 330223
Ponce, Puerto Rico 00730-0223
Telephone: 787-841-5055
Fax: 787-841-5110
Email: pnhs@coqui.net

One Stop Career Center of Puerto Rico

Cond. Plaza Universidad 2000
Calle Anasco 839 Local 5
San Juan, Puerto Rico 00928
Telephone: 787-296-1785
Fax: 787-767-5695
Email: onestoppr@yahoo.com

Rhode Island

CCCS Southern New England, A Division

of MMI

4 Richmond Square, Ste. 350

Providence, Rhode Island 02906

Telephone: 888-845-2227

Fax: 206-350-2227

Email: Daniel.fenton@
moneymanagement.org

Web site: **www.creditcounseling.org**

4 Richmond Square, Suite 350

Providence, Rhode Island 02906

Telephone: 401-468-7000

Toll-free: 800-308-2227

501 Centerville Rd, 2nd Floor

Warwick, Rhode Island 02886

Toll-free: 800-308-2227

Fax: 401-732-0250

www.creditcounseling.org

Acorn Housing

807 Broad Street, Suite 329

Providence, Rhode Island 02907

Telephone: 401-780-0509

Toll-free: 888-409-3557

Fax: 401-780-0548

Email: tnaylor@acornhousing.org

Web site: **www.acornhousing.org**

Elmwood Foundation

693 Broad Street

Providence, Rhode Island 02907

Telephone: 401-273-2330 Ext. 103

Fax: 401-274-3670

Email: nmunoz@elmwoodfoundation.org

Web site: **www.elmwoodfoundation.org**

The Housing Network of Rhode Island

48 Nashua Street

Providence, Rhode Island 02904

Telephone: 401-521-1461

Fax: 401-521-1478

Email: hiasimone@housingnetworkri.org

Web site: **www.housingnetworkri.org**

Neighborworks – Blackstone River Valley

719 Front Street, Suite 103

Woonsocket, Rhode Island 02895

Telephone: 401-762-0074 Ext. 208

Fax: 401-769-1010

Email: fdiaz@wndc.org

Web site: **www.wndc.org**

South Dakota

CCCS of LSS – South Dakota

202 S. Main Street, Suite 228

Aberdeen, South Dakota 57401

Telephone: 605-330-2700

Toll-free: 888-258-2227

Fax: 605-357-0150

Email: cccs@lsssd.org

Web site: **www.lsssd.org/services/cccs.
shtml**

1310 Main Ave S, Suite 107A

Brookings, South Dakota 57006
Telephone: 605-330-2700
Toll-free: 888-258-2227
Fax: 605-357-0150
Email: cccs@lsssd.org
www.lsssd.org/services/cccs.shtml

1371 Dakota Avenue South, Suite 202
Huron, South Dakota 57350
Telephone: 605-330-2700
Toll-free: 888-258-2227
Fax: 605-357-0150
Email: cccs@lsssd.org
www.lsssd.org/services/cccs.shtml

403 N. Lawler, Suite 206
Mitchell, South Dakota 57301
Telephone: 605-330-2700
Toll-free: 888-258-2227
Fax: 605-357-0150
Email: cccs@lsssd.org
www.lsssd.org/services/cccs.shtml

705 E 41st St Ste 100
Sioux Falls, South Dakota 57105-6025
Telephone: 605-330-2700
Toll-free: 888-258-2227
Fax: 605-357-0150
Email: cccs@lsssd.org
www.lsssd.org/services/cccs.shtml

816 E. Clark Street

Vermillion, South Dakota 57069
Telephone: 605-330-2700
Toll-free: 888-258-2227
Fax: 605-357-0150
Email: cccs@lsssd.org
www.lsssd.org/services/cccs.shtml

1424 9th Avenue SE, Suite 7
Watertown, South Dakota 57201
Telephone: 605-330-2700
Toll-free: 888-258-2227
Fax: 605-357-0150
Email: cccs@lsssd.org
www.lsssd.org/services/cccs.shtml

610 W. 23rd Street, Suite 104
Yankton, South Dakota 57078
Telephone: 605-330-2700
Toll-free: 888-258-2227
Fax: 605-357-0150
Email: cccs@lsssd.org
www.lsssd.org/services/cccs.shtml

CCCS of the Black Hills
209 1/2 Sioux Ave
PO Box 404
Pierre, South Dakota 57501
Telephone: 605-348-4550
Toll-free: 888-568-6568
Fax: 605-348-0107
Email: tmills@cccsbh.com
Web site: **www.cccsbh.com**

111 St. Joseph Street

PO Box 817

Rapid City, South Dakota 57701

Telephone: 605-348-4550

Toll-free: 888-568-6615

Fax: 605-348-0107

Email: jstone@cccsbh.com

www.cccsbh.com

Neighborhood Housing Services of the Black Hills

817-½ Main Street

Deadwood, South Dakota 57732

Telephone: 605-578-1401

Fax: 605-578-1405

Email: joy@nhsbh.org

Tennessee

Family Service Agency – CCCS

2855 Stage Village Cove

Bartlett, Tennessee 38134

Telephone: 901-383-2193

Toll-free: 800-255-2227

Fax: 901-377-9282

2400 Popular Avenue, Suite 445

Memphis, Tennessee 38112

Telephone: 901-323-4909

Toll-free: 800-255-2227

Fax: 501-812-4309

Partnership For Families, Children and

Adults/CCCS of Chattanooga

2221A Olan Mills Drive

Chattanooga, Tennessee 37421

Telephone: 423-490-5620

Toll-free: 800-459-2227

Fax: 423-490-5624

Email: tjohnson@partnershipfca.com

CCCS of Greater Atlanta

2111 Mountcastle Dr., Suite 2

Johnson City, Tennessee 37604

Telephone: 404-527-7630

Toll-free: 866-255-2227

Fax: 404-260-3338

Email: sue.hunt@cccsinc.org

Web site: **www.cccsinc.org**

521 Callahan Road, Suite 101

Knoxville, Tennessee 37912

Telephone: 404-527-7630

Toll-free: 866-255-2227

Fax: 404-260-3338

Email: sue.hunt@cccsinc.org

www.cccsinc.org

523 Lamar Alexander Ave, Suite 8

Maryville, Tennessee 37801

Telephone: 404-527-7630

Toll-free: 866-255-2227

Fax: 404-260-3338

Email: sue.hunt@cccsinc.org

www.cccsinc.org

221 Rutgers Avenue

Oak Ridge, Tennessee 37830

Telephone: 404-527-7630

Toll-free: 866-255-2227

Fax: 404-260-3338

Email: sue.hunt@cccsinc.org

www.cccsinc.org

CCCS of Southwestern VA/American Credit Counselors

1420 East Stone Drive

Kingsport, Tennessee 37660

Telephone: 888-845-5669

Fax: 713-592-0298

Email: virginia.garretson@
moneymanagement.org

CCCS of the Midwest

1101 Kermit Drive, Suite 204

Nashville, Tennessee 37130

Telephone: 800-355-2227

Fax: 614-552-4800

Email: info@cccservices.com

Web site: **www.cccservices.com/home.
asp**

Department of Human Services City of Chattanooga

501 West 12th Street

Chattanooga, Tennessee 37402-3852

Telephone: 421-757-5229

Fax: 423-757-4852

Email: chaney_thelma@mail.
chattanooga.gov

Web site: **www.chattanooga.gov**

West Tennessee Legal Services, Incorporated

P.O. Box 2066

Jackson, Tennessee 38302-2066

Telephone: 731-426-1307

Toll-free: 800-372-8346

Fax: 731-423-2600

Email: emma@wtls.org

Web site: **www.wtls.org**

Knoxville Area Urban League

1514 East Fifth Avenue

P.O. Box 1911

Knoxville, Tennessee 37917

Telephone: 865-524-5511 Ext. 120

Fax: 865-525-5154

Email: akyle@thekaul.org

Web site: **www.thekaul.org**

Legal Aid of East Tennessee

502 South Gay Street, Suite 404

Knoxville, Tennessee 37902

Telephone: 865-637-0484 Ext. 263

Toll-free: 800-821-1312

Fax: 865-252-1162

Email: jmoffett@laet.org

Web site: **www.laet.org**

Life of Victory International Christian Ministries

253A Old Nashville Highway

La – Vergne, Tennessee 37086

Telephone: 615-213-1468

Email: lifeofvictory@aol.com

Memphis Area Legal Services, Incorporated

109 North Main, 2nd Floor

Memphis, Tennessee 38103

Telephone: 901-432-4663

Fax: 901-529-8706

Email: sraj@malsi.org

Web site: **www.malsi.org**

Neighborhood Housing Opportunities

1548 Poplar Avenue

Memphis, Tennessee 38104

Telephone: 901-729-2934

Fax: 901-729-2933

Email: annie@mlfonline.org

NID-HCA Tate

3115 Park Avenue

Memphis, Tennessee 38111

Telephone: 901-507-1638

Fax: 901-458-9325

Email: nidmemphis@aol.com

Web site: **www.nidonline.org**

Vollintine Evergreen Community Association CDC

1680 Jackson Avenue

Memphis, Tennessee 38107-5044

Telephone: 901-276-1782

Fax: 901-276-1784

Email: wruth@vecacdc.org

Affordable Housing Resources of Nashville, Incorporated

1011 Cherry Avenue

Nashville, Tennessee 37203

Telephone: 615-251-0025 Ext. 234

Toll-free: 877-559-3377

Fax: 615-251-0143

Email: bholland@ahrhousing.org

Web site: **www.ahrhousing.org**

Woodbine Community Organization

222 Oriel Avenue

Nashville, Tennessee 37210

Telephone: 615-850-3453

Fax: 615-833-9727

Email: Rodwilliams47@yahoo.com

Web site: **www.woodbinecommunity.org**

Family Services Agency

628 West Broadway, Suite 203

North Little Rock, Tennessee 72114

Telephone: 501-753-0202 Ext. 209

Email: Daved@fsc-hsv.org

Legal Aid Society of Middle Tennessee and the Cumberlands, Incorporated

226 Broadway

P.O. Box 5209

Oak Ridge, Tennessee 37831

Telephone: 865-483-8454 Ext. 214

Toll-free: 800-483-8457

Fax: 865-483-8905

Email: nmcbride@las.org

Texas

CCCS of Fort Worth

500 Chestnut Street, 1511

Abilene, Texas 79602

Toll-free: 800-747-4222

Fax: 325-673-0405

Email: jim.savage@moneymanagment.org

Web site: **www.creditcounselingnetwork.org**

CCCS of Greater Dallas

6300 I 40 West, Suite 106

Amarillo, Texas 79106

Telephone: 806-358-2221

Toll-free: 800-878-2227

Fax: 806-356-0677

Email: info@cccs.net

Web site: **www.cccs.net**

1600 East Pioneer Parkway, Suite 345

Arlington, Texas 76010

Telephone: 817-461-2227

Toll-free: 800-249-2227

Fax: 817-460-0409

Email: info@cccs.net

www.cccs.net

5850 West I-20, Suite 110

Arlington, Texas 76017

Toll-free: 800-249-2227

Email: shouston@cccs.net

www.cccs.net

3705 W. Green Oaks Blvd Suite C

Arlington, Texas 76016

Telephone: 817-654-4200

Toll-free: 800-249-2227

Fax: 817-654-4203

Email: info@cccs.net

www.cccs.net

1106 Clayton Lane, Suite 490W

Austin, Texas 78723

Telephone: 512-447-0711

Toll-free: 866-901-2227

Fax: 512-444-2025

Email: info@cccs.net

www.cccs.net

4818 E. Ben White, Suite 101

Austin, Texas 78741

Telephone: 512-697-0875

Toll-free: 800-783-5018

Fax: 512-697-0879

Email: info@cccs.net

www.cccs.net

200 N. 13th Street, Ste 208

Corsicana, Texas 75110

Toll-free: 800-886-2227

Fax: 903-872-8097

Email: shouston@cccs.net

www.cccs.net

8737 King George Drive, Suite 200

Dallas, Texas 75235

Telephone: 214-638-2227

Toll-free: 800-249-2227

Fax: 214-630-6805

Email: info@cccs.net

www.cccs.net

8950 N Central Expressway, Ste 122

Dallas, Texas 75231

Telephone: 214-363-4357

Fax: 214-363-3538

Email: shouston@cccs.net

www.cccs.net

14110 Dallas Pkwy Plaza, Suite 280

Dallas, Texas 75240

Telephone: 972-387-2227

Toll-free: 866-957-2227

Fax: 972-866-6761

Email: info@cccs.net

www.cccs.net

6500 Greenville Suite 440

Dallas, Texas 75206

Telephone: 214-363-4357

Toll-free: 866-316-7476

Fax: 214-363-3538

Email: info@cccs.net

www.cccs.net

400 S Zang St., Suite 1004

Dallas, Texas 75208

Telephone: 214-943-2075

Toll-free: 800-249-2227

Fax: 214-943-4753

Email: info@cccs.net

www.cccs.net

1229 E. Pleasant Run Rd., Ste 214

DeSoto, Texas 75115

Telephone: 972-224-4786

Toll-free: 800-249-2227

Fax: 972-228-2992

Email: info@cccs.net

www.cccs.net

402 W. Wheatland Rd, Suite 116

Duncanville, Texas 75137

Telephone: 972-709-1723

Toll-free: 800-249-2227

Fax: 972-709-8974

Email: info@cccs.net

www.cccs.net

For more CCCS office in Texas, **visit www. hud.gov**

Catholic Charities of Corpus Christi

1322 Comanche Street

Corpus Christi, Texas 78401
Telephone: 361-884-0651 Ext. 215
Fax: 361-884-3956
Email: ddean@diocesecc.org
Web site: **www.catholiccharities-cc.org**

Acorn Housing

5353 Maple Avenue, Suite 200
Dallas, Texas 75235
Telephone: 214-823-9885
Fax: 214-823-0819
Email: srandall@acornhousing.org
Web site: **www.acornhousing.org**

6000 Welch Street, Suite 15
El Paso, Texas 79905
Telephone: 915-781-1303
Fax: 915-781-1315
Email: vstjohn@acornhousing.org
www.acornhousing.org

2600 South Loop West, Suite 270
Houston, Texas 77054
Telephone: 713-863-9002
Fax: 713-863-1964
Email: fakbar@acornhousing.org
www.acornhousing.org

2300 West Commerce Street, Suite 104
San Antonia, Texas 78207
Telephone: 210-432-4663
Fax: 210-432-4662

Email: Cdeleon@acornhousing.org
www.acornhousing.org

Urban League

4315 South Lancaster Road
Dallas, Texas 75216
Telephone: 214-915-4600 Ext. 4604
Fax: 214-915-4601
Email: cwhitfield@ulgdnctx.com
Web site: **www.dallasurbanleague.com**

1301 Texas Avenue
Houston, Texas 77002
Telephone: 713-393-8729
Fax: 713-393-8760
Email: jfair-payton@haul.org
Web site: **www.haul.org**

El Paso Community Action Program, Project Bravo, Incorporated

4838 Montana Avenue
El Paso, Texas 79903
Telephone: 915-562-4100
Fax: 915-562-8952
Email: apayton@projectnbravo.org
Web site: **www.projectbravo.org**

City of Fort Worth Housing Department

1000 Throckmorton Street
Fort Worth, Texas 76102
Telephone: 817-392-7322
Fax: 817-392-7508
Email: susan.fite@fortworth.org

Web site: **www.fortworthgov.org/housing**

Housing Opportunities of Fort Worth

1065 West Magnolia, Suite B
Fort Worth, Texas 76104-4345
Telephone: 817-923-9192
Fax: 817-924-8252
Email: hofw@swbell.net

NID-HCA

5504 Brentwood Stair Road
Fort Worth, Texas 76112
Telephone: 817-346-9990
Fax: 817-423-4207
Email: shirleye@prodigy.net
Web site: **www.nidonline.org**

4018 Chartres Street
Houston, Texas 77004
Telephone: 713-987-7003
Fax: 713-987-7004
Email: Acooksey67@aol.com
Web site: **www.nidonline.org**

7220 Homestead Road
Houston, Texas 77028
Telephone: 713-635-6941
Fax: 713-635-2877
Email: mdightman@hotmail.com
www.nidonline.org

2208 Blodgett Street

Houston, Texas 77004
Telephone: 713-521-3502
Fax: 713-523-4660
Email: Sheila@fryehoc.com
www.nidonline.org

Credit Coalition

3300 Lyons Avenue, Number 201/203A
Houston, Texas 77020
Telephone: 713-224-8100
Toll-free: 866-346-8100
Fax: 713-224-8102
Email: youngfam@flash.net
Web site: **www.creditcoalition.org**

Dominion Community Development Corporation

1102 Pinemont Drive, Suite B
Houston, Texas 77018
Telephone: 713-957-2789 Ext. 29
Fax: 713-957-3087
Email: lgibons@clearsail.net

Fifth-Ward Community Redevelopment Corporation

4300 Lyons Avenue, Suite 300
Houston, Texas 77226
Telephone: 713-674-0175
Fax: 713-674-0176
Email: kpayton@fifthwardcrc.org
Web site: **www.fifthwardcrc.org**

Gulf Coast Community Services

Association

5000 Gulf Freeway, Building # 1

Houston, Texas 77023

Telephone: 713-393-4787

Fax: 713-393-4760

Email: wallacej@gccsa.org

Web site: **www.gccsa.org**

Utah

CCCS of Southern Nevada DBA CCCS of Utah

720 South River Road C-235

St. George, Utah 84770

Telephone: 435-986-9223

Toll-free: 800-451-4505

Fax: 435-986-9410

Email: cccs@cccsnevada.org

Web site: **www.cccsutah.net**

Cedar City Housing Authority

364 South 100 East

Cedar City, Utah 84720

Telephone: 435-586-8462

Fax: 435-865-9397

Email: heidi@cedarcity.org

Utah State University – Family Life Center Housing and Financial Counseling

493 North 700 East

Logan, Utah 84321

Telephone: 435-797-7224

Fax: 435-797-7432

Email: flchfc@aggiemail.usu.edu

Web site: **www.usu.edu/fchd/hfc.cfm**

Your Community Connection

2261 Adams Avenue

Ogden, Utah 84401-1510

Telephone: 801-394-9456

Fax: 801-394-9457

Email: yccexec@aol.com

Community Action Services

815 South Freedom Boulevard, Suite 100

Provo, Utah 84601

Telephone: 801-373-8200 Ext. 241

Fax: 801-373-8228

Telephone: drusaw@unitedwayuc.org

Web site: **www.communityactionprovo. org**

Salt Lake Community Action Program

764 South 200 West

Salt Lake City, Utah 84101-2710

Telephone: 801-359-2444

Fax: 801-355-1798

Email: sabegglen@slcap.org

Vermont

Central Vermont Community Action Council, Incorporated

195 US Route 302 – Berlin

Barre, Vermont, 05641

Telephone: 802-728-9506

Toll-free: 800-846-9506

Fax: 802-728-4962

Email: cflint@cvcac.org

Web site: **www.cvcac.org**

HUD Employee HECM Counselor

159 Bank Street

Burlington, Vermont 05401

Telephone: 802-951-6290 Ext. 3008

Opportunities Credit Union

18 Pearl Street

Burlington, Vermont 05401

Telephone: 802-865-3404 Ext. 105

Toll-free: 800-865-8328

Fax: 802-862-8971

Email: cfatnassi@oppsvt.org

Web site: **www.ippsvt.org**

Gilman Housing Trust

101 Main Street

P.O. Box 259

Lyndonville, Vermont 05851

Telephone: 802-626-1175

Toll-free: 866-582-0337

Fax: 802-626-1184

Web site: **www.nekhome.com**

Rockingham Area Community Land Trust

90 Main Street, Suite 1

Springfield, Vermont 05156

Telephone: 802-855-3220 Ext. 222

Fax: 802-885-5811

Email: bwhitney@vermontel.net

Web site: **www.raclt.org**

Virginia

CCCS of Greater Washington

801 N Pitt Street Suite 117

Alexandria, Virginia 22314-1765

Telephone: 703-836-8772

Toll-free: 800-747-4222

Fax: 703-548-7704

Email: lori.johnson@moneymanagement.org

Web site: **www.creditcounselingnetwork.org**

604 South King Street, Suite 007

Leesburg, Virginia 20175

Toll-free: 800-747-4222

Fax: 703-777-7191

lori.johnson@moneymanagement.org

www.creditcounselingnetwork.org

10629 Crestwood Drive

Manassas, Virginia 20109-3433

Toll-free: 800-747-4222

Fax: 703-335-1632

lori.johnson@moneymanagement.org

www.creditcounselingnetwork.org

12662 B Lake Ridge Drive

Woodbridge, Virginia 22192

Telephone: 703-494-1014

Toll-free: 800-747-4222

Fax: 703-494-1594

lori.johnson@moneymanagement.org
www.creditcounselingnetwork.org

CCCS of Southwestern VA/American Credit Counselors
4846 Kings Mountain Rd.
Collinsville, Virginia 24078
Telephone: 800-646-0042
Fax: 540-366-7140
Email: virginia.garretson@
moneymanagement.org

700 Peters Creek Rd.
Roanoke, Virginia 24019
Telephone: 800-646-0042
virginia.garretson@moneymanagement.
org

CCCS of Greater Fort Worth
3927 Old Lee Highway, Suite 101 E
Fairfax, Virginia 22030-2422
Telephone: 703-591-9020
Toll-free: 800-747-4222
Fax: 703-591-3927
Email: jim.savage@moneymanagment.
org
Web site: www.moneymanagement.org

CCCS of Hampton Roads/Center for Child And Family Services
2021 Cunningham Drive, Suite 400
Hampton, Virginia 23666
Telephone: 757-826-2227
Fax: 757-838-8021

Email: hcobb@kidsandfamilies.com
Web site: www.debtfreeonline.com

312 Waller Mill Road
Williamsburg, Virginia 23185
Telephone: 757-826-2227
Fax: 757-838-8021
Email: hcobb@kidsandfamilies.com
www.debtfreeonline.com

Monticello Area Community Action Agency (MACAA)
1025 Park Street
Charlottesville, Virginia 22901-3934
Telephone: 434-295-3171
Fax: 434-296-0093
Email: mason@macaa.org
Web site: www.avenue.org/macaa

Piedmont Housing Alliance
111 Monticello Avenue, Suite 104
Charlottesville, Virginia 22902
Telephone: 434-817-2436 Ext. 104
Fax: 434-817-0664
Email: shelleym@piedmonthousing.org
Web site: www.piemonthousingalliance.org

Virginia Cooperative Northampton County Extension
5432-A Bayside Road
Exmore, Virginia 23350
Telephone: 757-414-0731

Fax: 757-414-0745

Email: vickiw@vt.edu

Telamon Corporation

111 Henry Street

P.O. Box 500

Gretna, Virginia 24557-0500

Telephone: 434-656-8357

Fax: 434-656-8356

Email: rroark@telamon.org

Web site: **www.telamon.org**

Lynchburg Community Action Group, Incorporated

926 Commerce Street

Lynchburg, Virginia 24504

Telephone: 434-846-2778 Ext. 41

Fax: 434-846-2759

Email: myuille@lyncag.org

Web site: **www.lyncag.org**

Prince William County Virginia Cooperative Extension

8033 Ashton Avenue, Suite 105

Manassas, Virginia 20109-8202

Telephone: 703-792-4799

Fax: 703-792-4630

Email: Jbotta@pwcgov.org

Web site: **www.pwcgov.org/vce/html/ personal_finance.html**

Newport News Office of Human Affairs

392 Maple Avenue

P.O. Box 37

Newport News, Virginia 23607

Telephone: 757-643-4086

Fax: 757-643-4087

Email: dbuchanan@ohainc.org

Web site: **www.ohainc.org**

Child & Family Services of Eastern Virginia, Incorporated

DBA The UP Center

222 West 19th Street

Norfolk, Virginia 23517

Telephone: 757-965-8639

Fax: 757-640-8402

Email: jallen@theupcenter.org

Web site: **www.theupcenter.org**

Homenet

201 Granby Street

Norfolk, Virginia 23510

Telephone: 757-624-8649

Fax: 757-314-1305

Email: lfortes@nrha.va.us

Web site: **www.nrha.us**

The Southeastern Tidewater Opportunity Project

2551 Almeda Avenue

Norfolk, Virginia 23513-2443

Telephone: 757-858-1360

Fax: 757-858-1389

Email: sharris@stopinc.org

Web site: **www.stopinc.org**

Urban League

3225 High Street

Portsmouth, Virginia 23707

Telephone: 757-627-0864 Ext. 107

Fax: 757-966-9613

Email: yyoung@ulhr.org

511 West Grace Street

Richmond, Virginia 23220

Telephone: 804-649-8407

Fax: 804-649-1745

Email: tvictory@urbanleaguerichmond.org

Catholic Charities

1512 Willow Lawn Drive

P.O. Box 6565

Richmond, Virginia 23230

Telephone: 804-545-5925

Toll-free: 800-528-1258

Fax: 804-285-9130

Email: letitia_brown@cccofvirginia.org

Web site: **www.cccofvirginia.org**

5361-A Virginia Beach Boulevard

Virginia Beach, Virginia 23462

Telephone: 757-484-0703

Fax: 757-484-1096

Email: rwoody@cceva.org

Web site: **www.cceva.org**

Housing Opportunities Made Equal of Virginia, Incorporated

700 East Franklin Street, Suite 3A

Richmond, Virginia 23219

Telephone: 804-354-0641

Fax: 804-354-0690

Email: lponder@phonehome.org

Web site: **www.phonehome.org**

Southside Community Development and Housing

1624 Hull Street

Richmond, Virginia 23224

Telephone: 804-231-4449 Ext. 103

Fax: 804-231-3959

Email: dianna@scdhc.com

Web site: **www.scdhc.com**

Total Action Against Poverty in Roanoke Valley

145 Campbell Avenue, Suite 700

Roanoke, Virginia 24011-2868

Telephone: 540-345-6781 Ext. 4390

Fax: 540-777-0422

Email: earl.reynolds@taproanoke.org

Web site: **www.taproanoke.org**

Skyline Community Action Program, Incorporated

31 Stanard Street

P.O. Box 508

Stanardsville, Virginia 22973

Telephone: 434-985-6066

Fax: 434-985-3793

Email: jnaylor@skylinecap.org

Washington

CCCS of the Tri-States
401 North Morain St. P.O. Box 6551
Kennewick, Washington 99336-2667
Telephone: 509-737-1973
Toll-free: 800-201-2181
Fax: 509-737-9722
Email: Lrue@cccswaor.org
Web site: **www.cccswaor.org**

CCCS of Yakima Valley
1115 West Lincoln Avenue Ste# 119
Yakima, Washington 98902-2571
Telephone: 509-248-5270
Toll-free: 800-273-6897
Fax: 509-248-5276
Email: merry@cccsyakima.org
www.cccsyakima.org

Neighborworks of Grays Harbor County (Aberdeen NHS)
710 East Market Street
Aberdeen, Washington 98520-3430
Telephone: 360-533-7828
Toll-free: 866-533-7828
Fax: 360-533-7851
Email: dmurnen@aberdeen-nhs.com
Web site: **www.aberdeen-nhs.com**

Acorn Housing
134 Southwest 153rd Street, Suite A
Burien, Washington 98166-2300

Telephone: 206-243-4663
Fax: 206-243-4676
Email: sgarcia@acornhousing.org
Web site: **www.acornhousing.org**

El Centro De La Raza
2524 16th Avenue South
Seattle, Washington 98144-5104
Telephone: 206-57-4639
Fax: 206-726-1529
Email: agonzalez@elcentrodelaraza.org
Web site: **www.elcentrodelaraza.org**

Solid Ground Washington
1501 North 45th Street
Seattle, Washington 98103-6708
Telephone: 206-694-6700
Toll-free: 866-297-4300
Fax: 206-694-6777
Email: donnad@solid-ground.org
Web site: **www.solid-ground.org**

Urban League of Metropolitan Seattle
105 – 14th Avenue
Seattle, Washington 98122-5558
Telephone: 206-461-3697
Fax: 206-461-8425
Email: ltaylor@urbanleague.org
Web site: **www.urbanleague.org**

Kitsap County Consolidated Housing Authority
9307 Bayshore Drive Northwest

Silverdale, Washington 98383-9113
Telephone: 360-535-6100
Toll-free: 800-693-7070
Fax: 360-535-6118
Email: howardd@kccha.org
Web site: **www.kccha.org**

Spokane Neighborhood Action Programs
500 South Stone Street
Spokane, Washington 99202-4150
Telephone: 509-456-7106
Fax: 509-456-7159
Email: burrell@snapwa.org
Web site: **www.snapwa.org**

Community Housing Resource Center
2700 Northeast Anderson Road, Suite D3
Vancouver, Washington 98661
Telephone: 360-690-4496 Ext. 101
Fax: 360-694-6665
Email: info@homecen.org
Web site: **www.homecen.org**

Washington DC

CCCS of Greater Washington
1250 Connecticut Avenue NW, Office 48
Washington, District of Columbia 20036
Telephone: 800-747-4222
Fax: 202-393-7373
Email: lori.johnson@moneymanagement.org
Web site: **www.creditcounselingnet-work.org**

AARP Foundation
601 E Street, Northwest
Washington, District of Columbia 20049
Telephone: 800-209-8085
Fax: 202-434-6068
Email: rmcounsel@aarp.org

Acorn Housing
737-½ 8th Street, Southeast
Washington, District of Columbia
20003-2802
Telephone: 202-547-9295
Fax: 202-546-6849
Email: ayoung@acornhousing.org
Web site: **www.acornhousing.org**

Greater Washington Urban League
2901 14th Street, Northwest
Washington, District of Columbia 20009
Telephone: 202-265-8200
Fax: 202-265-8929

Housing Counseling Services, Incorporated
2410 17th Street, Northwest
Washington, District of Columbia 20009
Telephone: 202-667-7006 Ext. 108
Fax: 202-667-1939
Email: mariansiegel@housingetc.org

Lydia's House
3939 South Capitol Street, Southwest
Washington, District of Columbia 20032

Telephone: 202-373-1050

Fax: 202-373-5270

Email: lydiashouse2@hotmail.com

Web site: **www.lydiashouse.com**

Marshall Heights Community Development Organization

3939 Benning Road, Northeast

Washington, District of Columbia 20019-2662

Telephone: 202-396-1201 Ext. 122

Fax: 202-396-4106

Email: bwilliams@mhcdo.org

Web site: **www.mhcdo.org**

National Credit Union Foundation

601 Pennsylvania Avenue, Northwest

South Building, Suite 600

Washington, District of Columbia 20004-2601

Telephone: 202-508-6751

Toll-free: 800-356-9655

Fax: 202-638-3912

Email: sbosack@ncuf.coop

Web site: **www.ncuf.coop**

Near Northeast Community Improvement Corporation

1326 Florida Avenue, Northeast

Washington, District of Columbia 20002-7108

Telephone: 202-399-6900

Fax: 202-399-6942

Email: ipholmes@nnecic.org

University Legal Services

220 I Street Northeast, Suite 130

Washington, District of Columbia 20002-4389

Telephone: 202-547-4747

Fax: 202-547-2083

Email: mbeard@uls-dc.org

3220 Pennsylvania Avenue Southwest, Suite 4

Washington, District of Columbia 20020

Telephone: 202-547-4747

Fax: 202-547-2083

Email: jbrown@uls-dc.com

West Virginia

CCCS of Southern West Virginia

111 Lebanon Lane

PO Box 2129

Beckley, West Virginia 25802

Telephone: 304-255-2499

Toll-free: 800-869-7758

Fax: 304-255-2412

Email: rcoleman@cccswv.com

Web site: **http://cccswv.com**

Green Valley Business Center

Blue Prince Rd

P.O. Box 6282

Bluefield, West Virginia 24701-6282

Telephone: 304-325-5143

Toll-free: 800-313-5097

Fax: 304-324-0375

Email: esimkins@cccswv.com
http://cccswv.com

1219 Ohio Ave.
Dunbar, West Virginia 25064-3019
Toll-free: 800-281-5969
Fax: 304-720-3644
Email: jwise@cccswv.com
http://cccswv.com

3983 Teays Valley Road, Box 15
Mount Vernon Plaza
Hurricane, West Virginia 25526
Telephone: 304-201-5017
Toll-free: 800-281-5969
Email: ckudlak@cccswv.com
http://cccswv.com

CCCS of North Central West Virginia

115 S 4th St
PO Box 1840
Clarksburg, West Virginia 26302-1840
Telephone: 304-623-0921
Toll-free: 800-498-6681
Fax: 304-624-4089
Email: cccsdir@criss-crosswv.org
Web site: www.criss-crosswv.org

1299 Pineview Drive, Suite 3
Morgantown, West Virginia 26505
Telephone: 304-291-6819
Toll-free: 800-498-6681
Fax: 304-291-3878

Email: cccsmotown@criss-crosswv.org
www.criss-crosswv.org

Religious Coalition for Community Renewal

1516 Washington Street East
Charleston, West Virginia 25311
Telephone: 304-346-6417
Fax: 304-346-6417
Email: kstatome@rccr.org
Web site: www.rccr.org

Family Service Credit Counseling
A Division of Family Service Upper Ohio Valley

51 11th Street
Wheeling, West Virginia 26006-2937
Telephone: 304-232-6733 Ext. 125
Toll-free: 800-220-3252
Fax: 304-233-7237
Email: jmarriner@ovrh.org
Web site: www.familyserviceuov.org

Wisconsin

Neighborhood Housing Services

156 St. Lawrence Avenue
Beloit, Wisconsin 53511
Telephone: 608-362-9051 Ext. 17
Fax: 608-362-7226
Email: cschlichting@nhsofbeloit.com
Web site: www.nhsofbeloit.com

1700 Mead Street

Racine, Wisconsin 53403

Telephone: 262-652-6766

Fax: 262-652-8108

Email: domenick@exepc.com

Neighborworks Green Bay

437 South Jackson Street

Green Bay, Wisconsin 54301

Telephone: 920-448-3075

Fax: 920-448-3078

Email: info@nwgreenbay.org

Web site: **www.nwgreenbay.org**

GreenPath Incorporated

4811 South 76th Street, Suite 5

Greenfield, Wisconsin 53220

Telephone: 800-550-1961

Email: sbriggs@greenpath.com

Web site: **www.greenpath.com**

802 West Broadway, Suite 202

Madison, Wisconsin 53713

Telephone: 888-776-6735

www.greenpath.com

HBC Services, Incorporated

118 South Main Street, Suite A

Jefferson, Wisconsin 53549

Telephone: 920-674-5611

Fax: 920-674-5631

Email: homebuyer@hbcservices.org

Web site: **www.hbservices.org**

217 Wisconsin Avenue, Suite 207

Waukesha, Wisconsin 53186

Telephone: 414-727-5700

Toll-free: 800-687-1680

Fax: 414-727-5701

Email: info@hbcservices.org

www.hbcservices.org

10533 West National Avenue, Suite 300

West Allis, Wisconsin 53227

Telephone: 414-727-5700

Fax: 414-727-5701

Email: info@hbcservices.org

www.hbcservices.org

Catholic Charities

3710 East Avenue, South

LaCrosse, Wisconsin 54601

Telephone: 608-782-0710 Ext. 222

Toll-free: 866-849-3311

Fax: 608-782-0702

Email: mcjacobson@cclse.org

Web site: **www.cclse.org**

1416 Cumming Avenue

Superior, Wisconsin 54880-1720

Telephone: 715-394-6617

Toll-free: 888-831-8446

Fax: 715-394-5951

Email: salqudah@ccbsuperior.org

Web site: **www.ccbsuperior.org**

Coalition of Wisconsin Aging Group, Incorporated

2850 Dairy Drive, Suite 100

Madison, Wisconsin 53718-6751

Telephone: 608-224-0606

Toll-free: 800-488-2596

Fax: 608-224-0607

Email: carolmat@cwag.org

Web site: www.cwag.org

Acorn Housing

3500 North Sherman Boulevard, # 302

Milwaukee, Wisconsin 53216

Telephone: 414-444-6902

Fax: 414-444-6968

Email: amilton@acornhousing.org

Web site: www.acornhousing.org

Housing Resources, Incorporated

8532 West Capitol Drive, Suite 201

Milwaukee, Wisconsin 53222

Telephone: 414-461-6330

Email: trenab@sbcglobal.net

Sci-Tech Development, Incorporated (SDI)

5401 North 76th Street, Suite 103

Milwaukee, Wisconsin 53218

Telephone: 414-364-3701

Fax: 414-760-9914

Email: info@knowledgeoutreach.org

Waukesha County Department of Senior Services

1320 Pewaukee Road, Room 130

Waukesha, Wisconsin 53188

Telephone: 262-548-7848

Fax: 262-896-8273

Email: sgjohnson@waukeshacounty.gov

Web site: www.senior.waukeshacounty.gov

Wyoming

CCCS of Northern and Western Wyoming

235 S David Street, Suite A

Casper, Wyoming 82601

Telephone: 406-761-8721

Toll-free: 877-275-2227

Email: timr@cccsmt.org

Web site: www.cccswyo.org

4 So. Main Street

Sheridan, Wyoming 82801

Telephone: 877-275-2227

Email: timr@cccsmt.org

www.cccswyo.org

CCCS of Northern Colorado and Southeast Wyoming

2113 Warren Ave

Cheyenne, Wyoming 82001-3739

Telephone: 800-424-2227

Toll-free: 800-424-2227

Fax: 970-229-0721

Email: general@cccsnc.org

Web site: www.cccsnc.org

Bibliography

Ballman, T. E. *The Reverse Mortgage Handbook*. Jawbone Publishing, 2004.

Boroson, Warren. *The Reverse Mortgage Advantage*. McGraw Hill, 2006.

Edmunds, Gillette, and Jim Keene. *Retire on the House*. John Wiley and Sons, Inc., 2006.

Kelly, Tom. *The Reverse Mortgage Formula*. John Wiley and Sons, Inc, 2005.

Kraemer, Tammy, and Tyler Kraemer. *The Complete Guide to Reverse Mortgages*. Adams Business, 2007.

Lyons, Sarah Glendon, and John E. Lucas. *Reverse Mortgages for Dummies*. Wiley Publishing, Inc, 2005.

Author Biography

Cindy Holcomb is a freelance writer and poet who was born and raised in Rome, Georgia. Acquiring a love of books from her mother, Cindy began reading at age 4 and writing at age 5. Cindy works as a freelance writer from her home in Cedar Bluff, Alabama, where she lives with her husband and children on beautiful Weiss Lake.

Cindy has published many articles via the Internet and was a staff writer for *Southern Families Magazine,* a regional magazine covering Louisiana, Mississippi, and Alabama. Cindy is currently pursuing a degree in business from Phoenix Online University.

"Learning is a treasure that will follow its owner everywhere."

— Chinese Proverb

Index